Dictionary Of Computer Terms

Second Edition

Michael Covington, Ph.D.
Advanced Computational Method Center
University of Georgia

Douglas Downing, Ph.D.
School of Business and Economics
Seattle Pacific University

BARRON'S

New York • London • Sydney • Toronto

© Copyright 1989 by Barron's Educational Series, Inc.
Prior edition © Copyright 1986 by Barron's Educational Series, Inc.

All inquiries should be addressed to:
Barron's Educational Series, Inc.
250 Wireless Boulevard
Hauppauge, New York 11788

Library of Congress Catalog Card No. 88-39671

International Standard Book No. 0-8120-4152-6

Library of Congress Cataloging-in-Publication Data

Downing, Douglas
Dictionary of computer terms / Douglas Downing, Michael Covington.
—2nd ed.
p. cm.
ISBN 0-8120-4152-6
1. Computers—Dictionaries. I. Covington, Michael. II. Title.
QA76.15.D67 1989
004'.03'21—dc19   88-39671
                                                        CIP

PRINTED IN THE UNITED STATES OF AMERICA

901 9770 9876543

CONTENTS

ABOUT THE AUTHORS

Michael Covington is a research scientist and teacher in the field of artificial intelligence and natural language processing at the University of Georgia. He is the author of *Prolog Programming in Depth* (with Donald Nute and Andre Vellino), *Astrophotography for the Amateur, Syntactic Theory in the High Middle Ages*, and numerous articles in computer magazines. He holds the Ph.D. degree in linguistics from Yale University.

Douglas Downing teaches economics at Seattle Pacific University. He is the author of several books in the Easy Way series: *Computer Programming in BASIC, Computer Programming in Pascal* (with Mark Yoshimi), *Algebra, Trigonometry, Calculus*, and *Statistics* (with Jeff Clark); he is also author of *Business Statistics* and *Quantitative Methods* (both with Jeff Clark for the Barron's Business Review series). He holds the Ph.D. degree in economics from Yale University.

PREFACE

This book is intended to help you understand what computers are, what they do, and how they do it. The entries cover a wide range of topics, including hardware, software, programming concepts and languages, operating systems, electronics, logic circuits, history of computers, and specific models of personal computers. The lists of terms by categories at the front of the book will help you find entries that relate to a particular topic.

Thousands of software packages are now available that allow computers to perform a wide variety of tasks, and new packages are constantly being introduced. We discuss some popular software packages (for example, we show how to set up a simple spreadsheet using the program Lotus 1-2-3). We also describe some of the general tasks that software packages perform and explain much of the terminology that appears in software advertisements. However, it would be impossible to include a listing for every worthwhile item of software or hardware. Instead, we have chosen to concentrate on those items that, in our judgment, have become especially common or were unusually innovative.

This book will also help you if you are interested in writing your own programs. We provide articles on nearly all of the programming languages in widespread use today, with sample programs in Ada, ALGOL, APL, BASIC, C, COBOL, FORTRAN, LISP, LOGO, Pascal, PL/I, and Prolog. Several features of the languages BASIC and Pascal are described in more detail. In addition, we include ready-to-run programs illustrating several important algorithms (selection sort, Quicksort, etc.) and quick-reference tables of information often used in programming (ASCII characters, hexadecimal numbers, Epson printer control codes).

We also include descriptions of the electronic components and logic circuits of which computers are made. For example, we describe how a transistor works and illustrate how a machine made with transistors can perform arithmetic calculations. You do not need to know much about how computers work in order to use one, but a knowledge of their inner workings can make them less mysterious and help you appreciate their capabilities.

The field of computers changes very rapidly, making this new edition of the book necessary. For example, desktop publishing systems have become widespread in recent years, so many new terms have been added in this area. Microcomputer hardware has rapidly improved, with much larger memories, faster processors, and improved graphics becoming available. Many entries have been added to reflect these improvements.

Michael Covington

September 1988   *Douglas Downing*

LOGIC SYMBOLS

In formulas:

$-x$, $\neg x$, $\sim x$, $\bar{x}$	not x
$x \,\&\, y$, $x \wedge y$, $x \cdot y$	x and y
$x \vee y$, $x + y$	x or y
$x \oplus y$	x or y, but not both
$x \rightarrow y$, $x \supset y$	x implies y
$x \leftrightarrow y$, $x \equiv y$	x is equivalent to y

In circuit diagrams:

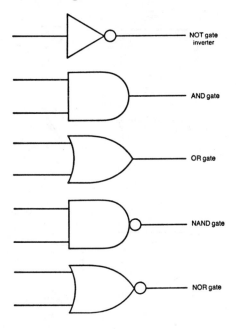

NOT gate
inverter

AND gate

OR gate

NAND gate

NOR gate

FLOWCHART SYMBOLS

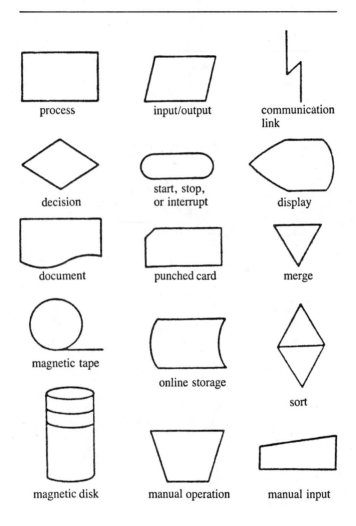

process

input/output

communication link

decision

start, stop, or interrupt

display

document

punched card

merge

magnetic tape

online storage

sort

magnetic disk

manual operation

manual input

READER'S GUIDE TO SELECTED TERMS
BY CATEGORY

Communication

ADM3A	Dow Jones	packet radio
ARPANET	download	parity
asynchronous	DTE	RBBS
bandwidth	electronic mail	RS-232
baud	EMAIL	RS-422
BBS	end user	RS-423A
Bell 103A	Ethernet	serial
Bell 202	FAX	server
Bell 212A	fiber optics	Source, The
BITNET	framing error	start bit
bps	full duplex	stop bit
call waiting	half duplex	SYSOP
CB simulator	handshaking	TBBS
CCITT	Hayes compatibility	telex
checksum	Kermit	token ring
cluster	LAN	USENET
CompuServe	local-area network	wide-area network
current loop	modem	X-OFF, X-ON
data bits	modem eliminator	XMODEM
data communication	modem null	YMODEM
data rate	network	ZMODEM
DCE	null modem	
DECNET	packet	

Desktop Publishing and Word Processing

ascender	document	justification
block move	elite	kerning
camera ready	em dash	landscape
clip art	en dash	leading
column move	fixed pitch	letter quality
courier	floating illustration	microspacing
cut	flush left	near letter quality
dash	flush right	orphan
descender	font	paste
desktop publishing	greeking	pica

pitch
point
portrait
Postscript
proportional pitch
ragged
required hyphen

required space
river
sans-serif
serif
style
TeX

typeface
typesetting mistakes
Ventura
widow
Word perfect
x-height

Electronics

ampere
base
bipolar transistor
brownout
capacitance
capacitor
chip
circuit
circuit diagram
clock
closed
CMOS
collector
conductor
coulomb
current
diode
doping
drain
electron
electronic compo-
    nents
emitter

farad
field-effect
    transistor
forward biased
germanium
grounding
henry
hole
impedance
inductance
inductor
insulator
integrated circuit
junction
Kirchhoff's law
large-scale
    integration
LED
magnetic bubble
    memory
medium-scale
    integration
microprocessor

N-type
ohm
Ohm's Law
P-type
parallel
power line
    protection
resistance
resistor
reverse biased
semiconductor
series
silicon
source
surge protector
transistor
TTL
uninterruptible
    power supply
vacuum tube
valence
VLSI
volt

Firms

Adobe
Aldus
Apple
Ashton-Tate
Atari

Borland
Commodore
Compaq
Control Data Corp.
CRAY

Digital Equipment Corp.
Digital Research Inc.
Epson
ETA
Hewlett-Packard

IBM	Micropro	Texas Instruments
Intel	Microsoft	Wang
Lotus Development	Radio Shack	Zilog, Inc.

Graphics

ANSI graphics	grid	palette
antialiasing	grid system	pixel
bit-mapped graphics	hercules graphics	resolution
CAD	card	sprite
CGA	MacDraw	three-dimensional
draw program	MacPaint	graphics
EGA	MCGA	VGA
fat bits	object-oriented	video modes (IBM PC)
graphics	graphics	windows draw
graphics card	paint program	windows paint

Hardware

acoustic coupler	disk drive	line printer
ADC	dot-matrix printer	liquid crystal
analog monitor	DRAM	display
analog-to-digital	drum	mainframe computer
converter	electrostatic printer	math coprocessor
bank switching	EPROM	matrix printer
board	file-protect ring	memory chips
bubble memory	fixed disk	Micro Channel
buffer	floppy disk	microfloppy disk
cache	full-height drive	minicomputer
CD ROM	gas plasma display	modem
Centronics interface	half-height drive	monitor
coaxial cable	hard card	monochrome monitor
composite video	hard disk	mouse
coprocessor	hardware	numeric keypad
CRT	ink-jet printer	optical character reader
daisywheel printer	jacket	plotter
dipswitch	joystick	port
direct-connect	laser printer	print spooler
modem	Laserwriter	printer
disk	light pen	PROM

History

Logic Gates and Computer Arithmetic

Machines

Mathematics

ABS	e	LOG
angle	EXP	logarithm
arcsin	exponent	numerical integration
arctan	exponential function	octal
argument	exponential notation	pi
base	factorial	precision
binary numbers	fixed-point number	radian measure
common logarithm	floating-point number	radix
COS	hexadecimal	real number
decimal number	integer	SIN
degree measure	LN	TAN
double precision		

Operating Systems and Operating System Concepts

auotexec	extended memory	protected mode
BAT file	extension	real mode
BIOS	filter	root directory
CMS	JCL	subdirectory
COM file	MS-DOS	TSO
CP/M	MVS	TYPE
DIR	operating system	UCSD P-System
directory	OS/2	UNIX
DOS	OS/360	VAX/VMS
EDLIN	path	VM/CMS
EXE file	presentation manager	VM/SP
expanded memory		

Programming Concepts

algorithm	Boolean variable	comment
archive	branch	compile-time error
array	bubble sort	concatenation
artificial intelligence	bug	conditional branch
assignment statement	CAD	constant
backtracking	CALL	context-sensitive help
benchmark	character string	data structures
binary search	circularity	data types

debug
declare
decryption
default
delimiter
dimension
documentation
dyadic operation
encryption
END
error trapping
expert system
expression
file
flowchart
function
global variable
hashing
help
heuristic
hierarchical
identifier
IF
incremental
  compiler
inference engine
information hiding
input
insertion sort
interpreter
interrupt
interrupt service
  routine

iteration
keyword
knowledge base
limits of computer
  power
linked list
list
literal
local variable
loop
macro assembler
memory resident
menu
merge
merge sort
mnemonic
module
monadic operation
Monte Carlo
multitasking
natural language
  processing
nest
node
object-oriented
  programming
outline
parallel processing
parameter
parsing
pointer
precedence

primitive
procedure
queue
Quicksort
radix sort
record
recursion
reserved word
run-time error
selection sort
Shell sort
side effect
simulation
software interrupt
sort
stack
string
string operations
structured programming
subroutine
symbolic algebra
syntax
table
top-down programming
transparent
trapping
tree
Turing machine
user friendly
user interface
variable
window

Programming Languages

Ada
ALGOL
APL
Backus-Naur form
BASIC

BASICA
C
COBOL
compiler
FORTH

FORTRAN
GW-BASIC
high-level language
LISP
LOGO

Modula-2
Pascal
PILOT
PL/I
programming
  language

PROLOG
QuickBASIC
RPG
SNOBOL

Turbo BASIC
Turbo Pascal
Turbo Prolog

Software

absolute address
accounting software
ARC
data base
data base manage-
  ment
dbase
desk accessory
Excel
HyperCard

Lotus 1-2-3
Microsoft Word
Norton Utilities
PageMaker
PLATO
pop-up utility
project manager
SideKick
software

spreadsheet
statistics program
TSR
Ventura
VisiCalc
Windows, Microsoft
Word Perfect
word processing
WordStar

Windows Interfaces and the Macintosh

desk accessory
desktop
double click
drag
draw program
finder
folder
hierarchical file
  system

HyperCard
icon
Laserwriter
MacDraw
Macintosh
MacPaint
MiniFinder
Motorola 68000
mouse

Presentation Manager
press
ResEdit
Send to Back
tiled windows
title bar
window
Windows, Microsoft

LIST OF TABLES

LIST OF PROGRAMS

a

ABS The function ABS(X) in BASIC and other programming languages calculates the absolute value of X. If X is positive, then ABS(X) = X; if X is negative, then ABS(X) = −X. For example, ABS(37) = 37; ABS(−37) = 37; ABS(−2.5) = 2.5; ABS(1985) = 1985. The absolute value of zero is zero. The absolute value of any other number is positive.

ABSOLUTE ADDRESS (1) An absolute address refers to a fixed location in the computer's memory. (See **computer design**.) (2) In a spreadsheet program, an absolute address is a cell address that refers to a fixed location that will not change when a formula is copied to another location. In Lotus 1-2-3, absolute addresses are indicated by placing a dollar sign before the column and row indicator. For example, if the formula 2*$D$7 is entered into a cell, then $D$7 is an absolute address. If this formula is copied to another cell, the $D$7 will not change. For contrast, see **relative address.** See also **segment; offset.**

ACCESS TIME The access time of a memory device is the amount of time required from the instant that the computer asks for data until those data are transferred to the computer. For example, the access time of a disk drive can be about 20 milliseconds, and the access time of an internal electronic memory can be less than 10^{-8} second.

ACCOUNTING SOFTWARE An accounting software package is a computer program designed to computerize the accounting process for a business. A complete system should include modules for the following functions: entering transactions data; posting that data to accounts at the appropriate times; presenting year-end reports, including balance sheets and income statements; and maintaining records of accounts receivable and accounts payable. Because of the importance of the data included in the system, a program should have a security mechanism, such as requiring the use of passwords, in order to prevent unauthorized users from altering the data. A system also should keep a record of transactions that have been entered (called an *audit trail*) so it is possible to trace how the figures that appear on the reports were derived. An example of an accounting program that has become widely used for small businesses is DAC Easy accounting, produced by DAC Software.

1

ACCUMULATOR The accumulator is the register where a computer stores the results of an arithmetic operation. For example, the assembly language command ADD 7 means to add the contents of memory address 7 to the number in the accumulator, and then store the result in the accumulator. (See **computer design; assembly language.**)

ACOUSTIC COUPLER An acoustic coupler is a type of modem that couples to the telephone line by means of a microphone and speaker arrangement into which the telephone handset is placed, as opposed to a direct-connect modem, which is wired to the telephone line. (See **modem.**)

ACRONYM An acronym is a word or name that is formed by joining the first letters (or first few letters) of a series of words. For example, NASA stands for National Aeronautics and Space Administration, and BASIC stands for Beginner's All-Purpose Symbolic Instruction Code.

ACTIVATE To activate a window is to make it the active window. This is done by moving the mouse pointer into it and clicking one button. (See **window.**)

To activate a piece of software is to start it by clicking on its name or icon. (See **click; icon.**)

ACTIVE WINDOW On the Macintosh or in Microsoft Windows or similar software environments, the active window is the window currently in use. (See **window.**)

ADA The programming language Ada was developed in the late 1970s for the U.S. Department of Defense. It is named for Augusta Ada Byron, Countess of Lovelace, who worked with Babbage's mechanical calculator in the nineteenth century.

Ada is based on Pascal, with some influence from PL/I and ALGOL 68. Comments begin with two hyphens and continue to the end of the line. Every statement ends with a semicolon even if it is embedded within another statement (such as an *if-then* or *loop-end loop* structure); in this respect Ada is like PL/I and C and unlike Pascal.

Like Pascal, Ada allows the programmer to create his own data types by specifying ranges or sets of possible values. For example:

```
type COLOR is (RED, GREEN, BLUE);
```

Ada subprograms can be compiled separately and linked together before execution; if only part of a program is changed, it is not necessary to recompile the whole program. This is an old FORTRAN feature that is missing from ALGOL 60 and Pascal. In the sample program, the *with* and *use* statements specify that this program uses a library of precompiled subroutines called I_O_PACKAGE.

Much of the original motivation for designing Ada was the need for a better language for real-time programming, that is, programming computers to control automatic or semiautomatic equipment. Toward this end, Ada allows the programmer to create multiple tasks that run concurrently (see **timesharing**), to pass signals from one task to another, and to introduce controlled time delays.

The Department of Defense has prepared an Ada compiler validation package that verifies that Ada has been implemented correctly on any given computer. Ada compilers that pass this test can be expected to be more reliable than compilers for other languages.

Here is a sample program written in Ada:

```
with I_O_PACKAGE;
procedure FACTORIAL is
   use I_O_PACKAGE;
   -- This program reads a number and
   -- computes its factorial.
   NUM, FACT, COUNT: INTEGER;
begin
   GET(NUM);
   FACT := 1;
   for COUNT in 2..NUM loop
      FACT := FACT * COUNT;
   end loop;
   PUT("The factorial of ");
   PUT(NUM);
   PUT(" is ");
   PUT(FACT);
end;
```

ADAPTIVE SYSTEM An adaptive system is a system that is able to learn from what has happened in the past.

ADC See **analog-to-digital converter**.

ADDRESS Each location in computer memory is identified by an address, which allows the computer to find the location of a specific data item (or instruction).

ADM3A The Lear Siegler ADM3A computer terminal was popular in the early 1980s. Like most terminals, it transmits and receives ASCII characters asynchronously through an RS-232 serial port. It is not VT-100 compatible (see **VT-100**), but it has its own simpler set of codes for controlling the screen.

ADOBE Adobe Systems, Inc. (Palo Alto, California), is a software company that produces the PostScript command language for laser printers. (See **PostScript.**)

AFT AFT is a protocol for detecting and correcting errors in data transmission. (For a description of another method in detail, see **XMODEM.**) AFT error correction is built into some high-speed modems so that erroneous data are never sent to the computer.

ALDUS Aldus is a software company located in Seattle, Washington, that produces products such as PageMaker, one of the pioneer programs for page layout and desktop publishing.

ALERT BOX An alert box is a small window that appears in order to advise the user of an error condition. When the user acknowledges reading the message by pressing a mouse button, the window disappears.

ALGOL ALGOL (for Algorithmic Language) is the name of two programming languages that had a strong impact on programming language design. The first of these, ALGOL 60, was designed by an international committee led by Peter Naur of the University of Copenhagen; the official description of it was published in final form in 1963.

Figure 1 shows a sample ALGOL 60 program. The words **begin** and **end** function like brackets to group statements together; a basic rule of the language is that, anywhere a statement can occur, a group of statements bracketed by **begin** and **end** can be substituted. This means that, whereas BASIC and FORTRAN programs are simply numbered lists of instructions, ALGOL programs consist of blocks of statements, grouped together to form larger blocks.

Note that in the example the *for* and *while* keywords together define a single loop with two termination conditions; in Pascal, a

```
begin
  comment
            Sieve of Eratosthenes -- sample
            ALGOL 60 program by Michael A. Covington.
            Prints the prime numbers from 1 to 1000 ;

  integer procedure next(last,limit,prime);
      value limit;
      integer last, limit;
      boolean array prime;
      begin
          integer i;
          boolean found;
          found := false;
          for last := last + 1
              while not found and last <= limit do
                  if prime [last] then found := true;
              if found then
                  begin
                      last := last - 1;
                      for i := last step last until limit do
                          prime [i] := false;
                      next := last
                  end
              else next := 0

      end;

  boolean array numbs [1:1000];
  integer latest, i;
  for i := 1 step 1 until 1000 do
      numbs [i] := true;
  latest := 1;
  for latest := next (latest,1000,numbs)
      while latest > 0 do
          output(61,`7 ZD',latest)
end
```

FIGURE 1 Sample ALGOL 60 Program. It is written in the form in which ALGOL programs are usually published (using **boldface** type for basic symbols, and *italic* for user-assigned names).

ALGORITHM 6

for-while combination creates a loop within a loop.

ALGOL 60 was the first language to have its syntax described in Backus-Naur form (See **Backus-Naur form**); it was also the first to allow subprograms to call themselves (see **recursion**). The programming languages JOVIAL, Pascal, and Modula-2, among others, are direct outgrowths of ALGOL 60.

The standard syntax of ALGOL 60 describes how programs are to be presented in published papers, but not how they are to be typed into a computer. In published papers, ALGOL keywords (called *basic symbols*) are printed in boldface type to distinguish them from variable names; on most computers, they are flanked by quotation marks or asterisks.

ALGOL 68 is quite different from ALGOL 60; it includes many new features and has a reputation for being powerful but difficult to learn. ALGOL 68 programs are easy to recognize because the ends of blocks of statements are marked by spelling keywords backward (*do. . .od, if. . .fi, case. . .esac*). The language allows a wide variety of data types, including combinations (called *united modes* or *unions*) that can take on values of more than one type; for example, if X is declared as the union of types *int* and *char*, then 2, 4, 32767, X, and '&' are among its possible values. In addition, data items can be declared as references (*ref*), which means that they refer to the location at which an item is stored rather than the value of the item itself.

An important principle of ALGOL 68 is *orthogonality*, which means that all meaningful combinations of features are allowed. (In geometry, two things are *orthogonal* if they meet at right angles; the use of the term in ALGOL 68 comes from the square tables in which combiantions of orthogonal features can be listed.)

Discontent with the complexity of ALGOL 68 led Niklaus Wirth to design first ALGOL W and then Pascal (see **Pascal**), which has almost completely replaced ALGOL in practical use today.

ALGORITHM An algorithm is a sequence of instructions that tell how to solve a particular problem. An algorithm must be specified exactly, so there can be no doubt about what to do next, and it must have a finite number of steps. A computer program is an algorithm written in a language that a computer can understand, but the same algorithm could be written in several different languages. An algorithm can also be a set of instructions for a

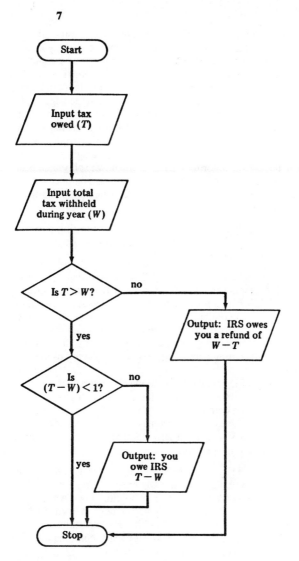

FIGURE 2

person to follow. Figure 2 is an algorithm (expressed as a flowchart) that tells how to calculate your income tax payment or refund, once you know the total amount of tax you owe and the total amount that has been withheld. (See **flowchart.**)

A set of instructions is not an algorithm if it does not have a definite stopping place, or if the instructions are too vague to be followed clearly. The stopping place may be at variable points in the general procedure, but something in the procedure must determine precisely where the stopping place is for a particular case.

If you study the game of tic-tac-toe long enough, you will be able to develop an algorithm that tells you how to play an unbeatable game. However, some problems are so complicated that there is no algorithm to solve them. (See **heuristic; limits of computer power.**)

ALPHA TEST Alpha testing is the first stage of testing of a new software product, carried out by the manufacturer's own staff. By way of contrast, see **beta test.**

ALPHANUMERIC CHARACTER The charaters that a computer can print or display are classified as alphabetic, numeric, special, and control. *Alphabetic* characters are the letters A to Z; *numeric* characters are the digits 0 to 9. *Special* characters are the other printable characters, that is, punctuation marks and other symbols. *Control* characters are codes that represent actions such as backspacing, starting a new line, or going to the top of the next page.

Alphanumeric characters are all the characters that are either alphabetic or numeric, that is, all the letters and digits.

On large IBM computers, the characters @, #, and $ count as alphabetic, and hence as alphanumeric. They are called *national* characters because they print differently on computers designed for use in different countries.

ALT KEY The Alt key on the IBM PC and PS/2 is used like a shift key; that is, you hold it down while pressing another key. For example, to type Alt-P, type P while holding down Alt.

The Alt key gives the other key a new meaning, which depends on the software being used. For example, in Word Perfect and Lotus 1-2-3, the Alt key is used in combination with various letters to call up macros (see **macro**).

Keys pressed while holding down Alt do not have ASCII

codes (see **ASCII**). Instead, each such key is read by the computer as 2 bytes. The first byte is zero, and the second byte serves to identify the key.

ALU ALU stands for <u>A</u>rithmetic/<u>L</u>ogic <u>U</u>nit, which is the part of a CPU (<u>C</u>entral <u>P</u>rocessing <u>U</u>nit) where arithmetic and logical operations are performed.

AMIGA The Amiga is a computer produced by Commodore especially suitable for graphics and sound generation. It is based on the Motorola 68000 microprocessor, and it contains three additional custom processors to improve its capabilities for sound generation and graphics, including animation. The Amiga provides the option of a menu-driven interface involving icons, or an interface where the user types commands.

The Amiga can be programmed in Microsoft Amiga BASIC, which is a version of BASIC that contains special commands for accomplishing tasks such as creating windows in different areas of the screen; displaying color pictures; drawing shapes on the screen and filling them in; and creating animation with images that move around the screen. The Amiga can also be used to generate sounds of specified frequences—in other words, it can create music. (See **MIDI**).

AMPERE An ampere (or amp, for short) is the unit for measuring electric current. A current of 1 ampere means that 6.25×10^{18} electrons are flowing by a point each second. A group of 6.25×10^{18} electrons has a charge of 1 coulomb, so 1 ampere = 1 coulomb per second.

ANALOG COMPUTER An analog computer is a computer in which information is stored in a form that can vary smoothly between certain limits rather than having discrete values. (By way of contrast, see **digital computer**.) A slide rule is an example of an analog computer, because it represents numbers as distances along a scale.

All modern, programmable computers are digital. Analog computer circuits are used in certain kinds of automatic machinery, such as automotive cruise controls and guided missiles. Also, a fundamental analog computer circuit called the operational amplifier is used extensively in audio, radio, and TV equipment.

ANALOG MONITOR An analog monitor is one that displays an unlimited range of brightnesses for each primary color, from fully on to fully off. As a result, a vast range of colors can be displayed. By contrast, with an ordinary RGB monitor, each of the primary colors (red, green, and blue) is either on or off. (See **RGB monitor.**)

ANALOG-TO-DIGITAL CONVERTER An analog-to-digital converter is a device that changes data from analog to digital form, making it possible to feed them into a computer. For example, the temperature in a room may be measured by a device that represents it as a continuously varying voltage. An analog-to-digital converter transforms this voltage into a set of signals representing decimal or binary digits.

"ANALYTICAL ENGINE" See **computers, history of.**

input 1 ——————

—————— output

input 2 ——————

FIGURE 3

AND GATE An AND gate (Figure 3) is a logic gate that produces an output of 1 only when all of its inputs are 1. The operation of a two-input AND gate is completely described by the following table:

Input 1	Input 2	Output
0	0	0
0	1	0
1	0	0
1	1	1

One simple way to make an AND gate is to use two switches connected in series (Figure 4). There will be an output voltage only if both switches are on (closed). Exactly the same principle can be used to make an AND gate with two transistors connected in series; each transistor acts as a switch.

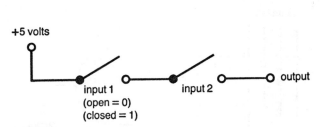

+5 volts

input 1
(open = 0)
(closed = 1)

input 2

output

FIGURE 4

Figure 5 shows how this works. In this circuit, logic level 0 is represented by 0 volts, and logic level 1 is represented by 5 volts. Each transistor conducts if its input is positive. However, the positive voltage cannot reach the output unless both transistors are conducting. (The resistors limit current flow to keep the transistors from overheating.)

FIGURE 5

AND gates are used in computer arithmetic. (See **binary addition.**) In addition, AND gates with 8 or 16 inputs are used to recognize signals coming in simultaneously on several wires, such as memory addresses. (See **parallel.**) NOT gates are used on inputs that are supposed to be zero, so that the input to the AND gate consists of all 1's when the desired signal is present. Figure 6 shows a four-input version of this kind of circuit.

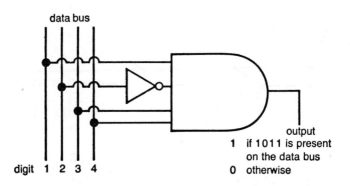

FIGURE 6

ANGLE The size of an angle can be measured by the number of degrees it contains. One complete rotation measures 360 degrees (written as 360°). A square corner (called a *right angle*) measures 90°. Angles can also be measured in radians. A complete rotation measures 2π radians, and a right angle measures $\pi/2$ radians.

ANSI The abbreviation ANSI stands for American National Standards Institute. There are official ANSI standards in almost all industries, and quite a few of them have to do with computers. In computer programming, ANSI most often refers to one of the following:

1 ANSI standard versions of FORTRAN, COBOL, or other programming languages. ANSI standard languages are designed to make it possible to run the same program on any computer without worrying about variations in the details of the language. Typically, a particular manufacturer's version of FORTRAN or COBOL will include all of the features defined in the ANSI standard, plus additional features devised by the manufacturer. To be easily transportable from one computer to another, a program should not use any features that are not in the ANSI standard.

2 ANSI standard escape sequences for controlling the screen of a computer terminal or microcomputer. An escape sequence is a series of character codes which, when sent to the screen, causes the screen to do something other than simply display

the characters to which the codes correspond. The ANSI escape sequences all begin with the ASCII Escape character (code 27). (See **ANSI screen control.**)

The advantage of using escape sequences for screen control is that any program can control the screen, even if it is is written in a language that has no statements for screen control. All the program need do is send a special sequence of characters to the screen exactly as if the characters were to be displayed.

ANSI GRAPHICS On BBSes, the use of ANSI terminal control codes in combination with the IBM PC special character set is sometimes called ANSI graphics. Strictly speaking, the term is inappropriate, because the computer is not in graphics mode and the special characters are not covered by an ANSI standard.

ANSI SCREEN CONTROL An ANSI standard specifies a set of sequences of characters (escape sequences) which, when sent to the screen of a computer, make it perform actions such as clearing the screen.

Some computers obey these codes at all times. These include the DEC Rainbow, the Texas Instruments Personal Computer, and all DEC VT-100-compatible terminals.

The IBM PC obeys ANSI screen control codes only if the CONFIG.SYS file contains a line of the form

```
DEVICE = ANSI.SYS
```

and the codes are sent to the screen using DOS services rather than BIOS services. (On the IBM PC, ANSI control codes can also be used to redefine keys; see the DOS Technical Reference Manual for details.)

Table 1 show some commonly used ANSI control code sequences.

All ANSI control sequences begin with Esc (code 27) followed by "["; many of them contain numbers that specify how far the cursor is to be moved or where it is to be placed. For example,

```
Esc [ 1 5 C
```

moves the cursor 15 spaces to the right, and

```
Esc [ 3 C
```

moves it only 3 spaces to the right.

TABLE 1 Commonly Used ANSI Screen Control Sequences

Characters sent	Effect
Esc [1 2 ; 3 5 H	Move cursor to row 12, column 35
Esc [1 2 ; 3 5 f	Same as above
Esc [4 A	Move cursor up 4 lines
Esc [3 B	Move cursor down 3 lines
Esc [6 C	Move cursor 6 columns to the right
Esc [7 D	Move cursor 7 columns to the left
Esc [s	Save current cursor position
Esc [u	Return cursor to where it was when you did Esc [s
Esc [2 J	Clear whole screen and home cursor
Esc [K	Erase from cursor position to end of line
Esc [0 m	Select normal type (white on black)
Esc [1 m	Select bold (bright white) type
Esc [4 m	Select underlined type (on VT-100 or IBM Monochrome Display; blue on other IBM displays). (Other numbers, all the way up to 47, alter the foreground and/or background color on IBM color displays.)
Esc [6 n	Place a cursor position report in the keyboard buffer. (For example, if the cursor is on row 3, column 4, then *Esc [3 ; 4 R* will appear in the keyboard buffer as if the user had typed it.)

ANTIALIASING Ordinarily, vertical and horizontal lines appear straight when drawn on computer screens, but lines in other directions have a stairstep appearance because the line is drawn by turning on pixels that are arranged in a square grid. Antialiasing is a way of smoothing out this stairstep effect. The line is thought of as cutting a swath across the grid of pixels, and pixels that are only partly covered by the line are only partly illuminated. This doubles the apparent resolution of the screen.

APL APL is an interactive programming language that is well suited for handling complex operations on arrays. APL(<u>A</u> <u>P</u>rogramming <u>L</u>anguage) uses several Greek letters and some other special symbols, so this language requires a specially designed terminal. Some features of APL are as follows:

1 A function, or program, is defined by the symbol ∇, as in ∇ FN1. To execute the function, just type FN1. The return key signifies the end of a statement. The APL system automatically keeps track of the statement numbers in a function.

2 Arithmetic operations are symbolized by the following: + addition, − subtraction, × multiplication, ÷ division, and * exponentiation. All operations are executed from right to left (if no parentheses are present). An assignment statement is written in the form

   X ← expression

such as

   X ← 4 × 20

3 The statement X ← □ in a function causes the computer to type a question mark, ?, and then wait for the user to type in a value for X. To display the value of X, either manually or as part of a function, just type X.

4 A regular branch statement is written as → S1, where S1 is the label of the statement where you want to go. A conditional branch is written as → (I < N)/S1, which will cause a jump to S1 if the condition in the parentheses (in this case I < N) is true.

5 APL has many facilities for handling arrays. For example, the expression X ← (3,3) ρ 5 causes X to become the 3 × 3 array

$$\begin{array}{ccc} 5 & 5 & 5 \\ 5 & 5 & 5 \\ 5 & 5 & 5 \end{array}$$

Subscripts of arrays are written with brackets, such as X[1;2]. The expression ∅X calculates the transpose of X, and the expression A + . × B calculates the matrix product **AB**. One of the advantages of APL is that this language makes it very easy to change the size of arrays in the middle of a program.

6 Some other features of APL are:

+ /X calculates the sum of all the elements in a vector X.

× /X calculates the product of all the elements in a vector X.

ι N is a vector of all the integers from 1 to N.

2 φ X is the vector formed by rotating all the elements of X two places to the left.

Here is a program written in APL. (Note that it is possible to write a complete APL program that is only one line long.)

```
∇ CHECK PRIME N
[1] ((1–L)/'PRIME'),(L←(v/LQ)=Q←N+1↓ι⌈(N*0.5)))/'NOT PRIME'
[2] ค THIS APL PROGRAM TESTS WHETHER A NUMBER IS PRIME
    ∇
```

Here are some examples of the use of this program. The user types the lines that are indented.

```
    CHECKPRIME 3
PRIME
    CHECKPRIME 45
NOT PRIME
    CHECKPRIME 77
NOT PRIME
    CHECKPRIME 101
PRIME
    CHECKPRIME 117
NOT PRIME
    CHECKPRIME 343
NOT PRIME
    CHECKPRIME 701
PRIME
    CHECKPRIME 1003
NOT PRIME
    CHECKPRIME 1007
NOT PRIME
    CHECKPRIME 1009
PRIME
    CHECKPRIME 1103
PRIME
```

APPLE Apple is one of the largest personal computer manufactuers. The Apple II, introduced in 1977, was one of the earliest popular microcomputers. A wide range of software was written for the Apple II and its followers, the Apple II+, the Apple IIe, the Apple IIC, and the Apple IIGS (with extra graphics and sound capabilities). More recent Apple products include the Macintosh (introduced in 1984), which contains innovations in graphics, word processing, and ease of use. The company, located in Cupertino, California, was founded by Steve Jobs and Steve Wozniak, who began work in a garage.

APPLICATION PROGRAM An application program is one that performs useful work not related to the computer itself. Examples of application programs include a word processor, a spreadsheet, an accounting system, or an engineering program. By way of contrast, see **utilities** and **operating system.**

APPLICATIONS PROGRAMMER An applications programmer is a person who writes programs that use the computer as a tool to solve particular applied problems. By way of contrast, see **systems programmer.**

ARC ARC is a popular data-compression program published by System Enhancement Associates. Two shareware programs written by Phil Katz, PKARC and PKXARC, do the same work and use the same file format. ARC originated on the IBM PC, but versions have been developed for UNIX and for the Amiga.

ARC takes one or more files, compresses them, and combines them into an "archive" file (with a name ending in .ARC), which ARC can later decompress. ARC is often used for files that are to be transmitted by telephone because the compressed file takes less time to transmit; also, a group of files is easily kept together by storing them in a single archive.

See also **data compression.**

ARCHIVAL STORAGE Archival storage is storage for data that must be kept for a long time but will seldom be used, such as backup copies of working programs. Microcomputers with hard disks often use tape cartridges or floppy disks for archival storage. Magnetic tape is usually the cheapest form of archival storage, but the tapes should be copied every 2 or 3 years if their contents are still needed, since tapes can become demagnetized with age.

ARCHIVE (1) An archive is a filing system for information designed to be kept for a long time.

(2) An archive file, or ARC file, is a file containing compressed information from other files. The original files can be reconstructed from it. (See **ARC.**)

(3) In MS-DOS (PC-DOS) and other operating systems, every file has an archive bit that says whether or not it has been backed up by copying to another disk or tape. The ATTRIB command can be used to examine or change archive bits. It is possible to back up only the files that have not already been backed up.

ARCSIN The arcsin function is the inverse of the sine function. If $y = \sin A$, then $A = \arcsin y$. (See **SIN.**) If you are using a programming language that does not have the arcsin function, then the value of the arcsin can be found by using this formula involving the arctan function:

$$\arcsin y = \arctan\left(\frac{y}{\sqrt{1 - y^2}}\right)$$

ARCTAN The arctan function is the inverse of the tangent function. If $y = \tan A$, then $A = \arctan y$. (See **TAN.**)

ARGUMENT The arguments of a function or subprogram are the value or values given to it by the main program. For example, in BASIC the SQR function finds the square root of a number. In the expression SQR(25), which asks for the square root of 25, the argument is the number 25.

ARPANET ARPANET is a wide area network established by the U.S. Defense Advanced Research Projects Agency. It links a wide variety of universities and research labs, and its main use is to transmit electronic mail among researchers who are working together. ARPANET has gateways to BITNET and USENET.

ARRAY An array is a collection of data that is given one name. An array is arranged so that each item in the array can be located when needed. An array is made up of a group of elements, which may be either numbers or character strings. Each element can be identified by a set of numbers known as subscripts, which indicate the row and column in which the element is located. The dimension of an array is the number of subscripts needed to locate a particular element. For example, it takes two subscripts to identify an element in a two-dimensional array.

If seven basketball players scored respectively 18, 10, 16, 20, 11, 7, and 14 in one game, these scores can be stored in a one-dimensional array containing seven elements. If we call the array name SCORE and write the subscripts in parentheses, then:

SCORE(1) = 18, SCORE(2) = 10, SCORE(3) = 16, and so on.

(Each programming language has its own rules for how to name arrays and where to write the subscripts.)

If we need to score four statistics for each player, then we can use a two-dimensional array, where the first subscript indicates the player and the second subscript indicates the statistic. For example:

SCORE(1,1) = 9,   SCORE(1,2) = 18, SCORE(1,3) = 0, SCORE(1,4) = 0,
SCORE(2,1) = 3,   SCORE(2,2) = 3,   SCORE(2,3) = 4, SCORE(2,4) = 4,
SCORE(3,1) = 7,   SCORE(3,2) = 15, SCORE(3,3) = 2, SCORE(3,4) = 6,
SCORE(4,1) = 10, SCORE(4,2) = 15, SCORE(4,3) = 0, SCORE(4,4) = 0,
SCORE(5,1) = 4,   SCORE(5,2) = 4,   SCORE(5,3) = 3, SCORE(5,4) = 4,
SCORE(6,1) = 3,   SCORE(6,2) = 5,   SCORE(6,3) = 1, SCORE(6,4) = 2,
SCORE(7,1) = 7,   SCORE(7,2) = 14, SCORE(7,3) = 0, SCORE(7,4) = 0,

where the first column represents field goals; the second column, field goal attempts; the third column, free throws; and the fourth column, free throw attempts.

By using a two-dimensional array, we can store all the statistics for all the players for one game. If we need to store statistics for more than one game, we can use a three-dimensional array, where the first subscript indicates the game number, the second subscript indicates the player number, and the third subscript indicates the statistic number.

ARRAY PROCESSOR An array processor (also known as a *vector processor*) is a computer that can perform an operation on an entire array in a single step. Presently available array processors are large mainframes, such as the Control Data Corporation CYBER 205.

Consider, for example, the problem of adding the corresponding members of two 100-element arrays A and B to produce a third array C (that is, C(1) = A(1) + B(1), C(2) = A(2) + B(2), and so forth). On an ordinary computer, this is done with instructions such as the following BASIC statements:

```
10   FOR I = 1 TO 100
20   LET C(I) = A(I) + B(I)
30   NEXT I
```

On an array processor, however, the entire operation is done in a single machine instruction. The additions may or may not be done simultaneously; the important thing is that time is saved because the CPU need not fetch another instruction each time or calculate values for the variable I.

ARROW KEYS Many computer keyboards have arrow keys that move the cursor up, down, or to the left or right. The effect of these keys depends on the software being used; some pieces of software ignore them or handle them incorrectly. You should be especially cautious about using the arrow keys when communicating with another computer; even if the cursor moves correctly, the other computer may not understand what you are doing.

On the IBM PC and PS/2, the arrow keys do not have ASCII codes. Instead, each of them is read as 2 bytes, a zero byte and a byte that identifies the key.

ARTIFICIAL INTELLIGENCE Artificial intelligence (AI) is the branch of computer science that deals with using computers to simulate human thinking. Artificial intelligence is concerned with building computer programs that can solve problems creatively, rather than simply working through the steps of a solution designed by the programmer.

For an example, consider computer game playing. Some games, such as tic-tac-toe, are so simple that the programmer can specify in advance a procedure that guarantees that the computer will play a perfect game. With a game such as chess, however, no such procedure is known; the computer must use, instead, a *heuristic*, that is, a procedure for discovering and evaluating good moves.

One possible heuristic for chess would be for the computer to identify every possible move from a given position, and then evaluate the moves by calculating, for each one, all the possible ways the game could proceed. Chess is so complicated that this would take an impossibly long time (on the order of millions of years with present-day computers).

A better strategy would be to take shortcuts. Calculating only five or six moves into the future is sufficient to eliminate most of the possible moves as not worth pursuing. The rest can be evaluated on the basis of general principles about board positions. In fact, an ideal heuristic chess-playing machine would be able to modify its own strategy on the basis of experience; like a human chess player, it would realize that its opponent is also following a heuristic and try to predict her behavior.

One of the main problems of AI is how to represent knowledge in the computer in a form such that it can be used rather than merely reproduced. In fact, some workers define AI as the construction of computer programs that utilize a *knowledge base*. A computer that tells you the call number of a library book is not displaying artificial intelligence; it is merely echoing back what was put into it. Artificial intelligence would come into play if the computer used its knowledge base to make generalizations about the library's holdings or construct bibliographies on selected subjects. (See **expert system**.)

Computer vision and robotics are important areas of AI. Although it is easy to take the image from a TV camera and store it in a computer's memory, it is hard to devise ways to make the computer recognize the objects it "sees." Likewise, there are many unsolved problems associated with getting computers to move about in three-dimensional space—to walk, for instance, and to find and grasp objects—even though human beings do these things naturally.

Another unsolved problem is natural language processing—getting computers to understand speech, or at least typewritten input, in a language such as English. In the late 1950s it was expected that computers would soon be programmed to accept natural-language input, translate Russian into English, and the like. But human languages have proved to be more complex than was expected, and progress has been slow. The English-speaking computers of *Star Wars* and *2001* are still some years away. (See **natural language processing**.)

The important philosophical question remains: Do computers really think? Artificial intelligence theorist Alan Turing proposed a criterion that has since become known as the *Turing test*: a computer is thinking if a human being, connected to it by teletype, cannot tell whether he is communicating with a machine or with another person. In response, Terry Rankin has pointed out that it makes little sense to build a machine whose purpose is to deceive human beings. Increasing numbers of AI workers are taking the position that computers are not artificial minds, but merely tools to assist the human mind, and that this is true no matter how closely they can be made to imitate human behavior.

ASC The ASC function in many versions of BASIC calculates the ASCII code number associated with a given character. (See **ASCII**.) For example, ASC("A") is 65 because the ASCII code of the character "A" is 65 (expressed in decimal).

Here is a short Microsoft BASIC program that reads in a string of characters and converts all of the lower-case letters to upper case letters, using the ASC function:

```
10  REM PROGRAM READS IN CHARACTER STRING
11  REM THEN PRINTS OUT THE STRING
12  REM WITH ALL OF THE LOWER CASE LETTERS
13  REM CHANGED TO CAPITAL LETTERS
14  REM NOTE THE USE OF THE MID$, ASC,
15  REM AND CHR$ FUNCTIONS
20  INPUT X$
30  FOR I = 1 TO LEN(X$)
40  C = ASC(MID$(X$,I,1))
50  IF (C>=97) AND (C<=122) THEN C=C-32
60  MID$(X$,I,1) = CHR$(C)
70  NEXT I
80  PRINT X$
90  END
```

ASCENDER An ascender is a part of a printed character that extends upward. For instance, the letter "d" has an ascender and the letter "o" does not. (See **descender; typeface**.)

ASCII ASCII is a standard code for representing characters as binary numbers, used on most microcomputers, computer terminals, and printers. ASCII stands for American Standard Code for Information Interchange. In addition to printable characters, the ASCII code includes control characters to indicate carriage return, backspace, etc. Table 2 shows a list of ASCII printable characters, and Table 3 lists ASCII control characters.

ASCII FILE An ASCII file is a text file on a machine that uses the ASCII character set. (See **text file**.) In MS-DOS (PC-DOS) and CP/M, each line ends with Carriage Return and Line Feed (hex 13 and 10).

TABLE 2 ASCII Printable Characters
(decimal, hexadecimal, and character representations)

Dec.	Hex.	Char.	Dec.	Hex.	Char.	Dec.	Hex.	Char.
32	20	space	64	40	@	96	60	`
33	21	!	65	41	A	97	61	a
34	22	"	66	42	B	98	62	b
35	23	#	67	43	C	99	63	c
36	24	$	68	44	D	100	64	d
37	25	%	69	45	E	101	65	e
38	26	&	70	46	F	102	66	f
39	27	'	71	47	G	103	67	g
40	28	(	72	48	H	104	68	h
41	29	)	73	49	I	105	69	i
42	2A	*	74	4A	J	106	6A	j
43	2B	+	75	4B	K	107	6B	k
44	2C	,	76	4C	L	108	6C	l
45	2D	−	77	4D	M	109	6D	m
46	2E	.	78	4E	N	110	6E	n
47	2F	/	79	4F	O	111	6F	o
48	30	0	80	50	P	112	70	p
49	31	1	81	51	Q	113	71	q
50	32	2	82	52	R	114	72	r
51	33	3	83	53	S	115	73	s
52	34	4	84	54	T	116	74	t
53	35	5	85	55	U	117	75	u
54	36	6	86	56	V	118	76	v
55	37	7	87	57	W	119	77	w
56	38	8	88	58	X	120	78	x
57	39	9	89	59	Y	121	79	y
58	3A	:	90	5A	Z	122	7A	z
59	3B	;	91	5B	[	123	7B	{
60	3C	<	92	5C	\	124	7C	¦
61	3D	=	93	5D	]	125	7D	}
62	3E	>	94	5E	∧	126	7E	~
63	3F	?	95	5F	_			

TABLE 3 ASCII Control Characters

| Numeric Value | | Code | How | Action |
Decimal	Hex	Name	Typed	(on most computers)
0	00	NUL	CTRL @	—
1	01	SOH	CTRL A	—
2	02	STX	CTRL B	—
3	03	ETX	CTRL C	Interrupt program
4	04	EOT	CTRL D	—
5	05	ENQ	CTRL E	—
6	06	ACK	CTRL F	—
7	07	BEL	CTRL G	Sound beeper
8	08	BS	CTRL H	Same as backspace key
9	09	HT	CTRL I	Same as tab key
10	0A	LF	CTRL J	Same as line feed key
11	0B	VT	CTRL K	—
12	0C	FF	CTRL L	Top of page (on printer)
13	0D	CR	CTRL M	Same as return key
14	0E	SO	CTRL N	Change typeface
15	0F	SI	CTRL O	Undo effect of CTRL N
16	10	DLE	CTRL P	—
17	11	DC1, X-ON	CTRL Q	Undo effect of CTRL S
18	12	DC2	CTRL R	—
19	13	DC3, X-OFF	CTRL S	Make computer stop typing
20	14	DC4	CTRL T	—
21	15	NAK	CTRL U	—
22	16	SYN	CTRL V	—
23	17	ETB	CTRL W	—
24	18	CAN	CTRL X	—
25	19	EM	CTRL Y	—
26	1A	SUB	CTRL Z	End of file mark
27	1B	ESC	CTRL [	Same as ESC key
28	1C	FS	CTRL \	—
29	1D	GS	CTRL]	—
30	1E	RS	CTRL ∧	—
31	1F	US	CTRL _	—
127	7F	DEL	DEL key	—

Note: The effects of these control characters vary widely from machine to machine; consult the appropriate manual for details and for instructions on how to type them. Many keyboards do not allow the use of the CTRL key with characters other than letters.

CTRL characters are often referred to by prefixing them with ∧; for example, ∧C indicates CTRL C. This is only a notation; the CTRL key is not at all equivalent to the character ∧.

ASHTON-TATE Ashton-Tate, a software company in Culver City, California, produces the data base management program dBASE III and the integrated software package Framework.

ASSEMBLER (1) An assembler is a program that translates assembly language into machine language. (See **assembly language; machine language; compiler.**) (2) The assembly language itself is sometimes called the assembler. The word is used in this sense mainly with the IBM 360 and 370.

ASSEMBLY LANGUAGE An assembly language is a computer language in which each statement corresponds to one machine language statement. Assembly languages are more cumbersome to use than regular (or high-level) programming languages, but they are much easier to use than pure machine languages, which require that all instructions be written in binary code.

See Page 26 for an example of a simple assembly language for an imaginary computer with only 16 different instructions. This language assumes that the computer has an accumulator register, an index register, and a 1-bit condition register.

Since this language has 16 instructions, it will take a 4-bit register to store the instructions ($2^4 = 16$). (See **computer design.**) Real microprocessors use 8-bit or 16-bit instruction registers.

Here is a BASIC program that will print the sum of the squares of N numbers:

```
10  INPUT N: FOR I = 1 TO N
20  INPUT A,B
30  C = A^2 + B^2 : PRINT A,B,C
40  NEXT I : END
```

Here is an assembly language program to do the same task:

Address	Instruction	Comment
11	READ I	;input the number N and place ;it in the index register
12	READ 2	;read in A
13	READ 3	;read in B
14	LOAD 2	
15	MPY 2	;the accumulator now holds A^2
16	STORE 4	
17	LOAD 3	
18	MPY 3	;the accumulator now holds B^2
19	ADD 4	;the accumulator now holds A^2 + B^2

Binary Code	Assembly Language Statement	
0 0 0 0	GO A	The next instruction executed will be the instruction located at the address stored in memory address A.
0 0 0 1	CGO A	Same as GO, except that A will be executed next only if the condition register is 1.
0 0 1 0	ST	Subtract 1 from the index register and set the condition register to 0 if the index register is 0 (used for loops).
0 0 1 1	STOP	Stop the machine.
0 1 0 0	ADD A	Add the number stored in memory address A to the number stored in the accumulator, and store the result in the accumulator.
0 1 0 1	SUB A	Subtract the number stored at A from the accumulator.
0 1 1 0	MPY A	Multiply the number stored at A by the accumulator.
0 1 1 1	DIV A	Divide the accumulator by the number stored at A.
1 0 0 0	EQU A	If the number stored in A is equal to the accumulator, set the condition register to 1.
1 0 0 1	GTR A	If the number stored in the accumulator is greater than the number stored in A, set the condition register to 1.
1 0 1 0	AND A	The accumulator will become 1 if both A and the accumulator are 1.
1 0 1 1	NOT	The accumulator will become 1 if it now holds 0, and vice versa.
1 1 0 0	LOAD A	Load the contents of memory location A in the accumulator.
1 1 0 1	STORE A	Load the contents of the accumulator in location A.
1 1 1 0	READ A	Read a number from an input device and store the result in A.
1 1 1 1	PRINT A	Send the contents of A to an output device.

20	STORE 5	
21	PRINT 2	
22	PRINT 3	
23	PRINT 5	
24	ST	
25	CGO 12	;go to 12 if all N numbers have not ;been read yet
26	STOP	

This is only a hypothetical example; the assembly language of an actual computer would have dozens or hundreds of different instructions, and operations such as READ and PRINT would be much more complex than they appear here. Assembly languages generally allow you to use symbolic addresses instead of actual machine addresses. This feature makes them easier to use.

The obvious disadvantages of assembly languages are that the programs are lengthy and hard to read, and that the same assembly language cannot be used on different types of computers. The main advantage is that, in general, assembly language programs run faster and occupy less memory than programs produced by compilation from a high-level language, since with an assembly language the programmer can be sure that nothing unnecessary is present.

ASSIGNMENT STATEMENT An assignment statement is a computer program statement that calculates the value of an expression and assigns that value to a particular variable name. An example of a BASIC assignment statement is

```
10 LET C = (A*A + B*B)^(0.5)
```

This statement will calculate the value of $\sqrt{A^2 + B^2}$ and then give that value to the name C.

Another example is

```
20 LET I = I + 1
```

This statement will cause I to take on a value one greater than its old value. (In most BASIC systems the keyword LET is optional.)

ASYNCHRONOUS The term *asynchronous* refers to processes that are not synchronized. For example, most computer terminals use asynchronous data transmission, in which the terminal or the computer is free to transmit any number of characters at any time. (The bits constituting each character are transmitted at a fixed rate, but the pauses betweeen characters can be of any duration.)

Synchronous terminals, by contrast, transmit data in packets of more than one character. This is faster than asynchronous communication because there is no need for a start bit or stop bit on each individual character.

ATARI Atari, Incorporated, is a manufacturer of home computers. In 1972, Atari manufactured the world's first coin-operated video game, called *Pong.* Subsequent products have included home video games and small home computers. The Atari 520 ST, announced in 1985, is a high-performance personal computer with a Motorola 68000 microprocessor and 512K of RAM; it resembles the Apple Macintosh but sells for a lower price. A more recent version is the ST1040.

ATTRIBUTES The attributes of a variable are the characteristics of that variable. For example, a variable may have the attributes of being a fixed point number, or a 3×3 array of floating point numbers, or a character string variable that is 7 characters long.

AUDIT TRAIL See **accounting software.**

AUTOEXEC In MS-DOS (PC-DOS), AUTOEXEC.BAT is the name of a file that contains commands to be executed whenever the computer boots up. For example, an AUTOEXEC.BAT file containing the following lines will set the date and time and then check the hard disk for lost clusters:

```
DATE
TIME
CHKDSK C: /F
```

AUTOMATION Automation refers to the use of machines to do work that was once done by people.

AUXILIARY STORAGE Auxiliary storage is a storage device that is under the control of the computer, but not directly a part of it. Disks and tapes are examples of auxiliary storage areas. The computer's own memory is called *internal storage.*

b

BABBAGE, CHARLES Charles Babbage was a nineteenth century inventor who designed several devices, such as the "analytical engine," that included concepts that were later used in computers. However, the technology of his day was not capable of building everything he designed.

BACKSLASH The backlash character is "\", as opposed to the forward slash "/".

BACKTRACKING Backtracking is a problem-solving method applicable to certain kinds of problems. The problem is to be solved by making a series of moves. Backtracking works as follows: First, choose a possible move and make it. Then, proceed from there by choosing a possible move, and so on, until a solution is found. If you reach a place where you have not found a solution but no more moves are possible, back up. That is, undo one or more moves until you get back to an alternative you did not take. Follow that different choice to see if the solution lies in that direction. If not, keep backing up until you find what you're looking for (you may have to try *all* possible moves).

Backtracking is built into the programming language Prolog, which uses it extensively (see **Prolog**). In this article we will discuss how to implement backtracking in a conventional language.

For example, consider this problem: Find three whole numbers $x[1]$, $x[2]$, and $x[3]$, each between 1 and 5, such that their sum is equal to their product. While you might try to solve this problem mathematically, it is easier just to try all the combinations. One way to get all the combinations would be to set up three nested loops, as follows:

```
for x[1]:=1 to 5 do
   for x[2]:=1 to 5 do
      for x[3]:=1 to 5 do
         if x[1]+x[2]+x[3] = x[1]*x[2]*x[3] then
            write (x[1],x[2],x[3],' is a solution');
```

This is possible because you know in advance that the solution will take three moves (choosing one number in each move), so you can set up three loops.

Backtracking occurs in this example because if the innermost loop doesn't find a solution, control returns to the middle loop, which increments $x[2]$ and starts the innermost loop over again. Similarly, the middle loop backtracks to the outer loop if it fails to find a solution. The loop counters keep track of untried alternatives, but it's important to understand that *any* method of generating alternatives one by one would work just as well.

With some problems, you don't know how many moves a solution will take. In such a case you must use recursion to nest the loops at run time. The following Pascal program solves the problem we've just discussed, but uses recursion so that it is a much more typical illustration of how backtracking is done.

```pascal
program backtrack;
var x: array[1 .. 3] of integer;

procedure choose (n:integer);
     { Chooses a value for x[n] }
var
   i: integer; { Must be local }
begin
   if n=4 then { we have chosen three values }
      begin
         if x[1] + x[2] + x[3] = x [1]* x [2]*x[3]
         then begin
            writeln('Solution found: ',
                 x[1]:3,x[2]:3,x[3]:3);
            halt
               {remove this line to get all solutions}
            end
         else
            writeln(x[1]:3,x[2]:3,x[3]:3,
               ' is not a solution; backtracking...')
      end
   else
   { recurse, trying all possible values for x[n] }
   for i:=1 to 5 do
      begin
         x[n]:=i;
         choose(n+1)
      end
end;
```

```
{ Main program }
begin
   choose(1)
end.
```

In Prolog, where backtracking is built in, all you have to do is specify possible values for the integers and specify the condition they must meet. You can solve our example problem by typing the query:

```
?-   member(X1, [1,2,3,4,5]),
     member(X2, [1,2,3,4,5]),
     member(X3, [1,2,3,4,5]),
     Sum is X1+X2+X3,
     Product is X1*X2*X3,
     Sum == Product,
     write([X1,X2,X3]).
```

Each clause in the query specifies a condition that the answer must meet. Whenever the computer encounters a clause whose condition cannot be satisfied, it backs up to an untried alternative in a previous clause and tries again.

BACKUP COPY A backup copy of a program or set of data is another copy of that program or those data that can be referred to if the original is lost. When working with a microcomputer, you should make backup copies of important disks and store them away from the working copies. On large computer systems, tape drives are often used to store backup copies of disk files. See also **archival storage**.

BACKUS-NAUR FORM (BNF) Backus-Naur is a notation used to describe the syntax of languages. BNF was devised by J. Backus and Peter Naur and introduced in the first official description of ALGOL 60 (see **ALGOL**); it is sometimes referred to as *Backus normal form*.

Each BNF statement describes some syntactic unit by giving one or more alternative expansions of it, separated by the symbol "|". For example, the following is a BNF description of the assignment statement in BASIC (we assume that <line number>, <variable name>, and <expression> have already been defined, and that <empty> stands for the absence of any written symbol):

```
<let keyword> ::= LET | <empty>
<assignment statement> ::=
    <line number> <let keyword>
    <variable name> = <expression>
```

The first statement defines <let keyword> as standing for either the word LET or no symbol, in order to indicate that the word LET is optional. The second statement defines <assignment statement> as consisting of a line number, an optional let keyword, a variable name, an equals sign, and an expression.

Many languages contain syntactic rules that cannot be expressed in BNF; for instance, BNF provides no way to say that (on most computers) a BASIC line number cannot exceed 32767. Still, BNF descriptions are handy because they are concise and definitive and because parsers can be generated directly from them. (See **parsing.**)

BACKUS NORMAL FORM See **Backus-Naur form (BNF).**

BANDWIDTH The bandwidth of an electronic system is the range of frequencies that it can transmit. In data-communication systems, high bandwidth allows fast transmission or the transmission of many signals at once. On a monitor screen, high bandwidth provides a sharp image.

BANK SWITCHING Bank switching is the ability to use more than one set of memory chips at different times, while giving them the same addresses. This makes it possible to equip a computer with more memory than it was originally designed for—simply store some data in one set of chips, then switch over and use the other set of chips.

Bank switching is used to give the IBM PC more than 640K of memory (see **expanded memory**). Bank switching is also used on the IBM EGA and other advanced color graphics cards.

BAR CODE A bar code is a pattern of wide and narrow bars, printed on paper or a similar material. A computer reads the bar code by scanning it with a laser beam or with a wand that contains a light source and a photocell.

The most familiar bar code is the Universal Product Code (see Figure 7), used with cash registers in supermarkets, but bar codes have been utilized to encode many kinds of data, including complete programs for some programmable calculators. Circular bar codes are sometimes used on boxes or pieces of luggage that may be scanned from many different directions.

FIGURE 7 An Example of a Bar Code (the Universal Product Code from the first edition of this book).

BASE (1) The base is one of the three parts of a bipolar transistor. (See **transistor.**)

(2) In the exponential function $y = a^x$, a is the base.

(3) The base of a number system is the number of digits used in that system. (See **binary numbers; decimal number; hexidecimal, octal.**)

BASIC BASIC is one of the easiest computer languages to learn, and one of the most popular languages for beginning students and for people with microcomputers. It was designed as an interactive language by John Kemeny and Thomas Kurtz in the 1960s. Since then many different versions of BASIC have been developed for different machines. Many computers are sold with the BASIC language already included.

Here are some features of most BASIC systems:

1 Each BASIC statement must be preceded by a line number. For example:

```
10 X = 25.5
20 PRINT X
```

Here 10 and 20 are line numbers. To execute the program, type RUN. To see the program displayed on the screen, type LIST. The command SAVE causes a program to be stored on a disk or tape, and the command LOAD causes the program to be read from the disk or tape into the computer's memory. However, the exact form of these two commands varies with different computers.

2 Some versions of BASIC require that numeric variable names be only one or two characters long. Many current versions, however, allow longer variable names, making it easier to give meaningful names to variables. A dollar sign, $, placed at the end of the variable name indicates that the variable is a character string variable.

3 Arithmetic operations in BASIC are as follows: ^ or ** exponentiation, * multiplication, / division, + addition, and − subtraction. In evaluating arithmetic expressions, operations surrounded by parentheses are done first, then exponentiations, then multiplications and divisions, and finally additions and subtractions. An assignment statement is of the form

LET X = expression

To execute this statement, the computer will calculate the value of the expression and assign that value to the name X. In most versions of BASIC the word LET is optional.

4 Input-output is handled as follows: The statement INPUT X,Y causes the computer to stop, type a question mark, and then wait for you to type in two values. It will call the first value X and the second value Y.

The statement READ A will cause the computer to look at the top of the data stack and assign that value to A. A data stack is created with a DATA statement, such as DATA 10, 15, 16.04, 30. The first time the computer hits a READ statement, such as READ A, it will give A the value 10. The next time it encounters a READ statement, such as READ B, it will give B the value 15.

The PRINT statement is used for output. The statement PRINT X,Y causes the values of X and Y to be displayed on the screen. The statement PRINT "WORD" causes the character string WORD to be printed. When a comma is used between the items in a print statement, the computer will space the items apart by a standard amount. When a semicolon is used in place of the comma, the computer will jam the items together.

In some versions of BASIC the LPRINT command works exactly the same as PRINT except that the output is directed to a printer instead of to the screen.

5 The GOTO command tells the computer to jump to the indicated statement number. For example, the GOTO 50 will cause the computer to jump to statement 50 and start executing at that point. The word IF is used to indicate conditional actions. For example:

```
100  IF X < 0 THEN PRINT "X IS LESS THAN 0"
```

or

```
110  IF A = 10 THEN GOTO 500
```

Loops can be constructed using FOR and NEXT statements. For example:

```
10     FOR I = 10 TO 20 STEP 2
       statements in middle, such as:
          20   J = SQR(I)
          30   PRINT I, J
100  NEXT I
```

This setup will cause the computer to execute the statements in the middle six times. The first time it will use the value I = 10, then the value I = 12, then I = 14, etc., through I = 20.

6 The sizes of arrays are defined with the DIM statement. For example, DIM A(25) defines A to be a one-dimensional array with 25 elements, and DIM B(6,18) defines B to be a two-dimensional array with 6 rows and 18 columns. Each element in the array can be identified by using subscripts, written in parentheses. For example, B(2,1) is the element of B located in row 2, column 1.

7 Subroutines can be defined in BASIC by using the statement GOSUB. Upon reaching the statement GOSUB 150, the computer will jump to statement 150 and start executing there. When the computer reaches a RETURN statement, it knows it has reached the end of the subroutine, so it will jump back to the statement immediately following the original GOSUB statement.

8 Comments can be inserted in a program by using the keyword REM (short for REMARK) at the beginning of the statement. When the computer comes to a statement such as

```
30    REM THIS REMARK IS HERE TO HELP
30    REM ME UNDERSTAND THIS PROGRAM
```

it will completely ignore it and proceed to the next statement.

BASIC is often the best language if you have a simple program that you would like to type and run quickly. Most BASIC systems use interpreters, rather than compilers. This means that a program can be run quickly and easily. Just type RUN, and the program starts executing immediately. However, interpreted programs generally run much slower than do compiled programs. Therefore, if you have a long program that needs to be executed often but does not require frequent changes, you probably will prefer a compiled language.

Many BASIC versions provide extensive graphics and sound-generation capabilities. However, the details of these commands vary greatly for different machines.

One disadvantage of BASIC is that it does not provide many of the features necessary for writing structured programs. (See **structured programming.**) Long BASIC programs can become very confusing to human readers. However, some versions partially remedy this deficiency by providing for IF/THEN/ELSE structures and WHILE loops. If you are writing a long BASIC program, you can help to clarify your meaning by breaking the program into subroutines and using a REM statement to clearly label the start of each subroutine.

More recent implementations of BASIC, such as Microsoft's QuickBasic and Borland's Turbo Basic, consist of compilers; they also contain other features to enhance the power of the language. Line numbers are not required in those versions.

Here is a sample program written in BASIC.

```
LIST
    1     REM BASIC PROGRAM TO TEST IF A
    5     REM NUMBER IS PRIME
   10     INPUT "N:"; N
   15     PRINT "----------"
   20     S = 1
   30     T = 1 + INT(SQR(N))
   40     I = 2
   50     R = N/I
   60     Q = R - INT(R)
   65     IF Q = 0 THEN GOTO 120
   67     REM IF Q = 0 NUMBER IS NOT PRIME
   70     I = I + S
   80     S = 2
   90     IF I < T THEN GOTO 50
```

```
 95   REM  IF I < T CHECK THE NEXT NUMBER
100   PRINT N;" IS PRIME"
110   GOTO 150
120   PRINT N;" IS NOT PRIME"
130   PRINT "IT IS DIVISIBLE BY ";I
150   END
```

BASICA In PC-DOS (MS-DOS) on the IBM PC family of computers, the command BASICA calls up an interpreter for a special
version of Microsoft BASIC (see **BASIC**). This interpreter uses
code stored on a ROM chip inside the computer; it works only on
IBM machines. A similar interpreter for clones is called GW-
BASIC.

BAT FILE In MS-DOS (PC-DOS), a BAT (batch) file is a file whose
name ends with ".BAT", and which contains a list of commands.
For instance, if you create a file called THREEDIR.BAT containing the lines

```
dir a:
dir b:
dir c:
```

then you can type THREEDIR and the three "dir" commands in
the file will all be executed in succession.

BATCH PROCESSING In batch processing, the user gives the
computer a "batch" of information, referred to as a *job*—for
example, a program and its input data on punched cards—and
waits for it to be processed as a whole. Batch processing contrasts
with *interactive processing*, in which the user communicates with
the computer by means of a terminal while his program is
running. The crucial difference is that with batch processing the
user must put all of the data into the computer before seeing any
of the results, while with interactive processing the user can
decide how to handle each item on the basis of the results obtained
with earlier items.

BAUD A baud is a unit that measures the speed with which information is transferred. The baud rate is the reciprocal of the length in
seconds of the shortest pulse used; for instance, a system whose
shortest pulses are 1/300 second is operating at 300 baud.
     On an RS-232 serial link, the baud rate is equal to the data rate
in bits per second (bps). With other kinds of communication, the

data rate may be considerably faster than the baud rate. For instance, a 2400-baud modem takes 2400-baud (2400-bps) serial data and encodes it into an audio signal whose true baud rate is about 1200, near the maximum rate at which a telephone line can transmit pulses. Each pulse carries more than one bit of information. At the receiving end, another modem transforms the signal back into 2400-baud serial data.

BBS A BBS (<u>B</u>ulletin <u>B</u>oard <u>S</u>ervice) is a computer that allows users to log in from remote terminals, exchange messages, and (usually) download programs. Many BBSs are run by microcomputer hobbyists and can be accessed free of charge by dialing a telephone number.

BELL 103A Bell 103A is the standard format for transmitting data by telephone at speeds of 300 baud or less.

BELL 202 Bell 202 is a standard format for transmitting data by telephone at a speed of 1200 baud. Bell 202 format is half duplex only and has now largely been replaced by Bell 212A. (See **half duplex.**)

BELL 212A Bell 212A is the standard format for transmitting data by telephone at a speed of 1200 baud.

BENCHMARK A benchmark program is a program used to test the performance of a computer or a piece of software. For example, the speed with which computers do arithmetic is often measured by running a prime-number-finding algorithm called the *Sieve of Eratosthenes* (see **ALGOL**).

Benchmark results are always somewhat untrustworthy because no single program tests all aspects of a computer's operation. A particular benchmark may exaggerate a difference between two machines that is unimportant in practice, or it may conceal an important difference.

BETA TEST Beta testing is the second stage of testing a new software product that is almost ready for market. Beta testing is carried out by volunteers in a wide variety of settings like those in which the finished product will be used. By contrast, see **alpha test.**

BIDIRECTIONAL PRINTER A bidirectional printer is capable of printing while the print head is traveling either forward or backward. It is faster than a single-direction printer because it does not need to return to the left margin each time it starts a new line.

BINARY ADDITION The first step in designing a computer that can do arithmetic is to develop a machine that can add two binary numbers. When we add decimal (i.e., regular) numbers, we proceed one digit at a time, starting with the rightmost digit. The table lists the results we would like our adding machine to give for each of the four possible combinations of the input digits:

Input 1	Input 2	Result
0	0	0
0	1	1
1	0	1
1	1	0 (with a carry of 1)

If we add together two zeros, the result is zero. The next two cases are also easy: $1 + 0 = 0 + 1 = 1$. The last case is trickier, since it involves a carry to the next digit to the left. The binary equation

$$1_{binary} + 1_{binary} = 10_{binary}$$

is the same as the decimal equation:

$$1_{decimal} + 1_{decimal} = 2_{decimal}$$

When the two input digits are 1, we must have a sum digit of 0, along with something that reminds us that we need to carry a

FIGURE 8 Half adder

1 to the next digit. A *half adder* (see Figure 8) is a circuit that accomplishes this function. It has two outputs; the sum output and the carry output.

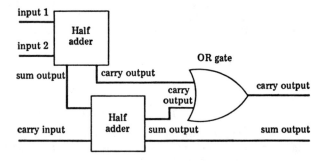

FIGURE 9 Full adder

A half adder can be constructed with standard logic gates. The carry output is the result of an AND gate. The sum output is the result of an OR gate, with a slight modification that sets the output equal to 0 when both inputs are 1.

The second step in binary addition involves propagating the carries from each digit to the left. A *full adder* (see Figure 9) is constructed to fulfill this function. A full adder consists of two half adders. It requires three inputs: the two digits to be added, plus the carry output from the next digit to the right. The full adder has two outputs: the sum output and the carry output. Figure 10 illustrates the sequence of full adders needed to complete the addition of two 5-bit binary numbers.

Before the addition is carried out, each of the two numbers is stored in a row of *flip-flops* called a *register*. (A flip-flop is a physical device that can flip between one state representing 0 and another state representing 1.) In order for the addition to be carried out, the two registers need to be connected to the computer's addition circuit. It is the job of the computer's boss—the CPU—to determine what numbers are to be added, find those numbers in the memory, load them in the appropriate registers, and then connect the registers to the addition circuit. After the

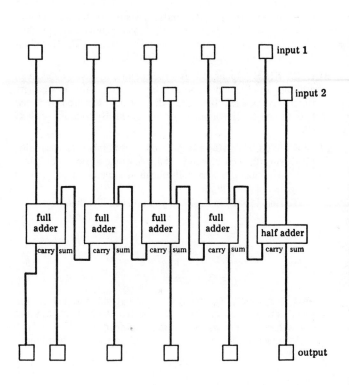

FIGURE 10

addition has been performed, the resulting sum is usually stored in a register called the *accumulator*.

BINARY DIVISION Division can be accomplished in computers by repeated subtraction. For example, 15/5 can be found by $15 - 5 = 10$, $10 - 5 = 5$, $5 - 5 = 0$. The answer is 3, since 3 subtractions were required. If we need to find a/b. where $a<b$, we can multiply a by a power of 2, perform the repeated subtraction, and then divide by the same power of 2 to find the answer. The flowchart in Figure 11 shows this division algorithm.

BINARY FILE A binary file is a file containing bits or bytes in an arbitrary arrangement. The term binary file usually denotes any file that is not a text file. Crucially, special software is required to print a binary file or view it on the screen. By contrast, see **text file.**

BINARY MULTIPLICATION Two binary numbers can be multiplied using the same principles that you would use to multiply two decimal numbers. Binary multiplication is even simpler, because there are only two digits.

To find 13×21 in decimal, you proceed like this:

$$
\begin{array}{r}
21 \\
\times\ 13 \\
\hline
63 \\
21 \\
\hline
273
\end{array}
$$

First, find 3×21. Then find 10×21, and add these two results together to get the final product. Note that the product has more digits than either of the two original numbers.

You can follow the same procedure to multiply two binary numbers:

10101	21	
× 01101	× 13	
10101	21	(21×2^0)
00000	0	
10101	84	(21×2^2)
10101	168	(21×2^3)
100010001	273	$(2^8 + 2^4 + 2^0)$

To design a multiplication machine, you'll need three registers, plus a binary addition circuit. (See **binary addition.**) The result

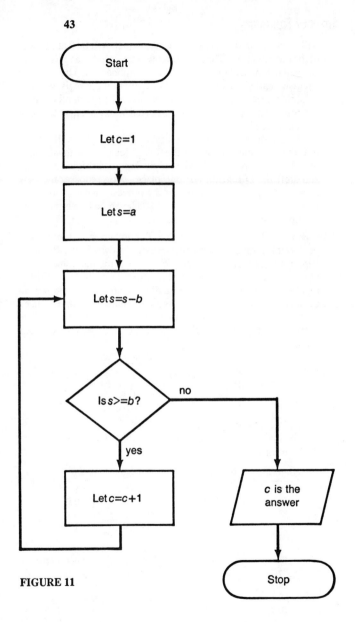

FIGURE 11

will be stored in the accumulator (A), which will be 0 at the start of the computation. The multiplier will be stored in a register you can call the multiplier (M), and the multiplicand will be stored in a register called the distributor (D). Both of these registers must be shift registers, meaning that you can shift the numbers they contain one place to the right or to the left when you give the right signal. (See **shift register.**)

First, look at the rightmost digit of the M register. If this bit is 1, then add the contents of the D register to A. If this bit is 0, then don't do anything. Next, shift the M register *right* one place, and shift the D register *left* one place. Now, look at the new rightmost digit of M, and repeat the process. Keep going until you've processed all the digits of M. The procedure is shown in the flowchart in Figure 12.

BINARY NUMBERS Binary (base-2) numbers are written in a positional number system that uses only two digits: 0 and 1. Binary numbers are well suited for use by computers, since many electrical devices have two distinct states: on and off. Writing numbers in binary requires more digits than writing numbers in decimal, so binary numbers are cumbersome for people to use.

Each digit of a binary number represents a power of 2. The rightmost digit is the 1's digit, the next digit to the left is the 2's digit, and so on.

Decimal	Binary
$2^0 = 1$	1
$2^1 = 2$	1 0
$2^2 = 4$	1 0 0
$2^3 = 8$	1 0 0 0
$2^4 = 16$	1 0 0 0 0

The table shows some numbers written in binary and decimal form.

Decimal	Binary	Decimal	Binary
0	0	11	1 0 1 1
1	1	12	1 1 0 0
2	1 0	13	1 1 0 1
3	1 1	14	1 1 1 0
4	1 0 0	15	1 1 1 1
5	1 0 1	16	1 0 0 0 0
6	1 1 0	17	1 0 0 0 1
7	1 1 1	18	1 0 0 1 0
8	1 0 0 0	19	1 0 0 1 1
9	1 0 0 1	20	1 0 1 0 0
10	1 0 1 0		

FIGURE 12

BINARY SEARCH A binary search is a method for locating a particular item from a list of items that is in order. Suppose that you need to find the location of a particular word in a list of alphabetized words. To execute a binary search, look first at the word that is the exact middle of the list. If the word you're looking for comes before the midpoint word, you know that your word is in the first half of the list; otherwise it is in the second half. Once you've determined which half of the list your word is in, repeat the procedure to determine which quarter, then which eighth, and so on, until you've finally found the exact position in the list of the word you're looking for. At the most, a binary search will take N steps to find the item you want if the list contains 2^N items.

Here is an example of a Pascal program that performs a binary search:

```
PROGRAM binsearch (INPUT,OUTPUT);
  {This program executes a binary search
   to determine if a number x is
   contained in the array a. The numbers
   in the array a must be in ascending
   order.}
VAR
  n : INTEGER;
  x : REAL;
  a : ARRAY[1..500] OF REAL;
PROCEDURE readin;
  {This procedure reads elements into
   the array a.}
VAR i : INTEGER;
BEGIN
  WRITELN('Input number of numbers in list:');
  READLN(n);
  FOR i := 1 TO n DO
    BEGIN
      WRITELN('Input number ',i);
      READLN (a[i])
    END
  END;
PROCEDURE binsearch;
  VAR
    lowbound, upbound, position : INTEGER;
    continue : BOOLEAN;
```

```
BEGIN
  lowbound := 1;
  upbound := n;
  continue := TRUE;
  WHILE continue DO
    BEGIN
      position :=
       (lowbound + upbound) DIV 2;
IF a[position] = x
THEN BEGIN
   WRITELN('In list at position ',
     position);
   continue := FALSE
     END
   ELSE BEGIN
IF a[position] > x
  THEN upbound := position
  ELSE lowbound := position;
IF (upbound-lowbound) = 1
  THEN BEGIN
    IF a[upbound] = x
  THEN WRITELN('In list at position ',
                      upbound)
  ELSE IF a[lowbound] = x
  THEN WRITELN('In list at position',
                      lowbound)
  ELSE WRITELN('Not in list');
   continue := FALSE
     END
     END
   END {end of WHILE loop}
  END; {end of procedure BINSEARCH}
BEGIN {Main program block}
  readin;
  REPEAT
   WRITELN('Type in number to search for:');
   READLN(x);
   binsearch;
  UNTIL x = -1
  {The program stops when you type -1.}
END.
```

BINARY SUBTRACTION The easiest way to teach a machine
how to subtract two binary numbers is to design a circuit so that
an addition circuit can be used. A binary adder can be readily constructed with logic gates. (See **binary addition**.)

Suppose that we have a number x, represented as a binary
number with k digits. The 2-complement of x (written as $\bar{x}$) is $\bar{x}$
$= 2^k - x$. Then, to find the difference $a - x$, we can write

$$a - x = a + \bar{x} - 2^k.$$

Therefore, to find $a - x$, we have to find $a + \bar{x}$, and then subtract
2^k from that result. This subtraction is very easy, since we ignore
the first digit of the result and keep the remaining k digits.

There is a simple way to change a number into its 2-comple-
ment. If we consider 3-bit numbers ($k = 3$), then we have

$$x = b_2 2^2 + b_1 2^1 + b_0 2^0$$

where b_0, b_1, and b_2 are the binary digits of x. Then, to find $\bar{x}$:

$$\begin{aligned}
\bar{x} &= 2^3 - x \\
&= 8 - x \\
&= 1 + 7 - b_2 2^2 - b_1 2^1 - b_0 2^0 \\
&= 1 + 2^2 + 2^1 + 2^0 - b_2 2^2 - b_1 2^1 - b_0 2^0 \\
&= 1 + (1 - b_2) 2^2 + (1 - b_1) 2^1 + (1 - b_0) 2^0
\end{aligned}$$

Therefore, to find the 2-complement of a binary number all we
need to do is reverse each digit (i.e., change all the 0's to 1's and
all the 1's to 0's) and then add 1 to the result. For example:

x (decimal)	x (binary)	$\bar{x}$ (binary)	$\bar{x} = 8 - x$ (decimal)
1	0 0 1	1 1 1	7
2	0 1 0	1 1 0	6
3	0 1 1	1 0 1	5
4	1 0 0	1 0 0	4
5	1 0 1	0 1 1	3
6	1 1 0	0 1 0	2
7	1 1 1	0 0 1	1

Now, to subtract $5 - 2$, we have:

$$
\begin{array}{rr}
5 & 1\,0\,1 \\
+\ 2 & +\ \ 1\,1\,0 \\
\hline
11 & 1\,0\,1\,1 \\
-\ 8 & -\ 1\,0\,0\,0 \\
\hline
3 & 0\,1\,1
\end{array}
$$

To subtract $7 - 1$:

$$
\begin{array}{r}
7 \\
+\ \overline{1} \\
\hline
14 \\
-\ 8 \\
\hline
6
\end{array}
\qquad
\begin{array}{r}
1\ 1\ 1 \\
+\quad 1\ 1\ 1 \\
\hline
1\ 1\ 1\ 0 \\
-\ 1\ 0\ 0\ 0 \\
\hline
1\ 1\ 0
\end{array}
$$

If we need to find $6 - 6$:

$$
\begin{array}{r}
6 \\
+\ \overline{6} \\
\hline
8 \\
-\ 8 \\
\hline
0
\end{array}
\qquad
\begin{array}{r}
1\ 1\ 0 \\
+\quad 0\ 1\ 0 \\
\hline
1\ 0\ 0\ 0 \\
-\ 1\ 0\ 0\ 0 \\
\hline
0\ 0\ 0
\end{array}
$$

This method for handling subtraction suggests a way to represent negative numbers. Suppose that we need to find $6 + (-3)$. We know that this is the same as $6 - 3$. Therefore the negative number -3 can be stored in the machine as $\overline{3}$, which is 1 0 1. There is one slight problem with this plan, though: 1 0 1 is already the binary representation for 5, so it can't also be the representation for -3. We need some way to tell these two numbers apart, so we'll put an extra bit in front of the number to act as the sign bit. In this notation 5 is represented by 0 1 0 1, and -3 is represented by 1 1 0 1. The leftmost bit is the sign bit, with 0 meaning "positive" and 1 meaning "negative."

The table shows how 4 bits can be used to represent the numbers from -8 to 7.

Positive Numbers		Negative Numbers	
Decimal	Binary	Decimal	Binary
0	0 0 0 0		
1	0 0 0 1	-1	1 1 1 1
2	0 0 1 0	-2	1 1 1 0
3	0 0 1 1	-3	1 1 0 1
4	0 1 0 0	-4	1 1 0 0
5	0 1 0 1	-5	1 0 1 1
6	0 1 1 0	-6	1 0 1 0
7	0 1 1 1	-7	1 0 0 1
		-8	1 0 0 0

Now, to find $2 - 5$, all we need to do is find $2 + \overline{5}$:

$$
\begin{array}{rr}
2 & 0\ 0\ 1\ 0 \\
+\ \overline{5} & +\ 1\ 0\ 1\ 1 \\
\hline
-3 & 1\ 1\ 0\ 1
\end{array}
$$

BINARY SYNCHRONOUS The IBM Binary Synchronous (Bi-Sync) protocol is a procedure for connecting computer terminals together. Many terminals can share a single link, and a controller determines which terminal can transmit at a particular moment.

BINARY-TO-DECIMAL CONVERSION Binary-to-decimal conversion is the process of calculating the decimal equivalents of binary numbers. Most computer calculations are performed on binary numbers, so the results need to be converted into decimal numbers before people can understand them.

BIOS In CP/M, the BIOS (Basic Input/Ouput System) is the part of the operating system that controls input and output.

On IBM PC-compatible machines, the BIOS is a set of routines stored on a ROM chip inside the computer. These routines handle all input-output functions, including screen graphics. By contrast, the routines provided by the operating system ("DOS calls") do not support graphics. Thus, most IBM PC software must call routines provided by the BIOS as well as those provided by DOS, and most IBM PC software will not run on a non-IBM-compatible machine that is running DOS (such as a DEC Rainbow).

OS/2 does not use the BIOS. Instead, all input-output services are provided by OS/2 itself.

BIPOLAR TRANSISTOR A bipolar transistor is formed by sand-wiching a thin layer of P- or N-type semiconductors between two regions of the opposite type of semiconductor. (See **transistor.**) The other general type of transistor is the *field-effect transistor.*

BISYNC See **Binary Synchronous.**

BIT *Bit* is a shorthand term for "binary digit." There are only two possible binary digits: 0 and 1. (See **binary numbers.**) Bits are represented in computers by two-state devices, such as flip-flops.

A *byte* is the number of bits (usually 8) that stand for one character. One kilobyte (K) is 1,024 bytes. A computer memory is a collection of physical objects that can represent bits. The size of a computer memory is the number of bits it can represent, usually measured in K's.

One important measure of the capability of a microprocessor is the number of bits that each internal register can contain. For example, the Z80 microprocessor is an 8-bit processor. The Intel 80286 processor found on many popular computers is a 16-bit processor. The Apple Macintosh contains the Motorola 68000 microprocessor, which has 32-bit registers although it can only transfer data 16 bits at a time. The Digital MicroVAX contains a full 32-bit processor. In general, a processor with a greater number of bits per instruction can process data more quickly (although there are other factors to consider that also determine a computer's speed). See also **microprocessor.**

BIT-MAPPED GRAPHICS Bit-mapped graphics offer a method of displaying pictures on a computer. The picture is treated as a large array of pixels (see **pixel**), each of which is stored in a specific memory location. The picture is drawn by specifying the color of each pixel. By contrast, see **vector graphics.** See also **draw program; paint program; memory-mapped video.**

BITNET BITNET is a wide-area network linking university computer centers all over the world. It originated in the northeastern U.S. in the early 1980s. Its most common use is to transmit electronic mail among scholars who are working together. BITNET has gateways to ARPANET and USENET.

BLOCK When data records are stored on magnetic tape, they are collected together in groups known as blocks. Each block is treated as a unit. Blocks are separated by blank areas called *interblock gaps.*

BLOCK MOVE The operation of moving a section of a file from one place to another within the file is known as a block move. (See **editor.**)

BLOCK PROTECT The block protect command in Word Perfect

marks a block of text so that it will not be split across pages. This is useful to prevent a table or formula from being broken up. Other word processors and desktop publishing packages have similar functions.

BOARD A printed circuit board is sometimes called a board or a card. Many computers, such as the IBM-PC, contain expansion slots where you can add additional boards to enhance the capability of the machine.

BOOLE, GEORGE George Boole was a nineteenth century mathematican who developed principles of mathematical logic that have become known as *Boolean algebra*. These principles are important in the design of computers.

BOOLEAN ALGEBRA Boolean algebra is the study of operations carried out on variables that can have only two values: 1(true) and 0 (false). Boolean algebra was developed by George Boole in the 1850s; it was useful originally in applications of the theory of logic, and has become of tremendous importance in that area since the development of the computer.

BOOLEAN VARIABLE A Boolean variable in ALGOL or Pascal (equivalent to a logical variable in FORTRAN) is a variable that can have one of two possible values, true or false. Boolean variables are named in honor of George Boole (d. 1864), who was the first to describe logical operations in algebraic notation.

In languages that have them, Boolean variables can be used in place of expressions such as "X is less than Y" and "Y equals Z." For example, in Pascal, the following two programs are equivalent:

```
PROGRAM one(INPUT,OUTPUT);
VAR x,y : INTEGER;
BEGIN
   READ(x,y);
   IF x = y
      THEN WRITELN('values are equal')
END.
```

```
PROGRAM two(INPUT,OUTPUT);
VAR x,y : INTEGER; b : BOOLEAN;
BEGIN
   READ(x,y);
```

```
   b := (x = y);
   IF b THEN WRITELN('values are equal')
END.
```

Boolean variables are useful when the results of a comparison must be saved for some time after the comparison is done. Also, they can be operated on repeatedly to change their values. For example, the following Pascal program reads numbers from the input file, prints them, and reports whether a number over 100 was encountered; the Boolean variable is used somewhat as an integer would be used to keep a running total.

```
PROGRAM booleandemo(INPUT,OUTPUT);
VAR x : INTEGER;
    b : BOOLEAN;
BEGIN
   b := false;
   REPEAT
     READ(x);
     WRITELN(x);
     b := b or (x > 100)
   UNTIL EOF;
   IF b THEN
   WRITELN('There was a number over 100.')
END.
```

BOOT To boot a computer is to start it up. The term *boot* (earlier *bootstrap*) derives from the idea that the computer has to "pull itself up by the bootstraps," that is, load into memory a small program that enables it to load larger programs. Some computers have to be bootstrapped, at least partly, every time a new disk is put into the main drive, so that a directory of the contents of the disk will be present in memory.

The operation of booting a computer that has been completely shut down is known as a *dead start, cold start,* or *cold boot.* A *warm start* or *warm boot* is a restarting operation in which some of the needed programs are already in memory.

BORLAND INTERNATIONAL Borland International, a small but influential manufacturer of microcomputer software, was founded by Philippe Kahn and is headquartered in Scotts Valley, California. Its first products were Turbo Pascal, an extremely popular Pascal compiler released in 1984 (see **Turbo Pascal**), and Sidekick, a set of IBM PC utilities that are always resident in RAM and can be called up at any time, even in the middle of another task. Later products include Superkey, which is a utility for redefining the keys on the IBM PC keyboard, compilers for BASIC, C, and other languages, the spreadsheet Quattro, and the database program Paradox.

BPS BPS stands for bits per second. (See **baud.**)

BRANCH A GOTO statement in a computer program is called a branch statement because it causes the computer to change its direction and branch to a new section of the program. A *regular branch* statement does not give the computer a choice, as in the BASIC statement GOTO 50. A *conditional branch* causes the computer to follow the branch only if a specified condition is met, as in the BASIC statement

IF I = N GOTO 200

BREAKPOINT A breakpoint is a place in a program where normal execution is interrupted to allow for manual intervention, often as an aid in debugging. For example, in many versions of BASIC the command STOP introduces a breakpoint in the program.

BRING TO FRONT In some graphical editing environments, the Bring to Front puts an object or window "in front," so that it hides other objects or windows that it overlaps. One way to hide part of an object in programs like MacDraw is to create a white object with invisible borders, then put it in front of what you want to hide.

See also **overlaid windows; Send to Back.**

BROWNOUT A brownout is an extended period of insufficient power line voltage. It can damage computer equipment. (See **power line protection.**)

BUBBLE MEMORY See **magnetic bubble memory.**

BUBBLE SORT The bubble-sort method is a way of arranging a group of *n* numbers in order. The method works like this. First, examine the first two numbers in the list. If they are in order, leave them alone; if not, interchange them. Do the same thing with the second and third numbers, then with the third and fourth numbers, until you have reached the last two numbers. At this point you are guaranteed that the largest number in the list has "bubbled" up the list so that it is now the last number in the list. Next, repeat the entire procedure for the first $(n-1)$ numbers. After doing this, you will be guaranteed that the second largest number will be in the second to last place. Keep repeating the procedure until eventually all the numbers are in order.

Here is an example of a BASIC program that performs a bubble sort.

```
10  REM BUBBLE SORT PROGRAM
20  REM A IS A LIST CONTAINING N NUMBERS
30  FOR I = 1 TO N
40    FOR J = 1 TO N - I
50  IF A(J) > A(J + 1) LET T = A(J + 1):A(J + 1)
    = A(J):A(J) = T
60    NEXT J
70  NEXT I
80  END
```

BUFFER A buffer is a holding area for data. Several different things are called buffers:

(1) Buffers are areas in memory that hold data being sent to a printer or received from an RS-232 port. The idea here is that the printer is much slower than the computer, and it is helpful if the computer can prepare the data all at once, then dole it out slowly from the buffer as needed. Similarly, an RS-232 port needs a buffer because data may come in when the computer is not ready.

(2) An edit buffer is an area in memory that holds a file that is being edited. Some editors allow you to edit more than one file at once, and each file occupies its own buffer.

(3) A disk buffer is an area in memory that holds data being sent to, or received from, a disk. Some operating systems allow you to adjust the size or number of disk buffers to fit the speed of your disk drive.

(4) A keyboard buffer holds signals from keys that have been pressed but have not yet been accepted by the computer. The IBM PC keyboard buffer holds 16 keystrokes.

BUG A bug is an error in a computer program. Bugs can be either syntax errors, meaning that the rules of the programming language were not followed, or logic errors, meaning that the program does not do what it is supposed to do.

BUNDLED SOFTWARE Bundled software is software that is sold in combination with hardware and cannot be purchased spearately.

BUS The bus is the main communication avenue in a computer. It consists of a set of parallel wires to which the CPU, the memory, and all input-output devices are connected.

The bus contains one wire for each bit needed to give the addresss of a device or a location in memory, plus one wire for each bit of data to be transmitted in a single step (usually 8 bits), and additional wires that indicate what operation is being performed. For example, if the CPU wants to place the value 0 0 0 1 1 0 0 1 into memory location 1 0 1 0 0 0 0 0, it places 0 0 0 1 1 0 0 1 on the data wires, places 1 0 1 0 0 0 0 0 on the address wires, and places 1 (rather than the usual 0) on the "write memory" wire. The memory unit is responsible for recognizing the "write memory" request, decoding the address, and storing the data in the right location.

The bus can transmit data in either direction between any two components of the system. If the computer did not have a bus, it would need separate wires for all possible connections between components.

See also **Micro Channel.**

BUTTON A button is a small circle within a window that represents a choice to be made. The user makes the choice by moving the mouse pointer to the button and clicking. (See **click; window; HyperCard.**)

BYTE A byte is the amount of memory space needed to store one character, which is normally 8 bits. A computer with 8-bit bytes can distinguish $2^8 = 256$ different characters. (See **ASCII** to learn the code that many computers use to represent characters.) The size of a computer's memory is measured in *kilobytes*, where 1 kilobyte (K) = 1,024 bytes.

C

C C is a programming language developed at Bell Laboratories in the 1970s, based on the two earlier languages B (1970) and BCPL (1967). A C compiler is provided as a part of the UNIX operating system (see **UNIX**), and C was used to write most of UNIX itself. In addition, C is becoming popular as an alternative to assembly language for writing highly efficient microcomputer programs.

C is a general-purpose language like Pascal and ALGOL; but, unlike other general-purpose languages, it gives the programmer complete access to the machine's internal (bit-by-bit) representation of all types of data. This makes it convenient to perform tasks that would ordinarily require assembly language, and to perform computations in the most efficient way of which the machine is capable.

Figure 13 shows a program written in C. This language encourages structured programming; the three loop constructs are *while*, *do* (like REPEAT in Pascal), and *for*. C uses curly brackets { }, to group statements together (like BEGIN and END in Pascal). The comment delimiters, /* */, are the same as in PL/I; and, like PL/I, C uses semicolons to terminate statements rather than to separate them.

Among the most useful operators in C are + +, which adds 1 to an integer, and – –, which subtracts 1. In other words, the C statement

```
++i;
```

is equivalent to "i : = i + 1" in Pascal. The + + and – – operators can even be used within expressions to add or subtract 1 from a variable before using it in a calculation.

Another noteworthy feature of C is the #define statement, which tells the compiler to transform a particular sequence of characters into another sequence of characters wherever it occurs in the program. For instance, the sample program begins with the statement:

```
#define N 256
```

This means, that, wherever a capital N occurs in the program, the compiler will act as if the number 256 were there instead.

CACHE A cache is a place where data can be stored to avoid having

```
/* Demonstration of the C language.   Program written by

        McLowery Elrod
        Advanced Computational Methods Center
        University of Georgia
        Athens, Georgia 30602

    The driving program, main, permits the user to enter a string
    of up to 256 characters.  The string is passed to function
    chksum where a check sum for the string is computed.   */

#define N 256

main()
{
int i, n;
char str[N], *p;

/* discard any characters that have already been typed */
    while (kbhit() != 0) n = getch();

    printf("Type a character string and hit Return. ");
    printf("To quit, hit Return by itself. ");

/* repeat until empty string is entered    */
    do {

/* input string and echo it    */
        i = 0;
        p = str;
        while (i < N  &&  (n = getch()) != 13) {
            str[i++] = n;
            putch(n);  }

/* call chksum and print results        */
        if (i > 0) {
            n = chksum(str, i);
            printf("The checksum is %d. Enter next string. ",n);  }
    } while (i > 0);
}

chksum(s, n)
int n;
char *s;
{
unsigned c;

  c = 0;
  while (n-- > 0) c = c + *s++;
  c = c % 256;
  return(c);
}
```

FIGURE 13 A Sample Program Written in C

to read the data from a slower device such as a disk. For instance, a disk cache stores copies of frequently used disk sectors in RAM so that they can be read without accessing the disk.

CAD CAD is an acronym for computer-aided design. This process occurs when a computer is used for design work in fields such as engineering or architecture, with the computer's graphics capabilities substituting for work that traditionally would have been done with pencil and paper. In order to do CAD, it is necessary to have a high-resolution monitor and a software package designed for the purpose.

In order to draw a building, for example, it is necessary to enter the plans by using a graphics input device, such as a mouse or light pen. There are several advantages to having the plans in the computer:

1 The computer can automatically calculate dimensions.
2 Changes can be made (for example, adding a new wall).
3 Repetitive structures can be added easily.
4 The image can be enlarged to obtain a closeup view of a particular part, or it can be shrunk to make it possible to obtain an overall view.

If the CAD program has dimensional capability, the image can be rotated to view it from many different perspectives. (See **three-dimensional graphics.**)

CALL The CALL statement in FORTRAN, PL/I, and some assembly languages transfers control of execution to a subprogram; when the subprogram ends, the main program resumes with the statement immediately after the CALL.

Languages such as ALGOL and Pascal perform calls by simply giving the name of the routine to be called. In BASIC subroutines are called with the GOSUB command.

CALL WAITING Call Waiting is a Bell System telephone service that causes your telephone to beep if someone tries to call you while you are already using the telephone. You can then put the previous call on hold and switch to the incoming call.

These beeps disrupt transmission of computer data by telephone. To make a call that will not be interrupted by beeps, dial * 7 0, wait for a dial tone, and then dial the call in the usual way. If you are using a Hayes-compatible auto-dial modem, then you would give the number 555-1212 as "*70W555-1212" or "*70,,555-1212".

CAM CAM stands for computer-aided manufacturing, which refers to the use of a computer in a manufacturing process. For example, a computer could store a 3-dimensional representation of an object, and then control the manufacture of the object. Some of the principles of CAM are the same as with computer-aided design (see **CAD**), and sometimes a system is referred to as CAD/CAM.

CAMERA-READY A piece of artwork or a printed page is camera-ready if it is ready to be photographed and offset printed. The camera will see only black and white, not shades of gray, so the camera-ready copy must be free of smudges, dust, and stray marks. Usually, pale blue marks do not photograph, and all other colors photograph as black.

CANNED PROGRAM A canned program is a prewritten program available for purchase.

CAPACITANCE The capacitance of a capacitor is a measure of how much electric charge can be stored on the capacitor. (See **capacitor**.)

CAPACITOR A capacitor is a device for storing an electric charge on two conducting plates separated by an insulating material. The symbol for a capacitor is shown in Figure 14. The capability of a capacitor to store charge is measured in a unit called the *farad*.

　　If a capacitor is connected to a direct-current (DC) circuit, a negative charge will develop on one plate and a positive charge will develop on the other plate. No current will flow. If the capacitor is connected to an alternating current (AC) circuit, current will flow because the capacitor will alternately be charged first in one way and then in the other. The higher the AC frequency, the easier it will be for current to flow through the capacitor.

FIGURE 14 Capacitor

CARD (1) See **punched card**.

(2) A card is a printed-circuit board, especially one designed to be added to a microcomputer to provide additional functions.

CARTRIDGE Some computers, such as the Commodore 64, allow you to buy programs stored in a ROM cartridge. The cartridge can then be connected to the computer, and you can run the program.

CASE The CASE command in Pascal directs a program to execute one particular action in a list of specific actions, depending on the value of a given variable. Here is an example:

```
CASE place OF
   1 : WRITELN ('First place ! ! ! !');
   2 : WRITELN ('Second place');
   3 : WRITELN ('Third place')
END;
```

If the variable "place" has the value 1, then the first WRITELN statement will be executed, and so on.

CATALOG A catalog is a list of the contents of a disk. (See **directory**.)

CB SIMULATOR On CompuServe, the CB Simulator is a mode in which dozens of people at different locations can converse with each other by typing on their computers, much as if they were using CB (citizen's band) radios.

CCITT The CCITT (Comité Consultatif Internationale Télegraphique et Téléphonique) sets international standards for data communication. (See **V series; X.21**.)

CD-ROM CD-ROM stands for compact disk read-only memory, which refers to the use of compact disks similar to audio compact disks as a computer storage medium. Audio compact disks became increasingly popular in the mid-1980s. In an audio CD, sound is "digitized" by representing it by a series of numbers corresponding to the amplitude of the sound at a particular time. The binary code for these numbers is then etched in the form of small pits on an aluminum disk about 4½ inches in diameter that is covered with a transparent plastic coating. In order to play the music, the compact disk is inserted in a player that uses a laser to detect which spots on the disk are reflective. Since there is no physical contact with the aluminum surface, there is less wear. By contrast, a traditional record represents sound in analog form, where the height of the groove corresponds to the amplitude of the sound.

A computer CD uses the same principle to store information. Computer CDs have capacities of several hundred megabytes (10 to 50 times as much information as can be stored on a typical hard disk, or a thousand times as much as can be stored on a typical 5 ¼-inch floppy disk). Computer CDs are "read-only" because the user cannot store information on the disk; they can only be used to retrieve the information that has been stored on them by the supplier. However, in the future it may be economical for microcomputer users to obtain compact disks that can be both read from and written to.

The information contained in an encyclopedia can be placed on a compact disk. With the appropriate software, you can search through the CD and find information on a specific topic. The CD might contain graphics as well as text. Other examples of information available from CD suppliers include indexes to periodicals and journals and financial data for corporations.

CENTRAL PROCESSING UNIT See CPU.

CENTRONICS INTERFACE Centronics interface is a standard format for parallel data transmission to and from microcomputer equipment, especially printers (originally used on Centronics printers).

CGA The IBM Color/Graphics Adapter (CGA) was for a long time the most popular video card for the IBM PC. Software written for the CGA will usually run on the EGA, VGA, and MCGA. (See **video modes [IBM PC]**.)

The CGA was designed for video games, not office applications. The lettering on the screen is too blurry for extended sessions of word processing or programming. Office workers who need graphics should use the EGA or VGA with a suitable high-resolution monitor.

CHARACTER A character is any symbol that can be stored and processed by a computer. For example, A, 3, : are computer characters. The ASCII coding system is one way of representing characters on a computer. (See **ASCII**.)

CHARACTER STRING A character string is a group of characters, such as "JOHN SMITH" or "R2D2". (See **string**.)

CHECKSUM When information is transferred from one computer to another, or is stored and then retrieved, it is important to verify that the information has been transmitted correctly. One way to do this would be to transmit all of the information twice; if there were an error, the two copies would almost certainly disagree. However, this is too time-consuming to be practical.

A better approach is to divide the information into small packets, such as lines of text or disk sectors, and compute a checksum for each packet. A checksum is a number that would almost certainly be different if the information were altered. One simple way to compute a checksum is to add up the ASCII codes for all the characters of data (see **ASCII**) and take the result modulo 256. (For a program that does this, see **C**.) Since this method gives only 256 possible checksums, it is quite possible for two different packets to have the same checksum. However, it is very unlikely that a transmission error would change a packet of information into another packet with the same checksum. Hence errors can be detected by transmitting the checksum along with each packet, and then testing whether the checksum matches the data actually received.

Checksums are used in the XMODEM protocol for error-free transmission of data by telephone. (See **XMODEM**.)

CHIP See **integrated circuit**.

CIRCUIT A circuit is a complete path for an electric current. A circuit must contain a power source, such as a battery or a generator. Electrons will flow from the negative power-supply terminal through a conducting medium (such as copper wire) to the positive power supply terminal. A useful circuit must also contain some sort of switch to determine whether or not it will be on, and some device that has resistance, known as the *load*. A circuit with no load is called a *short circuit*.

CIRCUIT DIAGRAM A circuit diagram is a schematic picture of an electronic circuit, using symbols to represent electronic components. The purpose of the diagram is to make it as easy as possible for people to trace the flow of current, rather than to exactly reproduce the physical locations of the components in the real circuit. (See **electronic components**.)

CIRCULARITY A problem of circularity arises when a computer cannot finish a task until it has already finished it—in other words, an impossible situation arises. For example, in Lotus 1-2-3, a circularity problem arises if you enter the formula 2*B1 into cell A1 and then enter the formula A1/2 into cell B1. In order to evaluate cell A1, the computer needs to have the value for cell B1; but in order to evaluate cell B1, it needs to evaluate cell A1. Therefore, a circularity warning message will be displayed.

CIRCUMFLEX The circumflex accent is the mark "^" written above a letter (e.g., ê). The ASCII character "^" is sometimes called a circumflex.

CLEAR (1) To clear a flip-flop or a memory location is to set it to zero.

(2) To clear the screen of a CRT means to cause it to go blank. In many versions of BASIC, the command CLS clears the screen.

(3) In some BASIC interpreters and other interactive environments, the CLEAR command either sets all variables to zero, or frees any memory that has been allocated to specific purposes, such as arrays.

CLICK To click a mouse is to press one button very briefly (usually the leftmost button if there is more than one). By contrast, see **press**. See also **double-click**.

CLIP ART Clip art is artwork that can be freely reproduced. Many of the pictures in newspaper advertisements come from clip art. Several clip art collections are available on disk for various drawing, painting, and desktop publishing programs.

CLIPBOARD On the Macintosh and in Microsoft Windows, the clipboard is an area to which information can be copied in order to transfer it from one application program to another. For instance, the clipboard can be used to transfer text from a word processor into a drawing program.

CLOCK (1) The clock of a computer is a circuit that generates a series of evenly spaced pulses. All the switching activity in the computer occurs while the clock is sending out a pulse. Between pulses the electronic devices in the computer are allowed to stabilize. A computer with a faster clock rate is able to perform more operations per second. Powerful computers are now capable of performing an operation every 10 to 20 nanoseconds, and a microprocessor can perform an operation in less than 0.5 microsecond. The clock speed of a computer is often given in megahertz (MHz), where 1 MHz = 1,000,000 cycles per second. The fastest mainframe computers have a clock speed of about 50 MHz. The original IBM PC had a clock speed of 4.77 MHz. More recent microcomputers run at speeds of up to 25 MHz.

(2) A real-time clock is a circuit within a computer that keeps track of the date and time. Some computers have real-time clocks that run even when the computers are turned off.

CLOCK/CALENDAR The original IBM PC and XT keep track of the time and date as long as they are running, but they lose this information as soon as they are shut down. The PC AT and PS/2 have built-in clock/calendars that are run by batteries independent of other power supplies.

Similar clock calendars have been built for the PC and XT. With these cards, it is necessary to run a special program every time the computer boots up. This program reads the battery-operated clock and sets the PC's original clock to match it. A command to run this program is usually placed in the AUTOEXEC.BAT file.

CLONE A clone is a computer that is an exact imitation of another (e.g., a clone of the IBM PC), or a software product that exactly imitates another. In biology, a clone is an organism that has exactly the same genetic material as another, such as a plant grown from a cutting.

CLOSED (1) A *switch* is closed when it is turned on, that is, when it is set so that current can flow through it. (see Figure 15).

(2) A *file* is closed when it is not available for data to be read from it or written to it.

FIGURE 15 Closed Switch. Current can flow.

CLUSTER A cluster is a group of disk sectors that are treated as a unit. (See **lost cluster**.)

CMOS CMOS (<u>C</u>omplementary <u>M</u>etal-<u>O</u>xide <u>S</u>emiconductor) is a type of integrated circuit noted for its extremely low power consumption and its vulnerability to damage from static electricity. CMOS devices are used in digital watches, pocket calculators, microprocessors, and computer memories.

CMOS RAM CMOS RAM is a special kind of low-power memory that stores information about the configuration of an IBM PC AT or PS/2. It is operated by a battery so that it does not go blank when the machine is turned off.

CMS CMS (Conversational Monitor System) is an operating system for IBM mainframe computers, usually used in combination with VM/SP (see **VM/SP**). The resulting combination, known as VM/CMS, gives the user a working environment much like a large, powerful microcomputer that will run software originally designed for other IBM mainframe operating systems (OS, DOS).

Each VM/CMS user has a virtual disk, that is, one large real disk file that simulates the function of a disk drive on which many small files can be stored. VM/CMS file names are of the form XXXXXXXX YYYYYYYY Z, where XXXXXXXX is an identifying name, YYYYYYYY indicates the type of file, and Z indicates which of several virtual disks the file is on (A for the user's own disk, or a letter such as S for a system disk accesible to all users). In addition, there is a virtual printer for sending files to the system printer, and a virtual card punch and card reader, used respectively to send files to, and receive them from, other users.

Some common CMS commands are as follows:
XEDIT XXXXXXXX YYYYYYYY Z
   Edit the file referred to. (Leave the editor by typing FILE
   in the command line at the bottom of the screen.)
FLIST (full-screen terminals only)
LISTFILE (all types of terminals)
   List the files on the user's virtual disk.
QUERY SEARCH
   List the virtual disks that the user has access to.
HELP Display information about other commands.

COAXIAL CABLE Coaxial cable consists of a single conductor surrounded by insulation and a conductive shield. The shield prevents the cable from picking up or emitting electrical noise. (By contrast, see **twisted pair**.)

Coaxial cables are rated for their impedance, given in ohms, which indicates how the inductance and capacitance of the cable interact. For instance, RG-58 cable is rated at 52 ohms. This impedance cannot be measured with an ohmmeter.

COBOL COBOL is a programming language for business data processing, developed in the early 1960s by several computer manufacturers and the U.S. Department of Defense. As the sample program (Figure 16) shows, COBOL statements resemble English sentences, and the structure of the program requires that some documentation be included. COBOL programs are long and wordy, but easy to read; this readability makes it easy for programmers other than the original author to make corrections or changes.

A COBOL program consists of the IDENTIFICATION DIVISION, which gives some mandatory documentation, such as the program name; the ENVIRONMENT DIVISION, which describes the machine environment; the DATA DIVISION, for data structures and input-output formats; and the PROCEDURE DIVISION, for the algorithm.

COBOL was the first programming language to introduce the record data structure (see **data structure**) and to recognize that the data structures used by a program are as important as the algorithm. In the file section of the program, each file is given not only a name, but also a record format specifying how the data on each line are to be arranged. In the sample program of Figure 16, each record of the input file contains a 4-digit number that is read into the variable X-IN, followed by 76 characters that are assigned the dummy name FILLER, indicating that they are to be discarded. Each record of the output file contains a 4-digit number called X-OUT, followed by a 50-character string called VERDICT.

In many COBOL programs, practically all of the variables are declared in this way. Programs that do a substantial amount of computation can also include a working-storage section to declare variables that are not associated with files.

COBOL is oriented toward reading and writing records of fixed length, each of whose components is also of fixed length. It is difficult to write a COBOL program that accepts input items consisting of variable numbers of characters. (Contrast, for example, the INPUT statement in BASIC, which makes no assumptions about the number of characters typed.) Complex numerical calculation is also difficult in COBOL. However, for applications that involve mostly reading and writing files, with small amounts of computation (e.g., rejecting certain records or keeping totals), COBOL programs can be quite efficient.

One important innovation of COBOL is the INCLUDE statement, which tells the compiler to read another file and treat its contents as part of the program. This makes it easy to use the same piece of code in more than one program. The INCLUDE statement is often used with complicated record descriptions; the programmer need write the record description of a file only once and then include it in every program that processes the file.

The procedure division of every COBOL program is divided into paragraphs, each of which has a name (START-UP, READ-A-NUMBER, etc., in the example). The PERFORM statement (not used in the sample program) makes it possible to treat any paragraph or group of paragraphs as a subroutine; this facilitates structure programming. *Structured COBOL* is a style of programming in which this technique and others are used to create a modular, easy-to-understand program. (See **structured programming**.)

CODEVIEW CodeView is a symbolic debugger produced by Microsoft. If allows the programmer to step through a program, interrupting it at any point and examining or changing the values of variables. CodeView analyzes the source code and object code and works through them together so that even though the program has been compiled, you can work with it as if you were editing the source program. This can only be done if the program was compiled with a Microsoft compiler or another compiler designed to be CodeView-compatible.

CODING Coding is the process of writing an algorithm or other problem-solving procedure in a computer programming language.

COLD BOOT, COLD START See boot.

COLLATING SEQUENCE The collating sequence of a computer is the "alphabetical order" of all its characters (including digits, punctuation marks, and other special characters). The collating sequence is important because it is often necessary to sort ("alphabetize") information that includes characters other than letters.

```
IDENTIFICATION DIVISION.                                              COB00010
                                                                      COB00020
PROGRAM-ID.        PRIME.                                             COB00030
AUTHOR.            M. A. COVINGTON.                                   COB00040
DATE-WRITTEN.      1982 FEBRUARY 15.                                  COB00050
REMARKS.                                                             COB00060
     THIS PROGRAM READS A LIST OF INTEGERS                           COB00070
     (EACH EXPRESSED AS FOUR DIGITS IN THE                           COB00080
     FIRST FOUR COLUMNS OF A CARD IMAGE)                             COB00090
     AND REPORTS ON WHETHER THEY ARE PRIME.                          COB00100
     THIS IS ANSI COBOL.                                            COB00110
                                                                      COB00120
ENVIRONMENT DIVISION.                                                 COB00130
                                                                      COB00140
INPUT-OUTPUT SECTION.                                                 COB00150
                                                                      COB00160
FILE-CONTROL.                                                         COB00170
     SELECT INFILE  ASSIGN TO UT-S-SYSIN.                            COB00180
     SELECT OUTFILE ASSIGN TO UT-S-SYSPRINT.                         COB00190
                                                                      COB00200
DATA DIVISION.                                                        COB00210
                                                                      COB00220
FILE SECTION.                                                         COB00230
                                                                      COB00240
FD   INFILE.                                                          COB00250
01   INRECORD.                                                        COB00260
     02  X-IN     PICTURE IS 9999.                                   COB00270
     02  FILLER   PICTURE IS X(76).                                  COB00280
                                                                      COB00290
FD   OUTFILE.                                                         COB00300
01   OUTRECORD.                                                       COB00310
     02  X-OUT    PICTURE IS ZZZ9.                                   COB00320
     02  VERDICT  PICTURE IS X(50).                                  COB00330
                                                                      COB00340
WORKING-STORAGE SECTION.                                              COB00350
                                                                      COB00360
77   X          PICTURE IS S9999999, USAGE IS COMPUTATIONAL.         COB00370
77   REM        PICTURE IS S9999999, USAGE IS COMPUTATIONAL.         COB00380
77   QUOT       PICTURE IS S9999999, USAGE IS COMPUTATIONAL.         COB00390
77   HALF       PICTURE IS S9999999, USAGE IS COMPUTATIONAL.         COB00400
77   DIV        PICTURE IS S9999999, USAGE IS COMPUTATIONAL.         COB00410
                                                                      COB00420
                                                                      COB00430
```

FIGURE 16

FIGURE 16 Continued

```
PROCEDURE DIVISION.                                               COB00440
                                                                 COB00450
START-UP.                                                        COB00460
    OPEN INPUT INFILE, OUTPUT OUTFILE.                           COB00470
    MOVE SPACES TO VERDICT.                                      COB00480
READ-A-NUMBER.                                                   COB00490
    READ INFILE, AT END GO TO FINISH.                           COB00500
    MOVE X-IN TO X.                                              COB00510
    IF X GREATER THAN 0 GO TO CHECK-IF-EVEN.                    COB00520
    MOVE ' IS NOT A NATURAL NUMBER.' TO VERDICT.                COB00530
    GO TO WRITE-IT.                                             COB00540
CHECK-IF-EVEN.                                                   COB00550
    IF X EQUAL TO 1 GO TO VERDICT-IS-YES.                       COB00560
    IF X EQUAL TO 2 GO TO VERDICT-IS-YES.                       COB00570
    DIVIDE X BY 2 GIVING HALF REMAINDER REM.                    COB00580
    IF REM EQUAL TO 0 GO TO VERDICT-IS-NO.                      COB00590
    MOVE 1 TO DIV.                                              COB00600
TRY-ANOTHER.                                                     COB00610
    ADD 2 TO DIV.                                               COB00620
    DIVIDE X BY DIV GIVING QUOT REMAINDER REM.                  COB00630
    IF REM EQUAL TO 0 GO TO VERDICT-IS-NO.                      COB00640
    IF DIV GREATER THAN HALF GO TO VERDICT-IS-YES.             COB00650
    GO TO TRY-ANOTHER.                                          COB00660
VERDICT-IS-YES.                                                  COB00670
    MOVE ' IS PRIME.             ' TO VERDICT.                  COB00680
    GO TO WRITE-IT.                                             COB00690
VERDICT-IS-NO.                                                   COB00700
    MOVE ' IS NOT PRIME.         ' TO VERDICT.                  COB00710
WRITE-IT.                                                        COB00720
    MOVE X TO X-OUT.                                            COB00730
    WRITE OUTRECORD.                                            COB00740
    GO TO READ-A-NUMBER.                                        COB00750
FINISH.                                                          COB00760
    CLOSE INFILE, OUTFILE.                                      COB00770
    STOP RUN.                                                   COB00780
```

The collating sequence of a computer is the same as the order of the numeric codes for the characters. (See **ASCII; EBCDIC.**)

COLLECTOR The collector is one of the three areas in a bipolar transistor. (See **transistor.**)

COLUMN MOVE The operation of moving material to the left or right within a file (e.g., moving the material in columns 10–20 into columns 5–15 on several consecutive lines in one step) is known as a column move. (See **editor.**)

COM FILE In CP/M and MS-DOS (PC-DOS), a COM file is a file whose name ends with ".COM" and which contains a nonrelocatable machine code program. To execute the program, type the name of the file without the final ".COM"; for example, to execute AAAA.COM, type AAAA.

In MS-DOS, COM files are usually used for small programs and for programs converted from CP/M. EXE files are used for larger programs and for programs that are OS/2 compatible. (See **EXE file.**)

In VAX/VMS, a COM file contains a list of commands to be executed, like a BAT file in MS-DOS (see **BAT file**).

COMDEX COMDEX (Computer Dealers' Exposition) is a major computer show sponsored by The Interface Group, Inc., and held annually in several locations. New microcomputer products are often introduced at COMDEX.

COMMAND KEY On the Macintosh, the Command key is the key marked with a cloverleaflike symbol. It is used like a shift key to change the meanings of other keys or to perform special functions. For example, you can print a picture of the current screen by holding down Command and Shift and pressing 4. If you press 3 instead, a picture of the current screen will be saved as a MacPaint document.

COMMENT A comment is information in a computer program that is ignored by the computer and is included only for the benefit of human readers. Here is how several computer languages identify comments:

BASIC	REM statements
Fortran	Lines beginning with the letter C in Column 1
C. PL/I	Material bracketed by /* */

Pascal   Material bracketed by { } or (* *)
Assembly languages   Material to the right of the statement,
                                often set off by a semicolon.

Comments reflect the fact that programs are written to be read by human beings, not computers—if we could write in the language that best suited the computer, we would not need compilers to translate BASIC, Pascal, and other programming languages into machine code.

Opinions vary as to how comments are best used. Some software engineers hold that a clearly written program needs few comments. This is certainly true in itself, but it is often impossible to write a program so clearly that another programmer—or even the author, months or years later—can tell at a glance how it works. Here are some general rules for using comments effectively, with the first four examples in Pascal:

1 Begin each program, procedure, or function with a comment stating exactly what it is supposed to do. For example:

```
PROCEDURE swap(VAR x,y : INTEGER);
   {Interchange values of x and y.}
VAR t : INTEGER;
BEGIN
   t := x; x:=y; y:=t
END;
```

A comment of this type may run to many lines or even pages.

2 Use comments to answer questions that the reader may have in mind. For example:

```
q := SIN(x/57.29578);
{x is in degrees,
   sine function expects radians.}
```

Here the comment explains the mysterious number 57.29578.

3 Do not state the obvious. This is an example of bad comment usage:

```
x := x + 1; {Add 1 to x.}
```

Here the comment adds no information.

4 Avoid misleading comments; in debugging a program, resist the temptation to believe that the statements do what the comments say they do. Here is an example of a misleading comment:

```
{ Interchange values of x and y. }
t :=x; x:= y; y:=x
```

In spite of the comments, x and y do not come out interchanged; both end up with the value that y had at the beginning.

5   In assembly language, explain step by step what the program is doing. Assembly language is never easy to read, and the reader needs all the help you can give. Again, however, don't state the obvious. The following example is in 8086 assembly language:

```
   MOV CX,5 ;  initialize loop counter
I: INT 10H   ;  perform video interrupt
   LOOP I    ;  decrement CX, repeat if
             ;  nonzero
```

Here the reader of the program may not remember that INT 10H requests video services on the IBM PC, or that the LOOP instruction uses the CX register for its counter. But to explain MOV CX,5 as "put 5 in CX" would be pointless.

COMMODORE Commodore Business Machines, Inc., of West Chester, Pennsylvania, has produced a popular home computer, the Commodore 64, and its successor, the Commodore 128. These computers can be programmed in BASIC and can run numerous educational and game programs. The Commodore 128 has 128K RAM, which is expandable. It can run programs designed to run on the Commodore 64 as well as programs written for the CP/M operating system. Commodore also produces the Amiga (see **Amiga**).

COMMON LOGARITHM See **logarithm**.

COMPAQ Compaq Computer Corporation of Houston, Texas, produces a number of IBM PC-compatible computers. The original Compaq was the first portable PC-compatible computer, and Compaq became one of the fastest-growing companies in history as its products developed a reputation for high quality. More recent products include the Deskpro 386/25, which contains an 80386 microprocessor with a very fast clock speed of 25 MHz;

and the Deskpro 386S, which is based on the 386SX microprocessor, a more economical version of the 386. In 1988 Compaq led a group of other computer companies in the development of an alternative bus to the Micro Channel used in some IBM PS/2 computers.

COMPATIBLE (1) Two *devices* are compatible if they can work together. For example, a particular brand of printer is compatible with a particular computer to which it can be connected. This type of compatibility might be called *hardware compatibility*.

(2) Two *computers* are said to be compatible if they can run the same programs. It is important to keep in mind that there are different degrees of compatibility. Many computers claim to be compatible with the IBM PC, but some IBM PC programs contain hardware-dependent features that will not run correctly on non-IBM computers. If you are interested in purchasing one of the compatible computers, you should check to make sure that the specific programs most important to you will run correctly on the machine you are considering. See also **PC compatibility**.

COMPILE-TIME ERROR A compile-time error is an error in a computer program that is caught in the process of compiling the program. For example, a compile-time error occurs if the syntax of the language has been violated. For contrast, see **run-time error**.

COMPILER A compiler is a computer program that translates FORTRAN, Pascal, or a similar high-level programming language into machine language. It contrasts with an *interpreter*, which executes high-level-language statements as it reads them. The high-level-langauge program fed into the compiler is called the *source program*; the generated machine language program is the *object program*.

On mainframe computers, almost all programming languages are compiled; interpreters are uncommon. However, most microcomputers run BASIC by means of an interpreter. The main reason is that a compiler must translate the entire program before executing any of it, a process that can take several minutes, whereas an interpreter can begin executing the program immediately.

On the other hand, compiled programs run 10 to 1,000 times faster than interpreted programs. Moreover, the machine-language program that the compiler produces usually requires no further help from the compiler; you do not need the compiler in order to run it. For this reason, most commercial software packages, such as Perfect Writer and WordStar, are distributed as compiled object programs.

Some criteria often used in evaluating the performance of compilers are the following:

1 Reliability. Is the compiler free of bugs? Does it conform to the official standards for the language that it implements?
2 Efficiency of compilation. How much memory and time are needed to compile a given program?
3 Efficiency of object code. How much memory and time are needed to run the object program? (This varies widely from compiler to compiler, even when the same program is compiled on the same computer. Memory requirements are especially variable because some compilers include large subroutine packages in all object programs, whether they are needed or not, while others are more selective.)
4 Optimization. Can the compiler detect unnecessary repetitions and other faults in the source program and rearrange the instructions to make computation more efficient? This feature is normally provided only on the most sophisticated compilers.
5 File size. With microcomputers, it is often important to know whether the entire compiler package will fit on one diskette. Also, object programs should occupy no more disk space than necessary.

COMPLEMENT The 2-complement of a k-digit binary number x is $2^k - x$. (See **binary subtraction**.) The 2-complement of a binary number can be found by reversing each digit and then adding 1 to the result. For example, the 2-complement of 1 1 0 1 0 1 is 0 0 1 0 1 1.

COMPOSITE VIDEO A composite video signal is the kind of video signal used in a TV set. The whole signal is transmitted on one wire. By contrast, an RGB signal has separate wires for red, green, and blue. (See **monitor**.)

COMPUSERVE The CompuServe Consumer Information Service, based in Columbus, Ohio, is accessible by telephone from anywhere in the United States. Users communicate with Compu-

Serve by using computer terminals or microcomputers with modems. (See **modem**.)

CompuServe offers information on a wide range of subjects, including weather forecasts, airline schedules, the stock market, and a medical question-and-answer service. In addition, CompuServe subscribers can send messages to each other, either in private or via many special-interest forums where anyone can read, and respond to, the messages.

Many CompuServe forums (or SIGs, "<u>S</u>pecial-<u>I</u>nterest <u>G</u>roups") deal with computing as a hobby or profession. Members can exchange programs by modem; CompuServe maintains large libraries of programs for this purpose.

COMPUTER A computer is a machine capable of executing instructions on data. The distinguishing feature of a computer is its ability to store its own instructions. This ability makes it possible for a computer to perform many operations without the need for a person to type in new instructions each time. Modern computers are made of high-speed electronic components that enable the computer to perform thousands of operations each second.

See **computers, history** of for a brief review of the history of computers, and **computer design** for a description of how computers are put together. Also see **word processing, spreadsheet,** and **graphics** for discussion of applications of computers, and **programming language, BASIC, C, COBOL, FORTH, FORTRAN, Pascal, PL/I** and **APL** for examples of how instructions are written for computers.

COMPUTER DESIGN A computer is best understood by viewing it at a series of levels (see Figure 17). At the basic level are the underlying electronic components, such as *transistors* and *integrated circuits*. These components are used to build logic circuits, such as *gates* and *flip-flops*. These logic circuits are used for simple arithmetic operations, such as arranging a circuit that can add two numbers (see **binary addition**). An adding circuit can serve as the basis for designing a computer that can perform complicated arithmetic instructions.

A machine language program is a set of instructions written in a binary code. These instructions tell the computer when to transfer data into and out of memory, and what operations to perform upon them. A translator can be added to convert programs written in a programming language such as BASIC into machine language, so that a person using the computer needs to

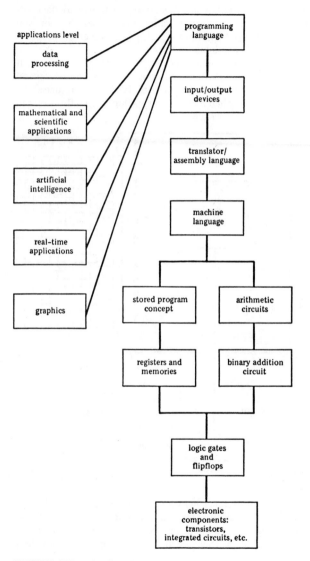

FIGURE 17 Levels of Understanding Computers

know only the program language, rather than the way the computer itself works. At the application level, a user does not even need to know how to program if a clearly documented, prepackaged program is available for use.

Figure 18 shows a schematic design for a simple computer. It consists of a memory (which can store 128 16-bit words), several registers, and a bus, or connecting wire. Each register, such as the accumulator, is formed by a row of flip-flops. Each flip-flop can be in either state 1 or state 0.

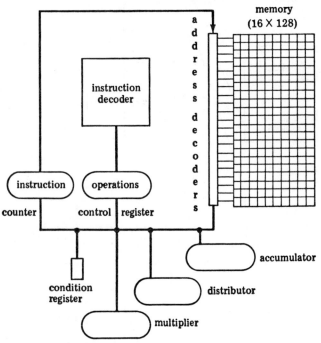

FIGURE 18

The major difference between a computer and a calculator is that a computer can store its own instructions. The instructions, written in machine language binary code, are stored in memory along with the data. (See **assembly language**.) The instruction counter register holds the address of the next instruction to be executed. A computer operates by alternating between two cycles; the fetch cycle and the execute cycle. During the fetch cycle, the computer checks the address stored in the instruction counter register. Then it transfers the contents of that memory address to the operations control register. The operations control register is connected to an instruction decoder circuit that figures out what the binary coded instruction means, and then tells the computer what to do. Then the computer goes into the execute cycle to carry out the instruction.

The simple computer of Figure 18 contains a 1-bit condition register. The value of the condition register will be 1 if some specified condition is true. If the computer faces a conditional branch instruction, it will execute that instruction only if the value of the condition register is 1. This computer also has a distributor register and a multiplier register to help with multiplication. A real computer will have several additional registers. Also, to be very useful a real computer must be connected to input and output devices, such as printers or terminals, so that it can communicate with the outside world.

COMPUTER SECURITY The advent of personal computers has made it easy for important business records or confidential data to be lost, sabotaged, or misused. Computers need protection from the following kinds of hazards:

1 *Machine failure.* Make backups of important files frequently. Every disk drive in the world *will* one day fail, losing all data.

2 *Physical hazards.* Protect the computer from fire, flood, and similar hazards, and store backups at a remote location. Remember, too, that the machine can be stolen.

3 *Operator error.* It is easy to delete information accidentally. This hazard can be minimized with software that retains original files while altered copies are being made.

4 *Computer tampering.* Can someone come in and alter your records without your knowing it? Bear in mind that large numbers of people know how to use popular business software packages. If possible, use software that keeps records of changes—recording who made them when—and requires validation (such as a password) to make large changes.

5 *Malicious programming.* Some computer crimes have been perpetrated by programmers who did such things as collect all the money that was lost by rounding interest payments to the nearest penny. A clever bookkeeping system, run by a dishonest programmer, can easily conceal abuse.

6 *Dial-up "break-ins."* This is a hazard only with computers that are physically connected to telephone lines and are programmed to answer incoming calls. Use software that requires users to type passwords and limits their access to the system. The UNIX operating system, designed originally for use in laboratories where no security was needed, is generally thought to be particularly vulnerable. Be aware of the possibility of break-ins through networks of computers.

7 *Easily guessed passwords.* The simplest approach to securing a computer is to require users to type passwords when they sign on. However, some users are sure to choose passwords that are excessively easy to guess, such as the names of their spouses or children. Also, if a user signs on the computer and then leaves the terminal unattended, others can tamper with it without typing the password.

8 *Excessive security measures.* Excessive attempts to build automated security into a computer can easily make the computer so hard to use that productivity is crippled. In the final analysis, all computer security depends on human trustworthiness. Concentrate on securing the people, not the machine. That is, ensure that employees are trustworthy and that strangers have no access to the machine, then give authorized users all the access they need to do their job effectively.

COMPUTERS, HISTORY OF Mechanical computation aids date back many centuries. The abacus, on which information is stored by moving beads along rods, was one of the earliest calculating devices. Blaise Pascal developed an adding machine in 1642 that used toothed wheels to handle carries from one digit to the next. Charles Babbage developed the concept of a stored program computer when he designed the "analytical engine" in 1833. Unfortunately, the mechanical devices of his day could not be made to work reliably, so the "analytical engine" was never completed.

An important data processing device, the punched card, was developed by Herman Hollerith to help the U.S. Census Bureau tabulate the census of 1890. (See **punched card**.) The first electronic digital computer was the ENIAC (Electronic Numerical Integrator and Calculator) which was built for the U.S. Army in 1946, largely because of the need to calculate ballistics tables. The ENIAC was programmed by plugging in cables to connect different units. In 1945 John von Neumann introduced the modern concept of a stored program computer, in which the computer memory can store both programs and data.

Once the concept was established, major improvements were made by developing smaller and more reliable electronic components. The ENIAC was a huge machine made with vacuum tubes. The invention of the transistor in the late 1940s made it possible to build much smaller computers that needed less cooling. Continued improvements in integrated circuits, which were first developed in the late 1950s, made it possible to continue the miniaturization of computers.

An important advance occurred in the mid 1970s when the first microcomputers were built. Previously, all computers had been large and expensive. Microcomputers are small enough and cheap enough that they can be purchased by small businesses and individuals. A microcomputer is built around a microprocessor chip, such as the Z80 or Intel 8088, which contains all of the logic circuits for the computer in a single integrated circuit. After microcomputers became common, innovation continued as new uses were developed for computers in businesses, schools, and homes. New software packages were developed to play games, teach children, perform spreadsheet calculations, and accomplish many other tasks.

CONCATENATION Concatenation is the operation of joining two (or more) character strings together, end to end. For example:

```
"ABC" concatenated with "DEF" equals
   "ABCDEF".
"GEORGE" concatenated with "WASHINGTON"
   equals "GEORGEWASHINGTON".
"ABRAHAM " concatenated with "LINCOLN"
   equals "ABRAHAM LINCOLN".
```

CONCURRENT PROCESSING Concurrent processing is what happens when 2 computations appear to be carried out at the same time, but in fact a single CPU is rapidly switching its attention back and forth between them. See also **timesharing; multi-tasking; parallel processing.**

CONDITIONAL BRANCH A conditional branch is a statement that causes a branch (GOTO) instruction to be executed only if a specified condition is true. An example of a conditional branch in BASIC is

```
60 IF N > 25 GOTO 120
```

First, the computer checks to see whether the condition $N > 25$ is true. If it is, then the computer will jump to statement number 120 and start executing there.

CONDUCTOR A conductor is a material in which electric current can flow. In order for a material to be a conductor the electrons must not be too tightly bound to their atoms.

CONFIG In MS-DOS (PC-DOS), the file CONFIG.SYS contains information about the machine configuration, including the type of keyboard (if not the standard U.S. model) and the amount of memory to be set aside for disk buffers. CONFIG.SYS is read only when the machine boots up.

CONFIGURE To configure a computer or program is to set it up to be used in a particular way. Many commerical software packages have to be "configured," or installed; this involves setting them up for a particular machine (including video card and printer) and for a particular user's preferences.

CONSTANT A constant is a value that remains unchanged during the execution of a program. Literal expressions, such as 3.5 and "GEORGE WASHINGTON", are constants because they always stand for the same value. In BASIC any item identified with a letter or other name is a variable whose value can be changed. In Pascal, however, it is possible to define names to represent constants.

CONTEXT-SENSITIVE HELP Many computer programs include a help key that gives you extra information. The help key is context-sensitive if its behavior depends on what you are doing at the time you press it. For example, a context-sensitive help key will give you information about how to edit if you press it while editing, or how to print if you press it while preparing to print.

CONTIGUOUS Two things are contiguous if they are next to each other. For instance, the states of North and South Dakota are contiguous, but Texas and Maine are not.

Most computers can store a disk file in either contiguous or noncontiguous sectors. (See **disk**.) Access is slower if the sectors are not contiguous, since to get from one part of the file to another, the computer must jump from one part of the disk to another.

In general, a copy of a noncontiguous file will be made on contiguous sectors if space is available.

CONTROL DATA CORPORATION Control Data Corporation is a computer manufacturer specializing in very large computers for complicated scientific purposes, such as weather forecasting. Control Data is also the developer of the computer-based education system called PLATO. The company is headquartered in Minneapolis. (See **CYBER**.)

CONTROL KEY The control (or CTRL or CNTL) key is a special key on the left-hand side of many computer keyboards. When it is pressed in conjunction with another key, it gives the other key a new meaning that depends on the program in use. For example, when you are using WordStar, pressing control-K-D causes the computer to save your document on the disk. If you are operating under CP/M or MS-DOS, typing control-P will cause everything that appears on the screen to be printed on the printer.

COPROCESSOR A coprocessor is a separate circuit inside a computer that adds additional functions to the CPU (central processing unit) or handles extra work while the CPU is doing something else.

Some computers have **graphics coprocessors** to do some of the computation necessary for displaying images on the screen. As a result, complex pictures can be displayed and changed more quickly than would be possible if the CPU had to do all the computation.

IBM-PC-compatible computers often use a **math coprocessor**, the Intel 8087, 80287, or 80387, to perform floating-point arithmetic. The coprocessor has no effect when the computer is running an ordinary program. However, programs that contain instructions for the math coprocessor can perform arithmetic much more quickly than programs that use the CPU alone.

In general, software that is designed to use the **math coprocessor** will not run at all if the coprocessor is not installed in the machine. However, some programs will sense whether the coprocessor is present and use the CPU alone if the coprocessor is not there.

Similar floating-point coprocessors exist for a variety of other computers, including the VAX.

COPY To copy information is to transfer it from one place to another, leaving the original unchanged. In many editing and drawing programs, "copy" means either of two things:
(1) To copy material from one place to another;
(2) To copy material from the document being edited into a holding area, from which you can then "paste" it elsewhere. (See **cut; paste.**)

COPY The COPY command under MS-DOS makes a copy of a disk file. For example, the command

```
COPY PGM.SRC PGMC2.SRC
```

takes the old file (PGM.SRC) and makes a copy of it under the name PGMC2.SRC. Two other examples are as follows:

```
COPY A:*.BAS B:
```

copies all files on drive A whose names end in .BAS onto drive B.

```
COPY A:*.* B:
```

copies all files from drive A onto drive B.

COPY PROTECTION A copy-protected disk cannot be copied by the software normally used to copy disks on a particular computer. Copy protection is usually achieved by changing the size of some of the sectors on the disk. Its purpose is to prevent unauthorized copying of computer programs.

Copy protection has several disadvantages and is becoming less common on newer programs. Because copy-protected disks use the disk drives in ways other than the way the manufacturer intended, they are often unreadable on later model machines. Further, if there is no way to make a backup disk, the software becomes unusable when the original disk wears out.

There are several commercial programs that enable you to duplicate copy-protected disks or to defeat the copy protection.

U.S. copyright law explicitly permits the making of backup disks, whether or not the original disks are copy protected.

COPYRIGHT Copyright law restricts the copying of books, magazines, recordings, computer programs, and other materials, in order to protect the original author's right to ownership of, and compensation for reproduction of, an original work. Most computer programs are protected not only by copyright but also by a software license (see **software license; free software**).

In the U.S., a program is protected by copyright if it contains a notice of the form

Copyright 1988 John Doe

or

© 1988 John Doe

in one or more prominent places. Unlike books and magazines, computer programs need not be registered with the Copyright Office or deposited in the Library of Congress.

U.S. copyright law allows limited copying of books and magazines for private study or classroom use. However, this does not apply to computer programs, which can only be copied with the permission of the copyright owner, or in order to make backup copies that will not be used as long as the original copy is intact.

Copyright protects expressions of ideas, not the ideas themselves. Copyrights do not cover algorithms, mathematical methods, techniques, or the design of machines. The design of a machine can be protected by a patent (see **patent**), but algorithms cannot be protected at all; they are considered to be basic mathematical discoveries free for anyone to use. There is some dispute as to whether copyrights can protect the visual appearance of a program, comprising such things as menus and icons.

CORE Core storage is the main memory of a computer. The term comes from the doughnut-shaped magnetic cores used as memory devices during the late 1950s and early 1960s.

COS If A is an angle in a right triangle, then the cosine of A (written as cos A) is equal to

$$\cos A = \frac{\text{length of adjacent side}}{\text{length of hypotenuse}}$$

The function COS(A) in BASIC and many other languages calculates the value of cos A. Many computers require that the value for *A* be expressed in radians. (See **angle.**)

COULOMB A group of 6.25×10^{18} electrons has a charge of 1 coulomb. (See **ampere.**)

COURIER Courier is a typewriterlike typeface often used on laser printers. Unlike other typefaces, Courier has fixed pitch; that is, all characters are the same width. For an illustration, see **typeface.**

CP/M (Control Program for Microcomputers) is an operating system for microcomputers. (See **operating system.**) It is produced by Digital Research of Pacific Grove, California. The original CP/M (now called CP/M-80) is widely employed on computers that use the 8-bit Z80 processor. Other versions, CP/M-86 and CP/M-68, have been developed for the Intel 8086 and Motorola 68000, respectively. However, CP/M is not commonly used on newer microcomputers. (see **MS-DOS.**)

When you first turn on a CP/M machine, you will usually see this prompt:

A>

The "A" means that disk drive A is the default drive. Whenever you type a file name, the computer will look for that file on the disk in the default drive unless you explicitly include a drive designation.

For example, if you are running BASIC under CP/M, the command LOAD "PROG" will tell the computer to look for the file PROG.BAS on the default drive. The command LOAD "B:PROG" will tell the computer to look for the file PROG.BAS on the disk in drive B.

If you are running WordStar under CP/M, the computer will ask you the name of the file you wish to edit. If you type a file name that includes an explicit drive designation, such as B:CHAP1.DOC, the computer will look for the file on the disk in drive B. If you leave out the drive designation, the computer will look for the file on the disk in the default drive.

The ">" in the prompt means that the computer is ready for you to type a command. For example, if you want to change the default drive to drive B, type B:. The computer will respond with

B>

File names in CP/M consist of up to eight characters followed by an optional file extension of up to three characters. (See **extension**.) Command files have the extension COM. For example, to enter Microsoft BASIC, type MBASIC, and the computer will execute the file MBASIC.COM.

A few CP/M commands are resident commands, that is, they can be typed at any time, regardless of what is on the disks in the machine. However, most commands consist of machine language programs stored on files with the extension COM. To invoke such a program, type its name (without including the COM extension). For example, if the file PIP.COM is on the disk in the default drive, then type PIP to begin executing this program. Here are some CP/M commands:

DIR	Display a directory of all files on the default drive.
DIR A: or DIR B:	Display a directory of all files on the indicated drive.
PIP	Copy a file to another file or from one disk to another.
STAT	Find out the status of a disk (e.g., how much space is left on the disk).
ERA	Erase a file.
COPY	Copy the contents of one disk onto another disk.

CPU The CPU (Central Processing Unit) is the part of a computer where arithmetic and logical operations are performed and instructions are decoded and executed. The CPU controls the operation of the computer. A microprocessor is an integrated circuit that contains a complete CPU on a single chip.

CRASH A computer is said to crash when a hardware failure or program error causes the computer to become inoperable. A well-designed operating system contains protection against inappropriate input, so that a user's program will not be able to cause a system crash.

CRAY Cray Research, Inc., founded by Seymour Cray, is a manufacturer of supercomputers (see **supercomputer**). Cray's first major product was the Cray-1, introduced in 1977, a vector processor designed for repetitious numeric calculations. See also **ETA**.

CRT CRT stands for Cathode Ray Tube, which is a device whereby electrons are sprayed onto a viewing screen, under the direction of magnetic fields, to form patterns. Examples of CRTs include television screens and computer terminals.

CSMA/CD See **Ethernet**.

CRTL-ALT-DEL On the IBM PC and PS/2, the computer reboots if you hold down the the Ctrl and Alt keys simultaneously and press the Del key.

CURRENT A current is a flow of electrons through a conductor. Current is measured in amperes; 1 ampere = 6.25×10^{18} electrons per second.

CURRENT LOOP Older teletypewriters use a high-voltage, constant-current loop instead of an RS-232 serial port to transmit data. (See **RS-232**.) Do not connect current loop equipment directly to RS-232 equipment; the high voltage may cause damage.

CURSOR The cursor is the symbol on a computer terminal that shows you where on the screen the next character you type will appear. Cursors often appear as blinking dashes or rectangles. Many computer have cursor movement (arrow) keys that allow you to move the cursor vertically or horizontally around the screen. This ability is essential for text-editing purposes such as word processing. If you are working with a computer equipped with a mouse, you can use the mouse to move the cursor quickly around the screen. (See **mouse**.)

CUT To "cut" material is to remove it from the document you are editing and to place it into a holding area. (See **copy; paste**.)

CYBER The name CYBER refers to several models of mainframe computers and supercomputers made by Control Data Corporation of Minneapolis. Examples include the CYBER 750, which performs very fast floating point arithmetic on 60-bit words; the CYBER 205 array processor; and the CYBERPLUS parallel processor. CYBER computers are used in scientific and engineering applications.

CYBERNETICS Cybernetics is the study of how complex systems are controlled. It includes the comparative study of the operations of computers and of the human nervous system.

CYLINDER See disk.

d

DAEMON In some computer systems, a program that runs continuously, or is activated by a particular event, is called a daemon because it is like a magical servant. The word *daemon* is Greek for "spirit" or "soul."

DAISYWHEEL PRINTER A daisywheel printer uses a rotating plastic wheel as a type element. Daisywheel printers are often used with microcomputers; they print relatively slowly (10 to 55 characters per second), but the quality of print is comparable to that of a good carbon-ribbon typewriter.

DASH A dash (—) is a punctuation mark similar to a hyphen, but longer. On a typewriter, a dash is typed as two hyphens. (In Word Perfect, it should be typed as two required hyphens; see **required hyphen**.)
  Proportional-pitch type often includes one or more kinds of dashes, such as an em dash, which is as wide as the letter M, or an en dash, which is as wide as the letter N.

DATA Data are factual information. *Data* is the plural of the word *datum*, which means "a single fact." Data processing is the act of using data for making calculations or decisions.

DATA BASE A data base is a collection of data stored on a computer storage medium, such as a disk, that can be used for more than one purpose. For example, a firm that maintains a data base containing information on its employees will be able to use the same data for payroll, personnel, and other purposes. (See **data base management**.)

DATA BASE MANAGEMENT Data base management is the task of storing data in a data base and retrieving information from those data. There are three aspects of data base management: entering data, modifying or updating data, and presenting output reports. In a well-designed data base system the user needs to know only the nature of the information that is available and the type of questions that must be asked, without having to know about the physical arrangement of the data on a storage medium (such as a disk or tape). Many mainframe computers are used by businesses for data base management purposes. Several programs are available for microcomputers that perform data base functions, such as dBASE II and its successor, dBASE III, and some data management capabilities are provided with integrated programs such as Lotus 1-2-3.

Some examples of data base applications including maintaining employee lists and preparing payrolls; maintaining parts order lists and keeping track of inventories; maintaining customer lists and preparing bills for credit customers; and keeping track of the students at a school.

Information in a data base system is generally stored in several different files. For example, a business will often have a file of regular customers and a file of employees. Each file consists of a series of records, with each record containing information on an individual case, such as one person or one transaction. Each record consists of several fields, with each field containing an individual data item. For example, in an employee file there would be one record for each employee, and there would be a field containing the person's name, a field for the address, a field for the Social Security number, and so on.

A data base management system must make provisions for adding new records (e.g., when an employee is hired); for deleting unneeded records (e.g., when an employee retires); and for modifying existing records. Some fields (such as the Social Security number) will not change; other fields (such as year-to-date pay) must be changed frequently.

When you create a file with a microcomputer data base program, you first need to define the structure of the records in that file. You must state how many fields will be in each record, what the label for each field will be, what type of data (numeric or character data) will be stored in the field, and what the width of the field will be. The program will make it as easy as possible for you to enter the data by placing carefully labeled prompts on the screen to tell you where to type each individual field. Each data base program has its own commands for adding new records, modifying existing records, or deleting records.

The main purpose of a data base management system is to make it possible to obtain meaningful information from the data contained in the data base. A data base program can respond to brief queries on the screen, or it can present detailed printed reports in a format chosen by the user. Here are some general functions that a data base management system should be able to fulfill:

1 Sort the records according to the order indicated by one specific field (e.g., sort in alphabetical order by name, or in numerical order by zip code). You should be able to designate a secondary field along which sorting will occur when there are ties in the primary field. For example, if you are sorting the records by the number of months the customers are overdue in their payments, you probably would like the names of all people 1 month overdue in alphabetical order, then the names of all people 2 months overdue in alphabetical order, and so on.

2 Set up selection criteria that allow you to examine only the records that meet a specific condition. For example, you may wish to look only at customers who live in your city, or you may wish to look at all employees whose job title is either "delivery driver" or "warehouse worker."

3 Count the number of records that meet a specific condition. For example, you may wish to count the number of employees who have been with the company for more than 10 years.

4 Perform calculations, such as computing the total amount owed on overdue accounts, or the year-to-date pay for each employee.

5 Connect together information from more than one file. For example, a data base system might contain an employee file that lists the job classification for each employee. A separate file for each job classification would contain information on wages, fringe benefits, and work schedules that apply to all workers in that classification. (See **relational data base.**)

The lists of terms by category in this book were prepared by a microcomputer data base program. Information on each entry was stored as a record, with each record containing four fields; the term itself, the category to which it belongs (electronics, programming concepts, etc.), the author, and the current status of the entry (in other words, whether or not the entry was finished). It was then easy to print a list of all of the electronics terms, then all of the communications terms, and so on. It was also possible to prepare a tabulation to see how many terms were done by each author. While the book was in progress, it was possible to prepare lists of the terms that remained to be done. Whenever an entry was finished, the status of that entry was changed from "not done" to "done."

DATA BITS In RS-232 serial communication, either 7 or 8 bits are used for each character. Mainframe computers usually use 7 data bits, and microcomputers usually use 8. (See **RS-232; XMODEM; Kermit.**)

DATA COMMUNICATION Data communication is the transfer of information from one computer to another. In order for communication to take place, several aspects of the communication process must be standardized. The international OSI (Open Systems Interconnection) standard (ISO Standard 7498) defines seven layers at which decisions have to be made:

1 *Physical layer.* What kind of electrical signals are sent from machine to machine? For examples of standards on this level, see **RS-232; modem.**

2 *Link layer.* How do the two machines coordinate the physical sending and receiving of signals? For examples, see **handshaking; packet.**

3 *Network layer.* How does one machine establish a connection with the other? This covers such things as telephone dialing and the routing of packets. For examples, see **Hayes compatibility** (command chart); **packet.**

4 *Transport layer.* How can the sender be sure the message has been received correctly? For examples, see **XMODEM** and **Kermit.**

5 *Session layer.* How do the machines identify each other? How do users sign on and identify themselves?

6 *Presentation layer.* What does the information look like when received on the user's machine?

7 *Application layer.* How does the information fit into the system of software that will be used to process it?

The OSI standard does not specify what any of these layers should look like; it merely defines a framework in terms of which future standards can be expressed. In a simple system, some of the layers are handled manually or are trivially simple.

DATA COMPRESSION To compresss data is to express data in such a way that they occupy less space. For example, long repetitive passages in a text can be replaced with short codes that mean "The following character is repeated 35 times" or the like. A more thorough form of data compression involves using codes of different lengths for different characters so that the most common characters take up less space.

Most text files can be compressed to about half their normal size. Digitized images can often be compressed to 10% of their original size, but machine-language programs often cannot be compressed at all because they contain no recurrent patterns.

See also **ARC**.

DATA RATE See **baud**.

DATA SET (1) A modem is sometimes called a data set. (See **modem**.)

(2) In OS/360 and related IBM operating systems, a data set is a file, referred to under the name by which it is known to the operating system. (The "file name" in such an operating system is the name by which the file is known to a program and is specified by the JCL DD statement, TSO ALLOCATE command, or CMS FILEDEF command.)

DATA STRUCTURES In computer programming, it is often necessary to store large numbers of items in memory in such a manner as to reflect a relationship between them. There are three basic ways of doing this, called *data structures*: arrays, records and linked lists.

An *array* consists of many items of the same type, identified by number. For example, the examination scores of a college class might be represented as an array of numbers. A picture can be represented as a large array of brightness readings, one for each of the thousands of cells into which the picture is divided.

A *record* consists of items of different types, stored together. For example, the teacher's record of an individual student might consist of a name (character data), number of absences (an integer), and a grade average (a floating point number).

Records and arrays can be combined. For instance, the teacher's records of the entire class would be an array of individual records; an individual record might contain, among other things, an array of test scores.

A *linked list* is like an array except that the physical memory locations in which the items are stored are not necessarily consecutive; this makes it possible to insert items in the middle of the list without moving other items to make room.

See **array; record; linked list**.

DATA TYPES The type of a data item indicates the range of possible values that the data item might have. Some possible data types include integers, real numbers, Boolean values, or character strings. Some languages, such as Pascal, are very strict about requiring that the type of each variable be declared before it can be used, and an error message occurs if a program attempts to assign an inappropriate value to a variable. Other languages make default assumptions about the types for variables if they are not declared. (For example, see **FORTRAN**.) The advantage of requiring data types to be declared is that it forces programmers to be more disciplined with their use of variables, and the computer can detect certain types of errors. There also can be disadvantages with a language requiring strict declaration of data types. For example, some operations (such as swapping the values of two variables) are essentially the same for any data type, so it should not be necessary to include separate subroutines for each type.

Individual data items can be arranged into various types of structures. (See **data structures**.)

dBASE dBASE II and its successors, dBASE III and dBASE III+, are popular data base management programs produced by Ashton-Tate. To start work with dBASE II, use the CREATE command to create a new file. For example, the command

CREATE NAMES

creates a file called *names*. Then the computer will ask you to define the structure of each record in the file. For example, you will need to specify how many fields each record will contain, the name of each field, and the size of each field. For example, a file that is a list of people might need one field for the name, one field for the address, one field for the city and state, one field for the zip code, and other fields that contain specific information about the person.

After you have defined the structure of the file, you must enter the data. Once the file has been entered, you may print all of the records in the file, you may print all of the records that meet a specific condition, you may sort the records along a specific field (e.g., you may like the names printed in alphabetical or in zip-code order), you may sum the total of numeric data, or you may use one of the other dBASE options. dBASE II also allows you to modify existing data or even change the structure of the records in a file.

There are two ways of working with dBASE II. At one level, the user types in dBASE II commands and the computer immediately begins executing the commands. It is also possible to use dBASE II as a programming language. Writing a dBASE II program enables the user to perform more elaborate calculations involving the data and provide more careful checks against erroneous data.

DCE The term DCE (Data Communications Equipment) applies to equipment that uses RS-232 serial communication, with conductor 2 for input and conductor 3 for output. Equipment that uses conductor 3 for input and 2 for output is called DTE (Data Terminal Equipment). A standard RS-232 cable can link two pieces of equipment only if one of them is DTE and the other is DCE; otherwise, both will try to transmit and receive on the same conductors, and a special cable that interchanges conductors 2 and 3 must be used. Most computer terminals are configured as DTE; most modems, as DCE.

DEAD START See **boot**.

DEBUG To debug a program is to remove errors from it. With a complicated program, it often takes longer to correct errors than it did to write the program in the first place.

In MS-DOS (PC-DOS), the DEBUG command allows you to manipulate the contents of memory and modify disk sectors. Considerable knowledge of machine language programming is needed in order to use DEBUG effectively. Symbolic debuggers, which show you the source program as well as the machine code, are generally easier to use. (See **symbolic debugger**.)

DECIMAL NUMBER A decimal number is a number expressed in ordinary base-10 notation, using the digits 0, 1, 2, 3, 4, 5, 6, 7, 8, 9.

DECLARE To declare a variable is to state its attributes. In PL/I the keyword DECLARE is used to declare a variable. For example, the statement

```
DECLARE X FLOAT;
```

means that X will be a floating point real number.

Arrays in BASIC are declared using a DIM command. Pascal requires that all variables be declared before they are used. (See **Pascal**.)

DECNET DECNET is a software product for networking computers

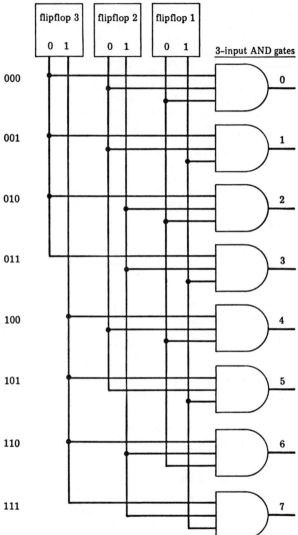

FIGURE 19 Decoder

made by Digital Equipment Corporation. It is widely used on VAX systems. (See **local-area network; VAX.**)

DECODER A decoder is a circuit that changes machine numbers (written in binary) into regular decimal numbers. Figure 19 shows an example of a decoder that will convert a 3-bit binary number into one of the eight decimal digits $0, 1, \ldots, 8$.

DECRYPTION Decryption means decoding—that is, translating information from an unreadable or secret format into a form in which it can be used. (See **encryption.**)

DEDICATED A piece of hardware is said to be dedicated if it performs only one function. For instance, a dedicated phone line is always connected to the same equipment. A dedicated word processor is a computer that performs only word processing.

DEFAULT A default option is an assumption that a computer makes unless it is given specific instructions to the contrary. For example, a word processing program may start out assuming a particular default combination of margins, page length, and so on, which the user can change by issuing specific commands.

FORTRAN makes default assumptions about the type of a variable if that variable is not declared explicitly. Variables whose names begin with I, J, K, L, M, or N are assumed to be integers; variables with other names are assumed to be real numbers.

DEFAULT DIRECTORY In MS-DOS (PC-DOS), OS/2, UNIX, and some other operating systems, the default directory of each disk is the directory in which the operating system looks for files if no directory is specified. The user chooses the directory with the command "cd" or "chdir." (See **directory.**)

DEFAULT DRIVE When a microcomputer is operated under CP/M or MS-DOS, one of the disk drives is designated as the default drive. Any time the computer executes a command that causes it to use a disk file, it will look for that file on the disk in the default drive unless an explicit drive designator was included with the file name. (See **CP/M; MS-DOS.**)

DEGREE MEASURE Degree measure is a way of measuring the size of angles in which a complete rotation has a measure of 360 degrees (written as 360°). (See **angle.**)

DELIMITER A delimiter is a symbol that marks the beginning or end of a special part of a program. For instance, { and } are the delimiters for comments in Pascal (see **Pascal**).

DESCENDER A descender is a part of a character that extends below the line. For instance, the letter "p" has a descender; the letter "o" does not. (See **ascender; typeface.**)

DESK ACCESSORY On the Apple Macintosh, desk accessories are programs, such as a calculator, that can be accessed from a menu at any time no matter what other program is running. They correspond to pop-up utilities on other computers.

DESKTOP The opening screen of a window-oriented operating system is called a desktop because it is a blank space on which various objects can be placed. (See **Finder; Macintosh; Presentation Manager; Windows, Microsoft.**)

DESKTOP PUBLISHING Desktop publishing is the use of personal computers to design and print professional-quality typeset documents. (See **typeface.**) A desktop publishing program such as PageMaker or Ventura is much more versatile than a word processor; in addition to typing documents, the user can specify the layout in great detail, use multiple typefaces, insert pictures, and preview the appearance of the printed document on the screen. (See **PageMaker; Ventura; TeX.**)

Desktop publishing is considerably more complicated than word processing, and anyone contemplating it should be prepared to learn the basics of typography and graphic design. (See **typesetting mistakes.**)

DESTRUCTIVE READ A destructive read occurs when the act of reading the information stored in a memory device causes the information stored there to be lost. For example, when the state of a magnetic core memory is read, the polarity of the core is changed, thereby destroying that information. For the opposite, see **nondestructive read.**

DEVICE DRIVER A device driver is a program that extends the operating system in order to support a specific device, such as a disk or tape drive or a special graphics display. In MS-DOS (PC-DOS), device drivers are usually installed by referring to them in the CONFIG.SYS file (see **CONFIG**).

The term *device driver* also refers to programs or configuration files that enable a word processor or other applications program to use a particular device, such as a printer driver in Word Perfect.

DIAGNOSTIC MESSAGE A diagnostic message is a message the computer prints in case of an error to help the programmer identify the cause of the error.

DIALOG BOX A dialog box is a small window that appears in order to ask the user a question—for instance, to find out the name of a file to be edited. When the user has answered the question, the window disappears.

DIGITAL COMPUTER A digital computer represents information in discrete form, as opposed to an *analog computer*, which allows representations to vary along a continuum. For example, the temperature of a room might be any value between 0° and 100°F. An analog computer could represent this as a continuously varying voltage between 0 and 100 volts. A digital computer, on the other hand, would have to represent it as a decimal or binary number with a specific number of digits (e.g., 68.80 or 68.81).

All modern general-purpose computers are digital. Analog computer circuits are, however, frequently used in industrial control equipment.

DIGITAL EQUIPMENT CORPORATION Digital Equipment Corporation (DEC) is a large manufacturer of computer equipment, particularly minicomputers. Digital has manufactured several popular minicomputers, including the PDP-8, introduced in 1965, and the PDP-11, introduced in 1970. Digital introduced the first computer in the VAX line of 32-bit minicomputers in 1977. Other products include VT100 computer terminals, DECNET networking software, and Rainbow and DECmate microcomputers. The company is headquartered in Maynard, Massachusetts.

DIGITAL RESEARCH, INC. Digital Research, Inc., of Pacific Grove, California, is a software company that has produced, among other products, the CP/M operating system and the MT-Plus version of Pascal.

DIM The DIM command in BASIC defines the size of an array. For example, the statements

```
10 DIM A(15)
20 DIM X(10,20)
```

tell the computer that A will be a 15-element, one-dimensional array, and that X will be a two-dimensional array with 10 rows and 20 columns. (See **array**.)

DIMENSION The number of dimensions of an array is the number of subscripts needed to identify a particular element in the array. A list of objects is a one-dimensional array, while a table is a two-dimensional array.

DIODE A diode is a device that allows electric current to pass in one direction, but not in the other (see Figure 20). A diode is forward biased when the voltage applied to it is the right way for current to flow; otherwise it is reverse biased. The symbol for a diode is a small arrow. Electrons flow in the direction opposite the way that the arrow points.

    Diodes are formed by joining two types of doped semiconductors: P type, with a deficiency of free electrons (and an excess of holes), and N type, with a surplus of free electrons. (See **semiconductor**.) The place where the two regions are joined is called the junction.

direction of electron flow

←←←←←←←←←←←←←←←

P region   N region

FIGURE 20 Diode

    If a negative voltage is applied to the N region, the electrons wil be driven away from the negative voltage and toward the junction. When a positive voltage is applied to the P region, the holes will be driven away from the positive voltage and toward the junction. At the junction, the electrons from the N region will jump into the holes from the P region, with the result that current can flow across the diode (see Figure 21).

If a positive voltage is applied to the N region, then the free electrons in the N region will be pulled away from the junction. Likewise, a negative voltage applied to the P region will pull all the holes away from the junction. The result is that no current flows across the junction, so the diode does not conduct at all. The only way to make current flow would be to apply a large enough voltage to the P region so that electrons are broken out of their crystal structure. This effect is called *breakdown*, and once it happens most diodes are ruined. Diodes come with ratings that indicate the maximum reverse bias voltage they can withstand before breaking down.

Suppose that the current is turned off. What keeps the extra electrons in the N region from filling up the holes in the P region? If the electrons did that, the N region would acquire a net positive charge, and the P region would acquire a net negative charge. Then all the electrons would be repelled from the P region and attracted back to the N region. Each of the phosphorus atoms in the N region contains 15 protons, while each silicon atom contains 14 protons. If the N region as a whole is to remain electri-

Current can flow.

Current cannot flow.

FIGURE 21

cally neutral, it must contain one free electron for every phosphorus atom.

Diodes are used in rectifier circuits and in some logic circuits. Transistors consist of three semiconductor regions separated by two junctions. A special type of diode is the light-emitting diode (or LED), which is used for the readout on some calculators.

DIP SWITCH A DIP switch is a miniature switch or set of switches often used in computer equipment. DIP, or dual-in-line package, means that the switch is the same size and shape as an integrated circuit.

DIR The DIR command under CP/M, MS-DOS (PC-DOS), and OS/2 causes a list of all of the files on the current disk to be displayed. DIR stands for "directory." If drive A is the current drive and you want to see the directory of the files on drive B, then type

DIR B:

To see a directory of all of the files on the current drive that have the file extension BAS, type

DIR *.BAS

The asterisk acts as a "wild card."

The DIR command is also used in VAX/VMS and some other operating systems. The equivalent commands in TSO and CMS are LISTCAT and LISTFILE, respectively. The equivalent command in UNIX is LS.

DIRECT-CONNECT MODEM A direct-connect modem is a modem connected by wires to the telephone line, as opposed to an acoustic coupler (see **acoustic coupler**).

DIRECTORY The directory of a disk is an area where the names and locations of files are stored. On the Macintosh, directories are called *folders*. Each disk has at least one directory (the main, or root, directory), and an operating system has a command that allows the user to see the names of the files on the disk (see DIR). Under MS-DOS (PC-DOS) version 2.0 and higher, OS/2, UNIX, VAX/VMS, and many other operating systems, a disk can have more than one directory arranged in a hierarchy (see **hierarchical**).

Subordinate directories are listed in the directory they are contained in as if they were a special type of file. If you are working with a floppy disk, you will not need to create subordinate directories, since the number of files on the disk is relatively small. However, the number of files on a hard disk rapidly becomes so large that you will have difficulty finding particular files if you have not created subdirectories. For example, you could create a directory called FINANCE to hold all of your financial records, another directory called WORDS to hold word processing files, and so on. Under the WORDS directory you could create further directories: LETTERS for letters to friends, BUSINESS for business correspondence, and so on. If you look at the root directory (assuming you are using MS-DOS), you will see:

```
Directory of G:\
FINANCE    <DIR>      8-25-88    3:00p
WORDS      <DIR>      8-25-88    3:00p
    2 File(s)       636928 bytes free
```

The names of the two subordinate directories are given, but names of the files in those directories are not given. If you now use the CD command to change the directory to WORDS, you will see:

```
Directory of G:\WORDS
           <DIR>      8-25-88    3:00p
           <DIR>      8-25-88    3:00p
LETTERS    <DIR>      8-25-88    3:00p
BUSINESS   <DIR>      8-25-88    3:45p
    4 File(s)       636928 bytes free
```

If you now switch to the LETTERS directory, you will see:

```
Directory of G:\WORDS\LETTERS
            <DIR>      8-25-88    3:00p
..          <DIR>      8-25-88    3:00p
FRED1  LET   896       8-25-88    3:49p
JANE1  LET  1280       8-25-88    3:50p
    4 File(s)        636928 bytes free
```

In this case, FRED1.LET and JANE1.LET are the names of the two files in this directory. (See also **path**.)

DISK A magnetic disk is a computer data storage device. Large computers store information on large disk packs consisting of several disks joined together on one spindle. Microcomputers use floppy disks (*diskettes*) or hard disks. A *floppy disk* looks a bit like a small phonograph record, except that it is covered with a magnetic coating, such as iron oxide, and encased in a square covering of stiff plastic. (The 3½-inch diskettes used on computers such as the Apple Macintosh have a very rigid covering; they can hardly be called floppy at all.) A *hard disk* (fixed disk) is permanently mounted in the computer and cannot be removed. The part of the computer that reads and writes the disk is known as the *disk drive*.

The iron oxide on the disk consists of microscopically small needles, each of which acts like a tiny bar magnet. Information is stored by magnetizing these needles. The *read-write head*, which skims the surface of the disk, can either generate a magnetic field to magnetize the needles, or detect the magnetic field of needles that are already magnetized. The binary digits 0 and 1 are represented by changes in the direction of magnetization.

Data on disks are stored in many concentric circles, each of which is called a *track*. Each track is divided into *sectors*, which are the amount of data that the computer reads into memory in a single step. On a double-sided or multilayer disk pack, the set of tracks in corresponding positions on different layers is known as a *cylinder*. The *directory* of a disk is a special area in which the computer records the names and locations of all the files on the disk. In some operating systems, such as MS-DOS and UNIX, the user can create many directories on a single disk.

As a typical example, the 5¼-inch floppy disks for the IBM PC have 40 tracks on each of two sides, and each track contains nine 512-byte sectors; with allowances for space taken up by the directory, the capacity of the disk is about 360 kilobytes. Hard disks with capacities ranging from 5 to 100 megabytes are available for the same computer; hard disks for mainframe computers have capacities as large as 2.5 gigabytes (more than 2.5 billion bytes).

Data stored on a magnetic disk cannot be read as quickly as data stored in the main memory of the computer, but disk storage has larger capacity and is not erased when the computer is turned off. Storing data on magnetic tape is even cheaper than using disks, but retrieving data from tape storage takes longer becasue the computer cannot jump from one location on the tape to another without going through all the tape in between.

In general, two computers cannot read each other's diskettes unless the computers are designed to be compatible. For example, an IBM PC cannot read diskettes recorded by an Apple II. However, the same kind of blank diskettes can be used on many different computers; each computer formats the diskette in its own way before recording on it (see **format**).

In purchasing diskettes for microcomputers, you need to know the following:

1   What size (3 ½-inch, 5 ¼-inch, or 8-inch) is needed.
2   Whether the diskettes are single- or double-sided. A double-sided diskette can be used in a single-sided drive, but not necessarily vice versa. In practice, most single-sided 5 ¼-inch diskettes can be used in double-sided drives, but they are not guaranteed to work.
3   Whether the diskettes are to be recorded at single, double, quad, or high-density. A double-density diskette can be used in a single-density drive, but not vice versa; the same goes for quad-density diskettes in double-density drives.
4   Whether the diskettes are hard or soft sectored. Almost all microcomputers use soft-sectored diskettes, meaning that the computer decides for itself where each sector is located. A few older computers and word processors use hard-sectored diskettes, in which a ring of small holes near the center is used to line up the sectors.

When in doubt, order 5 ¼-inch, double-sided, double-density, soft-sectored diskettes; these are suitable for the IBM PC, Kaypro, and most other popular microcomputers. The DEC Rainbow and a number of newer computers require quad-density diskettes, and the IBM PC AT uses special high-density floppy disks that hold 1.2 MB (see **IBM PC** and **PS/2**). There are three common types of 3½-inch diskettes: single-sided double density (360K to 400K capacity), double-sided double density (720K to 1 megabyte), and double-sided high density (1.4 to 2 megabytes). The exact capacity depends on the type of computer.

An interesting new development is the *optical disk*, on which information is stored by etching a transparent plastic medium with a laser beam. An optical disk stores about ten times as much information as a magnetic disk of the same size, but it cannot be erased. Optical disks are used mainly for large data files that are often read but seldom changed. (See **CD-ROM**.)

DISK DRIVE A disk drive is a device that enables a computer to read and write data on disks. (See **disk**.)

DO The keyword DO is used to identify loops in FORTRAN, PL/I, and Pascal. (See **loop; FORTRAN; PL/I; Pascal; FOR**.)

DOCUMENT A document is a file containing a text to be printed (e.g., a letter, term paper, or book chapter) or a drawing.

DOCUMENT MODE In WordStar and other word processors, document mode is the normal way of typing documents that are to be printed. The word processor includes codes that indicate hyphenation, page breaks, and the like, thereby producing a special word processing file rather than a text file. (See **nondocument mode; text file**.)

DOCUMENTATION A written description of a computer program is known as documentation. Documentation falls into several categories:

1 Internal documentation, consisting of comments, within the program. (See **comment**.) Internal documentation is addressed mostly to future programmers who may have to make corrections or other modifications.

2 On-line documentation, that is, information that is displayed as the program runs or that can be called up with a command such as HELP. The user should be able to control the amount of information displayed (more for beginners, and less as the user's experience increases). Also, HELP commands should be sensitive to the context in which they are invoked; for instance, typing HELP within an editor should call up information about the editor, not the whole operating system.

3 Reference cards, containing easily forgotten details for quick reference. A reference card assumes that the user is already familiar with the general principles of the program.

4 Reference manuals, setting out complete instructions for the program in a systematic way. Related information should be grouped together, and a good index should be provided.

5 Tutorials, serving as introductions for new users. Unlike a reference manual, a tutorial gives the information in the order in which the user will want to learn it; items are grouped by importance rather than by function or logical category.

DOPING Doping is the process of adding impurities to a silicon crystal to form either a P-type or an N-type semiconductor region. (See **semiconductor**.)

DOS DOS (Disk Operating System) has been used by many computer manufacturers as a name for various operating systems, including an early operating system for the IBM 360; the disk operating system for the Apple II (Apple DOS); MS-DOS, developed by Microsoft for 16-bit microcomputers; and PC-DOS, a version of MS-DOS commonly sold with the IBM PC.

DOT-MATRIX PRINTER A dot-matrix printer forms characters as patterns of dots. These printers are generally speedy and inexpensive. The quality of the print depends on the number of pins used (for example, a 24-pin printer will produce better looking characters than a 9-pin printer). Some dot-matrix printers allow the user to switch between a fast single-pass mode and a slower double-pass mode that produces higher quality characters. Dot-matrix printers are a good choice for many microcomputer buyers. However, if you only print important correspondence (with no graphics), and you don't mind a slower printer, then you should consider a daisywheel printer. If you need to print both high-quality text and graphics, consider a laser printer (although laser printers are more expensive than dot matrix printers).

DOTS PER INCH See **resolution**.

DOUBLE-CLICK To double-click a mouse is to depress one button (usually the leftmost button) twice very rapidly. By contrast, see **click** and **press**.

DOUBLE DENSITY A double-density floppy diskette is recorded in a format that puts twice as many bits into a given area as the earlier single-density format. (See **disk**.)

DOUBLE PRECISION Double precision means that the computer will carry out arithmetic calculations keeping track of twice as many digits as it usually does. For example, if a computer normally keeps track of 6 digits for floating point numbers, it will keep track of 12 digits when it is operating in double-precision mode.

DOUBLE-SIDED DISK A double-sided disk has magnetic coating on both sides and therefore can have data stored on both sides.

DOW JONES Dow Jones Information Service is a computer data bank containing current information on stock prices and other financial news. It can be accessed by subscribers with microcomputers and modems.

DOWN A computer system is down when it is not available to users for some reason, such as when it malfunctions or when it is being tested.

DOWNLOAD To download is to transmit a file or program from a central computer to a smaller computer or a computer at a remote site.

DOWNWARD COMPATIBILITY A computer program or accessory is downward compatible if it works not only on the machine for which it was designed but also on earlier models. By contrast, see **upward compatibility**.

DRAG To drag an object is to move it by using a mouse. To do this, move the mouse pointer to the object, then hold down a mouse button (usually the leftmost button if there is more than one), and move the mouse. The object will move along with the pointer. When you are finished moving it, release the button.

DRAIN The drain is one of the three regions in a field-effect transistor.

DRAM DRAM (Dynamic Random Access Memory) is a computer memory that requires a refresh signal to be sent to it periodically. Most computers use DRAM chips for memory. (See **memory; RAM**.)

DRAW PROGRAM A draw program is one type of program for drawing pictures on a personal computer. Unlike a paint program, a draw program treats the picture as a collection of objects, each of which will be printed as sharply as the printer can print. Thus, the sharpness of the picture is not limited by the resolution of the screen. Also, individual circles, lines, rectangles, and other shapes can be moved around without affecting other objects they overlap. On the other hand, individual pixels cannot be edited. Draw programs are sometimes called *object-oriented graphics programs.*

Draw programs are preferred for drawing diagrams, while paint programs are sometimes superior for pictorial artwork.

Some popular draw programs include MacDraw (for the Macintosh) and Micrografx Windows Draw (for Microsoft Windows). See also **paint program**.

DRIVER See **device driver**.

DRUM A magnetic drum is a computer storage device in which data items are stored on rotating metal cylinders.

DTE See **DCE**.

DUMP To dump is to transfer data from one place to another without regard for its significance.

A dump (on paper) is a printout of contents of a computer's memory or disk file, shown byte by byte, usually in both hexa-decimal and character form. Dumps are usually very hard to read and are used only when there is no other convenient way to get access to the data.

Large-scale copying of files from disk to tape, or vice versa, is sometimes referred to as dumping.

DYADIC OPERATION A dyadic operation requires two oper-ands. For example, addition, multiplication, subtraction, and division are all dyadic operations because each of them operates on two numbers. Negation is not a dyadic operation because it operates on only one number.

e

e The letter *e* is used in mathematics to stand for a number whose value is approximately 2.71828. The reaon why *e* is important is that the function e^x is its own derivative. In BASIC and other pro-gramming languages, the function EXP(X) computes e^x. If $y = e^x$, then x is the natural logarithm of y.

EBCDIC The acronym EDCDIC (Extended Binary Coded Decimal Information Code) refers to the numeric representation of charac-ters on large IBM computers. (By way of contrast, see **ASCII**, which applies to most other computers.) The decimal and hexadecimal numbers corresponding to the most commonly used EBCDIC characters are shown in Table 4. Note that the number-

TABLE 4 EBCDIC (IBM Mainframe) Character Codes

Decimal	Hex	Character	Decimal	Hex	Character
129	81	a	193	C1	A
130	82	b	194	C2	B
131	83	c	195	C3	C
132	84	d	196	C4	D
133	85	e	197	C5	E
134	86	f	198	C6	F
135	87	g	199	C7	G
136	88	h	200	C8	H
137	89	i	201	C9	I
145	91	j	209	D1	J
146	92	k	210	D2	K
147	93	l	211	D3	L
148	94	m	212	D4	M
149	95	n	213	D5	N
150	96	o	214	D6	O
151	97	p	215	D7	P
152	98	q	216	D8	Q
153	99	r	217	D9	R
162	A2	s	226	E2	S
163	A3	t	227	E3	T
164	A4	u	228	E4	U
165	A5	v	229	E5	V
166	A6	w	230	E6	W
167	A7	x	231	E7	X
168	A8	y	232	E8	Y
169	A9	z	233	E9	Z
240	F0	0	64	40	blank
241	F1	1	76	4C	<
242	F2	2	77	4D	(
243	F3	3	78	4E	+
244	F4	4	79	4F		
245	F5	5	80	50	&
246	F6	6	90	5A	!
247	F7	7	91	5B	$
248	F8	8	92	5C	*
249	F9	9	93	5D	)
			94	5E	;
122	7A	:	96	60	−
123	7B	#	97	61	/
124	7C	@	107	6B	,
125	7D	'	108	6C	%
126	7E	=	109	6D	_
127	7F	"	110	6E	$>$
			111	6F	?

ing of the letters of the alphabet is discontinuous. Some EBCDIC devices support a variety of additional characters.

ECHO To echo information is to send it back where it came from. With computers, this refers to two things:

(1) When communicating by modem, a computer echoes typed characters if it sends them to its own screen as well as to the other computer. If you can't see what you're typing, turn echoing on; if what you type appears twice, turn echoing off.

(2) In MS-DOS (PC-DOS) and OS/2, the ECHO command sends a message to the screen. In a BAT file, the command

```
ECHO OFF
```

tells DOS not to print commands on the screen as they are executed. In DOS 3.3 and higher, you can prevent the ECHO OFF command from itself being echoed by prefixing it with '@':

```
@ECHO OFF
```

There is a similar ECHO command in UNIX.

EDIT To edit a file is to examine it and make changes in it, usually with the aid of an editor. (See **editor**.)

EDITOR An editor is a computer program that enables the user to sit at a console or terminal, view the contents of a file, and add material or make other changes. There are two types of editors: full-screen and line.

Full-screen editors use the entire screen as a "window" through which to look at the file; the user can move the cursor around and type anywhere on the screen, or perform scrolling, that is, move the window up or down relative to the contents of the file in order to reach parts of the file that were not originally on the screen. *Line editors* do not allow such free movement of the cursor; instead, line numbers or an imaginary "current line pointer" are used to indicate what line is being worked on, and the user types only at the bottom of the screen.

Full-screen editors are used mostly with microcomputers; practically all word processing packages (e.g., WordStar) include them. It is possible to support full-screen editing at terminals on a large computer (e.g., XEDIT in IBM's VM/CMS), but the data transmission rate must be at least 1,200 baud, since one keystroke may require the entire screen to be retransmitted. Line editors are usually used on slower terminals and are mandatory on terminals that print on paper (e.g., teletypes).

Some questions to ask in evaluating a full-screen editor, particularly on a microcomputer, are the following:

1 What will the editor be used for? Word processing? Modifying existing files? Typing programs? (Does the progamming language have fixed margin requirements or a preferred style of indentation?)

2 In the case of a word processor, does it use the operating system's standard file format? (WordStar does not, unless you ask for nondocument mode.) The answer determines whether you can use the editor to create files for purposes other than word processing.

3 Are there limits on the size of the file—either the total size, or the line length? How does the editor handle lines longer than the width of the screen?

4 How fast does the editor run? Does the screen display move fast enough when scrolling? Are there noticeable delays at any point?

5 How easy is it to find and change all occurrences of a particular word or phrase (a *search and replace*)? To move several consecutive lines from one place to another (a *block move*)? Is it possible to shift a column of material sideways (a *column move*)? Can you insert material from another file or view more than one file at a time?

6 Are the keystrokes and commands easy to remember?

7 Does the editor protect your data? Will it prevent you from forgetting to save your file when you end the session? Will it save your file periodically while you are typing?

8 To what extent can you customize the editor to suit your specific needs?

EDLIN EDLIN, the editor provided with MS-DOS, is efficient but not especially easy to use. Some common commands are as follows:

5L	List a screenful of lines beginning with line 5.
5D	Delete line 5.
5,7D	Delete lines 5 through 7 inclusive.
	(Warning! Lines are automatically renumbered whenever any lines are inserted or deleted.)
8I	Start inserting lines after line 8. (End by hitting Ctrl-Break.)
E	Save the edited file and quit.

Q   Quit, ignoring the changes made and leaving the file in its original form.

EDSAC The EDSAC (Electronic Delayed Storage Automatic Computer) was a stored program computer developed at Cambridge University in 1949.

EDVAC The EDVAC (Electronic Discrete Variable Automatic Computer) was a computer developed at the University of Pennsylvania in 1949.

EGA The IBM Enhanced Graphics Adapter (EGA) provides all of the graphics modes of the Color/Graphics Adapter (CGA), as well as additional high-resolution modes and sharper text. (See **video modes [IBM PC].**)

EIA EIA stands for Electronics Industries Association and is occasionally used to refer to the EIA RS-232C standard. (See **RS-232.**)

ELECTRON An electron is a subatomic particle with a negative electric charge. An atom is made up of a nucleus (consisting of protons and neutrons) surrounded by an orbiting cloud of electrons. Two objects with negative charges will repel each other, but an object with a negative charge will be attracted to an object with a positive charge. An electric current is a flow of electrons.

ELECTRONIC COMPONENTS The basic electronic components that make up computers are *wires*, *transistors*, *diodes*, *resistors*, *capacitors*, and *inductors*. Their schematic symbols are shown in Figure 22. An integrated circuit is a device consisting of many transistors and other circuit elements on a single silicon chip.

ELECTRONIC MAIL An electronic mail system allows a person to type a message at one computer or terminal and then send that message to someone at another terminal or computer. The message will be stored until the receiver chooses to read it.

ELECTROSTATIC PRINTER A printer that prints by using an electric charge to deposit toner on paper, in the same way as a Xerox copier, is known as an electrostatic printer.

ELEMENT An element of an array is one of the items in that array. For example, in the two-dimensional array

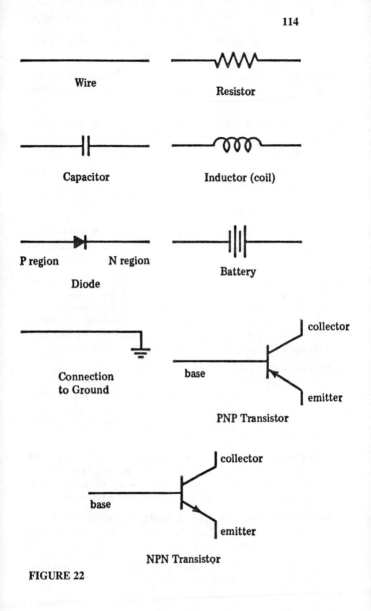

FIGURE 22

$$\begin{pmatrix} 11 & 12 & 13 \\ 10 & 20 & 40 \\ 50 & 80 & 0 \end{pmatrix}$$

the number 10 is the element in position (2,1).

ELITE An elite typewriter prints 12 characters per inch. (See **pitch; pica.**)

EM DASH See **dash.**

EMAIL EMAIL is an abbreviation for "<u>e</u>lectronic <u>mail</u>." (See **electronic mail.**)

EMITTER The emitter is one of the three areas in a bipolar transistor (See **transistor.**)

EMS See **expanded memory.**

EMULATION One machine emulates another if it achieves the same results as the machine being emulated. For example, VT-100 emulation means making a computer act exactly like a VT-100 terminal.

Emulation is different from simulation, which involves imitating the internal processes, not just the results, of the thing being simulated.

EN DASH See **dash.**

ENCRYPTION To encrypt information is to covert it into a code or cipher so that people will be unable to read it. A secret *key*, or password, is required to decrypt (decode) the information.

END The word END is used in several programming languages to indicate the end of a particular program structure. In BASIC the END command tells the computer to stop executing the program. In Pascal the keyword END followed by a period is placed at the end of a program. The word END is also used to mark the end of Pascal procedures, functions, and compound statements that are started with the word BEGIN.

END-OF-FILE MARK In some operating systems, every file ends with a special symbol. For example, in CP/M, ASCII character 26 (control-Z) marks the end of a text file. In MS-DOS and OS/2, control-Z is normally used in the same way, but it is not strictly necessary because the directory keeps track of the exact length of the file in bytes.

END USER An end user of a product is the person ultimately intended to use it, as opposed to people involved in developing or marketing it.

ENIAC The ENIAC (Electronic Numerical Integrator and Calculator), an early computer built in the mid 1940s, was the first electronic computer. It contained about 18,000 vacuum tubes. Initially, the ENIAC was programmed by plugging cables into circuit boards.

ENTER KEY The enter key on a computer terminal is the key you press at the end of each line in order to enter the contents of that line into the computer. On some terminals, this key is called the *return key.*

ENVIRONMENT (1) On a computer, an environment defines what you can do with the computer. For instance, the operating system, a word processor, and a spreadsheet provide (at least) 3 different environments that respond to different commands. For example, if you type a word processing command while you are in the operating system environment, or vice versa, the command will not be understood.

(2) In PC-DOS (MS-DOS) and OS/2, the environment is a data area in which you can leave messages for programs by using the SET command. To see the contents of the environment area, type SET by itself.

EPROM EPROM stands for Erasable Programmable Read Only Memory. A PROM is a memory chip that can be programmed once but cannot be reprogrammed. An EPROM is a special type of PROM that can be erased by exposing the chip to ultraviolet light. Then it can be reprogrammed.

EPSON Epson is a prominent Japanese manufacturer of dot-matrix printers, distributed in the United States, by Epson America, Inc., of Torrance, California. The Epson MX-80 printer received wide acceptance during the early 1980s and set many standards to which other manufacturers now adhere. Epson printers are capable of many special effects, including dot-by-dot graphics. Table 5 lists a number of control codes that work on the MX-80, RX-80, FX-80, and other Epson-compatible printers.

TABLE 5 Epson Printer Control Codes

These codes are the same on the MX-80, RX-80, and FX-80; they can be expected to work on virtually all printers claiming Epson compatibility. There are many other codes, each specific to a particular model of printer. In each case, the numbers given below are the ASCII codes for the sequence of characters to be transmitted (see **ASCII**).

7	Sound buzzer on printer.
10	Line feed
12	Go to top of next page.
13	Carriage return
27 48	Set line spacing to $\frac{1}{8}$ inch.
27 50	Set line spacing to $\frac{1}{6}$ inch (normal).
27 51 X	Set line spacing to $\frac{X}{216}$ inch.
27 67 X	Set form length. X is number of lines.
27 67 0 X	Set form length. X is number of inches.
27 78 X	Skip X lines at perforation between pages.
27 79	Cancel skip-over-perforation.
15	Condensed mode (narrow type) on
18	Condensed mode off
14	Double width mode until end of line
20	Double width mode off
27 87 1	Double width mode on until canceled
27 87 0	Double width mode canceled
27 69	Emphasized (heavy print) mode on
27 70	Emphasized mode off
27 45 1	Underlined mode on
27 45 0	Underlined mode off
27 83 1	Subscript mode on
27 83 0	Superscript mode on
27 84	Subscript or superscript mode off

Some printers also offer italics and/or elite type. All mode combinations are legal except the following:

Emphasized condensed	Emphasized elite
Emphasized subscript	Condensed elite
Emphasized superscript	

In particular, condensed double width is permissible and prints 8.5 characters per inch.

ERASE In PC-DOS (MS-DOS), the ERASE command deletes a file from disk. See also **recovering erased files.**

ERGONOMICS Ergonomics is the science of designing machines and working environments to suit human needs. An ergonomically designed machine is one whose design is based on the scientific study of human requirements such as vision, posture, and the like.

ERROR TRAPPING See **trapping.**

ESCAPE KEY The escape key is a key on a computer keyboard that has a special meaning depending on what software is being used. In a typical program, such as Lotus 1-2-3, the escape key means "get out of where you are now and get back to where you were before." The escape key is represented by ASCII character code 27, which is a character used to send special messages to devices. (See **escape sequence.**)

ESCAPE SEQUENCE An escape sequence is a special series of character codes that causes a screen or printer to perform some action (such as changing type styles) rather than displaying the characters. (See **ANSI screen control; Epson.**)

ETA ETA Systems, Inc., a subsidiary of Control Data Corporation, is a leading manufacturer of vector processing supercomputers. (See also **Cray.**)

ETHERNET Ethernet is a type of local area network originally developed by Xerox Corporation. Communication takes place by means of radio frequency signals carried by a coaxial cable. The name "Ethernet" apparently comes from "ether," the nineteenth-century name for the medium through which light waves were thought to travel. (See l**ocal-area network; data communication.**)

On the physical level, there are three types of Ethernet connections. *Thin-wire Ethernet* uses RG-58 coaxial cable. Conventional *baseband Ethernet* uses a thicker cable about 3/8 inch in diameter, and *broadband Ethernet* modulates the whole Ethernet signal on a higher-frequency carrier so that several signals can be carried simultaneously on a single cable, as is the case with TV channels.

The control strategy of Ethernet is called *CSMA/CD* (Carrier Sense, Multiple Access, Collision Detection). Each node listens to see if another node is transmitting. If so, it waits its turn to transmit. If two nodes inadvertently transmit at the same time, the collision is detected and they retransmit one at a time.

Different Ethernet systems use different software protocols, including TCP/IP and DECNET.

EXCEL Excel is an integrated program produced by Microsoft for the Apple Macintosh that combines a spreadsheet, a data base manager, and a graphics program.

EXE FILE In MS-DOS (PC-DOS), OS/2, and VAX/VMS, an EXE (executable) file is a file that contains a relocatable machine code program and has a name ending with ".EXE". To execute the program, type the name of the file without the final ".EXE"; for example, to execute AAAA.EXE, type AAAA. In VAX/VMS, however, an .EXE file is executed by the RUN command (e.g., RUN AAAAA.EXE.)

Most application programs are distributed as EXE files. Most compilers translate source code into EXE files (see **compiler**).

EXECUTE To execute an instruction is to do what the instruction says to do. A computer alternates between a fetch cycle, when it locates the next instruction, and an execute cycle, when it carries the instruction out. (See **computer design**.)

EXP In many programming languages the function EXP(X) calculates the value of e^x. The letter e represents a special number approximately equal to 2.71828.

EXPANDED MEMORY Expanded memory is a method of equipping an IBM PC with many megabytes of memory. Ordinarily, the 8088 processor in the PC can address only one megabyte (1024K) of memory. The upper 384K of this is reserved for special purposes, leaving only 640K available for ordinary use. Expanded memory uses bank switching to swap many different sets of memory chips into a single block of addresses within this 640K region. The Lotus-Intel-Microsoft Expanded Memory Specification (LIM-EMS) specifies how this is done. Special software is required to take advantage of it.

By contrast, extended memory (on the PC AT and PS/2) is directly accessible at addresses higher than one megabyte. This requires an 80286 or 80386 processor and, under DOS, a different type of special software. The OS/2 and UNIX operating systems use extended memory automatically.

EXPERT SYSTEM An expert system is a computer program that uses stored information to draw conclusions about a particular case. It differs from a database, which merely calls up stored information and presents it to the user unchanged. Expert systems are widely used to troubleshoot defects in machines; they have also been used successfully to diagnose diseases or recommend manufactured products.

Every expert system consists of three parts: (1) a user *interface*, which is a way of communicating with the user through such devices as menus, commands, or short-answer questions (See **user interface**); (2) a *knowledge base* containing stored expertise; and (3) an *inference engine*, which draws conclusions by performing simple logical operations on the knowledge base and the information supplied by the user.

Figure 23 shows a complete (though small) expert system written in Prolog. It has several features that would be hard to implement in a conventional programming language. The entire knowledge base is expressed in a notation that a human being can easily understand and verify. The program asks only the questions that are relevant to the diagnosis being considered, and it never asks the same question twice, even if it is needed for more than one diagnosis. You can easily expand this expert system, or adapt it to other purposes, by changing only the knowledge base, even if you do not know very much about Prolog.

See also **prolog; artificial intelligence**.

EXPONENT An exponent is a number or letter that indicates repeated multiplication. Thus a^n means to multiply n number of a's together. For example, $3^2 = 3 \times 3 = 9$, $4^5 = 4 \times 4 \times 4 \times 4 \times 4 = 1,024$, and $10^6 = 10 \times 10 \times 10 \times 10 \times 10 \times 10 = 1,000,000$.

Also, $a^2 = a \times a$ is called a to the second power, or a squared. The number that when multiplied by itself gives a is called the square root of a (written as $\sqrt{a}$). That means $\sqrt{a} \times \sqrt{a} = a$. For example, $\sqrt{9} = 3$, since $3 \times 3 = 9$.

EXPONENTIAL FUNCTION An exponential function is a function of the form $y = a^x$, where a can be any positive number except 1 and is called the *base* of the function. The most common exponential function is e^x. (See *e*.)

EXPONENTIAL NOTATION Exponential notation is a way of expressing very big and very small numbers on computers. It is the same as scientific notation. A number in exponential notation

```
/* Demonstration expert system    M. Covington 1988 */

/************************
 *** INFERENCE ENGINE ***
 ************************/

/* The built-in Prolog inference engine is used. */
/* The following procedure makes it backtrack    */
/* through all possible diagnoses.               */

main :-
  write('This program tells you why your car won''t start.'), nl,
  write('Answer all questions ''y'' or ''n'' (lower case).'), nl,
  nl,
  abolish(recorded_answer/2),
  possible_diagnosis(D),
  give_explanation(D),
  fail.

main.

/***********************
 *** USER INTERFACE ***
 **********************/

/*
 * answer(Q,A)
 *    checks whether question Q has already been answered,
 *    and if so, whether the answer was A.
 *    If Q has not already been asked, it is asked and
 *    the user's answer is recorded.
 */

answer(Q,A) :- call(recorded_answer(Q,A)).

answer(Q,A) :- not recorded_answer(Q,_),
               question_text(Q,Text), write(Text), nl,
               get_y_or_n(Resp),
               assert(recorded_answer(Q,Resp)),
               !,
               A = Resp.

/*
 * get_y_or_n(Resp)
 *    instantiates Resp to "y" or "n".
 */

get_y_or_n(Resp) :-
        get(Char), nl,
        check_y_or_n([Char],Resp).

check_y_or_n("y","y") :- !.
check_y_or_n("n","n") :- !.
check_y_or_n(_,Response) :-
        write('(Type y or n) '),
        get_y_or_n(Response).
```

FIGURE 23

```
/***********************
 *** KNOWLEDGE BASE ***
 ***********************/

/*  Table of questions that can be asked  */

question_text(starter_worked,
  'Did the engine turn over when you first tried to start it?').

question_text(starter_still_working,
  'Does the engine turn over when you try starting it now?').

question_text(fuel_in_carb,
  'Is there fuel reaching the carburetor?').


/*  Possible diagnoses, with conditions for each */

possible_diagnosis(electrical) :-
      answer(starter_worked,"n").

possible_diagnosis(drained_battery) :-
      answer(starter_worked,"y"),
      answer(starter_still_working,"n").

possible_diagnosis(fuel) :-
      answer(fuel_in_carb,"n").

possible_diagnosis(ignition) :-
      answer(fuel_in_carb,"y"),
      answer(starter_worked,"y").

/*  Explanations for the diagnoses */

give_explanation(electrical) :-
  write('The defect may be in the battery, alternator,'), nl,
  write('or voltage regulator. Jump-starting may get'), nl,
  write('the car going temporarily.'), nl, nl.

give_explanation(drained_battery) :-
  write('The battery has become drained during your'), nl,
  write('attempts to start the car. Jump-starting or'), nl,
  write('recharging may be necessary.'), nl, nl.

give_explanation(fuel) :-
  write('Either the car has run out of fuel, or there'), nl,
  write('is a defect in the fuel line or fuel pump.'), nl, nl.

give_explanation(ignition) :-
  write('The defect may be in the ignition system.'), nl, nl.
```

FIGURE 23

```
C:\>api
Arity/Prolog Interpreter Version 4.0
Copyright (C) 1986 Arity Corporation
?- consult(carstart).

yes
?- main.
This program tells you why your car won't start.
Answer all questions 'y' or 'n' (lower case).

Did the engine turn over when you first tried to start it?
y
Does the engine turn over when you try starting it now?
n
The battery has become drained during your
attempts to start the car. Jump-starting or
recharging may be necessary.

Is there fuel reaching the carburetor?
n
Either the car has run out of fuel, or there
is a defect in the fuel line or fuel pump.

yes
?- halt.
```

FIGURE 24

is written as the product of a number from 1 to 10 and a power of 10. The letter E is used to indicate what power of 10 is needed. For example, 5.4 E 6 means 5.4×10^6, which in turn means 5,400,000. The number of meters in a light year is 9,460,000,000,000,000, which can be written in exponential notation as 9.46 E 15. The wavelength of red light is 0.0000007 meter, which is 7 E –7.

EXPRESSION In a programming language, an expression is a set of symbols that can be evaluated to have a particular value. For example, the following are numeric expressions (i.e., their values are numbers):

```
3.5
(4/3)*PI*R**3
SQRT (A**2 + B**2)
```

Some programming languages have expressions whose values are character strings or Boolean (true-false) values. For example,

```
"WALLA" + "WALLA"
```

is a character string expression, and

```
(P OR Q) AND R
```

is a Boolean expression.

EXTENDED MEMORY Extended memory is memory at addresses higher than 1 megabyte on IBM PC AT and PS/2 computers. It contrasts with expanded memory, which is bank-switched. The OS/2 and UNIX operating systems use extended memory. (See **expanded memory; bank switching**.)

EXTENSION A file name in CP/M, MS-DOS, and some other operating systems can be followed by a three-letter file extension that often indicates the nature of the file. When typing the file name, a period is used to separate the name from the extension. For example, in the file name

```
PROG1.BAS
```

BAS is the file extension. Some file extensions have standard meanings. For example, BAS designates BASIC program files; COM or EXE, command files; and BAK, backup files.

f

F KEYS See **function keys**.

FACTORIAL The factorial of a positive integer is equal to the product of all the integers from 1 up to that number. The factorial of a number n is symbolized by an exclamation point: *n!*. For example:

$$2! = 2 \times 1 = 2$$
$$3! = 3 \times 2 \times 1 = 6$$
$$4! = 4 \times 3 \times 2 \times 1 = 24$$
$$5! = 5 \times 4 \times 3 \times 2 \times 1 = 120$$

FARAD The farad is the unit of measure of capacitance. A 1-farad capacitor will store a charge of 1 coulomb when 1 volt is applied across it. Capacitors in common use range in values from about 1 picofarad (10^{-12} farad) to 250,000 microfarads (0.25 farad). Capacitors as large as 3 farads can be made, but they have high internal resistance and are used only to back up CMOS memories when power is turned off.

FAT BITS In MacPaint, Fat Bits is a mode in which the user can edit individual pixels (the small black or white squares of which the picture is composed). The pixels are shown greatly magnified on the screen.

FAX A FAX, or facsimile machine, transmits copies of paper documents over telephone lines by converting the appearance of the document into an electronic signal. The output looks much like a photocopy. Some computers have the ability to send and receive FAX signals.

FEED HOLES Feed holes are the holes along the sides of computer printer paper that allow the paper to be driven by a sprocket wheel.

FEEDBACK Feedback occurs when a control device uses information about the current state of the system to determine the next control action. For example, when a thermostat controls the temperature in a house, it needs to know the current temperature in the house before it decides whether to turn on the furnace.

FIBER OPTICS A fiber-optic cable carries light rather than electrical energy. It is made of a thin fiber of glass. Large amounts of data can be carried by a single fiber-optic cable.

FIELD A group of adjacent characters is called a field. For example, in a company payroll system the information about a single individual can be stored as one record. Each record will be divided into several fields. One field will contain the employee's name; another field, his Social Security number; a third field, his salary or rate per hour; and so on.

FIELD-EFFECT TRANSISTOR A field-effect transistor consists of two islands of N-type semiconductor inside a P-type region. One island is called the *source*, and the other is called the *drain*. A thin insulating layer of silicon dioxide is placed over the P-type region between the drain and the source, and a thin layer of metal, called the *gate,* is placed over this insulating material. Field-effect transistors can perform the same switching and amplification functions as bipolar transistors, and they can be packed more densely on a chip of silicon.

FIFTH-GENERATION COMPUTERS Fifth-generation computers, predicted by some to be available in the 1990s, will be capable of knowledge processing instead of merely data processing. These computers will be able to understand languages that are much closer to natural languages than are current programming languages. The advent of fifth-generation computers will require significant advancements in artificial intelligence and the development of enhanced supercomputers that perform logical operations many times faster than do the computers currently available. In 1981 Japan announced a concerted national effort directed toward producing fifth-generation computers by the 1990s. (See **artificial intelligence.**)

FILE A file is a collection of information stored as records. The information in a file is stored in such a way that the computer can read information from the file or write information to the file.

For example, the U.S. Census Bureau stores vast amounts of information. Suppose that the bureau is keeping information on a monthly sample of 130,000 people. The information on each person can be stored in one record. The entire set of information can be stored in a file containing 130,000 records. The file will be stored on a magnetic tape.

Microcomputers can store files on floppy disks. Here is an

example of storing information on a disk file in Microsoft BASIC. First, we must open the file with an OPEN command, such as:

```
10 OPEN "O",1,"HELLO"
```

The "O" means that the file will be an output file (in other words, the computer will be writing information out to the file). The number 1 means that this file will be referred to as file #1 in all subsequent statements. In this case "HELLO" will be the name of the file.

Now we can write information to the file:

```
20 A$ = "Hi! How are you doing today?"
30 PRINT#1,A$
```

The command PRINT#1,A$ tells the computer that the string variable A$ is to be written to file #1. Now that we have finished writing output to the file, we must close the file:

```
40 CLOSE#1
```

To read information from the file, we must first open it again, but this time we will specify that we are opening it for input instead of output:

```
50 OPEN "I",3,"HELLO"
```

The "I" stands for input. This time we will open the file as #3. (You should check with your computer to find what numbers it allows for file numbers.)

Now we can read from the file.

```
60 INPUT#3,X$
```

The command INPUT#3,X$ tells the computer to read the next item from file #3 and store the item it finds there under the name X$. Now, if the computer finds the command

```
70 PRINT X$
```

The screen will display:

Hi! How are you doing today?

Now that we are done with the file we can close it:

```
80 CLOSE#3
```

FILE-PROTECT RING A file-protect ring is used to prevent the information on a magnetic tape from being accidentally overwritten or erased. Information can be stored on the tape only when the ring is in place. When the ring is removed, recording cannot take place. A similar system works for audio cassette tapes. When the tabs at the end of the tape are broken, recording becomes impossible.

FILTER See **UNIX**.

FINDER The Finder is part of the operating system of the Apple Macintosh. It allows users to copy and manipulate files by moving icons on the screen.

FIRMWARE The term *firmware* refers to software (i.e., computer programs) that are stored in some fixed form, such as a read-only memory (ROM).

FIRST-GENERATION COMPUTERS First-generation computers are the computers that were built in the late 1940s and early 1950s, using vacuum tubes.

FIXED DISK See **hard disk**.

FIXED PITCH Fixed-pitch type is type in which all letters are the same width (e.g., "I" the same width as "M"). Most typewriters, low-cost printers, and computer screens use fixed-pitch type. By contrast, see **proportional pitch**. For illustration, see **typeface**.

FIXED-POINT NUMBER A fixed-point number is a number in which the decimal point is fixed. For example, the population of a city can be represented by a fixed point number with no digits to the right of the decimal point. An amount of money in U.S. currency can be represented by a fixed point number with two digits to the right of the decimal point. By way of contrast, see **floating-point number**.

FLIP-FLOP A flip-flop is the basic component of which computer registers are composed. A flip-flop can flip between two states, called 1 and 0. Figure 25 shows how to construct a flip-flop using two NOR gates. (A NOR gate is the opposite of an OR gate.) A simple flip-flop has two inputs; the set input and the clear input. The two outputs correspond to 1 and 0. When the 1 output is at high voltage, the state of the flip-flop is 1. When the 0 output is at high voltage, the state of the flip-flop is 0. (Both outputs cannot be at high voltage at the same time, because of the way the NOR gates are connected.) The following table describes the operation of the flip-flop:

FIGURE 25 Flip-flop

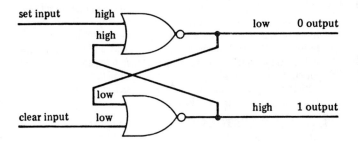

FIGURE 26

Set Input	Clear Input	Old State	New State
0	0	0	0
0	0	1	1
1	0	0	1
1	0	1	1
0	1	0	0
0	1	1	0

If neither the set input nor the clear input is pulsed, the flip-flop will stay the same way it was. Figure 26 shows what will happen if the set input is at high voltage. The state of the flip-flop will become 1, regardless of its old state. If the clear input is at high voltage, the opposite will happen and the state of the flip-flop will become 0.

When reading information into flip-flop (see Figure 27), you need to have a data input, telling what state you want the

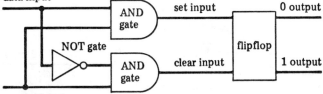

FIGURE 27

flip-flop to be in, and a control input, telling whether or not you want the flip-flop to pay attention to the data input. If the control input is 0, then neither the clear input nor the set input will be pulsed, so the flip-flop will stay the way it was. If the control input is 1, then the state of the flip-flop will match the state of the data input. This control structure is used to control the transfer of data between different registers. A register, such as the accumulator, is composed of a row of flip-flops.

FLOATING ILLUSTRATION In desktop publishing, a floating illustration is a picture that should appear near a particular position, but need not be at a particular point in the text. For instance, the figures in this book are floating illustrations; they appear near the articles that refer to them, but not between particular words. The page-layout software places the illustrations wherever it is convenient to put them.

FLOATING-POINT NUMBER A floating-point number is a number in which the decimal point can be in any position. For instance, a memory location set aside for a floating-point number can store 0.735, 62.3, or 1200. By contrast, a fixed-point memory location can only accommodate a specific number of decimal places, usually 2 (for currency) or none (for integers).

Floating-point numbers are often written in scientific notation, such as 4.65E4, which means 4.65×10^4, or 46,500.

FLOPPY DISK A floppy disk is a computer storage medium made of plastic covered with a magnetic coating. Floppy disks are one of the most popular storage devices for microcomputers because of their convenience. There are two common sizes of floppy disks: 5¼ inches and 8 inches in diameter. The 5¼-inch size is the most popular. Each floppy disk is covered with a jacket containing holes that allow the disk drive access to the disk. When the disk is not being used, it should be kept in the envelope that comes with it. Floppy disks should be stored in a dry, cool container away from magnetic fields. (See **disk; hard disk; microfloppy disk.**)

FLOWCHART A flowchart is a chart consisting of symbols and words that completely describe an algorithm (i.e., how to solve a problem). Each step in the flowchart is followed by an arrow that indicates which step to do next. The flowchart in Figure 28 describes how to solve the quadratic equation $ax^2 + bx + c = 0$.

Flowcharts can also be used to represent procedures that contain loops. The flowchart in Figure 29 shows how to calculate the cube root of a number (a) using Newton's method. If x is the guess for the cube root of a, and δ indicates how accurate the result must be, then the procedure will follow around the loop until $|x^3 - a| < \delta$.

"Start" and "stop" statements are written with ovals; action statements are written with squares; and decision statements are written in diamonds. A decision statement asks a yes or no question. If the answer is yes, the path labeled "yes" is followed; otherwise the other path is followed.

Writing a flowchart often helps to solve a complex programming problem, although flowcharts are used less often now that structured programming has become popular.

FLUSH LEFT To align type flush left is to start each line at the same horizontal position, allowing the lengths of the lines to vary.

> This is
> an example of
> flush-left
> type.

FIGURE 28

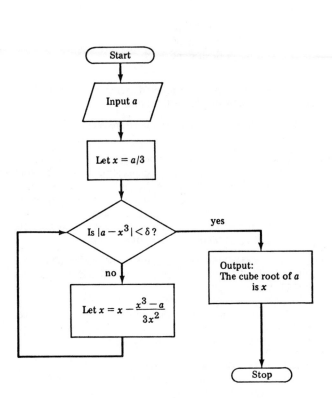

FIGURE 29

Note that the left margin is smooth and right margin is irregular ("ragged").

This is how type is ordinarily arranged on a typewriter. By contrast, see **justification; flush right.**

FLUSH RIGHT To align type flush right is to make each line end at the same horizontal position. The beginnings of the lines are not lined up.

This is
an example of
flush-right
type.

Flush-right alignment is seldom used except in charts or tables. By contrast, see **flush left; justification.**

FOLDER Subdirectories on the Macintosh are called folders. (See **directory.**)

FONT A font is a collection of characters with a consistent size and style. Most desktop publishing systems allow you to use more than one font in a single document. For example, you could have some words printed in italics and some other words printed in boldface. Figure 30 shows a sample of different fonts (these are the internal fonts that come with a Hewlett-Packard LaserJet printer). See also **typeface; style; pitch;** and **point.**

FOR The keyword FOR is used to identify the beginning of one kind of loop in BASIC and Pascal. (It corresponds to DO in PL/I and FORTRAN.)

A FOR loop causes a certain variable, known as the *loop variable,* to take on several values in sequence. For example, these groups of statements, in BASIC and Pascal, respectively, print out the whole numbers from 1 to 10:

```
BASIC: 10  FOR I = 1 TO 10
       20  PRINT I
       30  NEXT I
```

```
Pascal: FOR i:= 1 TO 10 DO WRITELN(i);
```

A FOR loop can be used either to obtain repetition or to make the values of the variable available for some purpose. For example, here is how to calculate the sum of the whole numbers from 1 to

FONT ID	NAME	PITCH	POINT SIZE	SYMBOL SET	PRINT SAMPLE

RIGHT FONT CARTRIDGE

FONT ID	NAME	PITCH	POINT SIZE	SYMBOL SET	PRINT SAMPLE
R15	SPECIAL	16.6	7	0Q	ABΓΔΕ ζηθικˆα·ςϛ√Σ:w∞∾123
R16	SPECIAL	16.6	7	1Q	σθθωω⌠∮∫│∠↓↑⊖↓∂3X∫∖ ∓±∇∃т

INTERNAL FONTS

FONT ID	NAME	PITCH	POINT SIZE	SYMBOL SET	PRINT SAMPLE
I00	COURIER	10	12	8U	ABCDEfghij#$@[\]^'(|)~123 ÀÂ˚ÇÑ¡¿£§êéàèëöÄØÅæÄÜßÁÐÒ
I01	COURIER	10	12	10U	ABCDEfghij#$@[\]^`(|)˜123 íó|¦╡╢╖╕╣║╗╝╜╛┐└┴┬├─┼╞╟╚╔╩╦╠═╬╧╨╤╥╙╘╒╓╫╪┘┌█▄▌▐▀απΦ
I02	COURIER	10	12	11U	ABCDEfghij#$@[\]^`(|)˜123 íó|¦╡╢╖╕╣║╗╝╜╛┐└┴┬├─┼╞╟╚╔╩╦╠═╬╧╨╤╥╙╘╒╓╫╪┘┌█▄▌▐▀απΦ
I03	COURIER	10	12	0N	ABCDEfghij#$@[\]^`(|)˜123 ¡¢³´¶.¹»½ÅÀÈÉÍÎÐÒÓ×ØÚÞàãë
I04	COURIER BOLD	10	12	8U	**ABCDEfghij#$@[\]^'(|)~123 ÀÂ˚ÇÑ¡¿£§êéàèëöÄØÅæÄÜßÁÐÒ**
I05	COURIER BOLD	10	12	10U	**ABCDEfghij#$@[\]^`(|)˜123 íó|¦╡╢╖╕╣║╗╝╜╛┐└┴┬├─┼╞╟╚╔╩╦╠═╬╧╨╤╥╙╘╒╓╫╪┘┌█▄▌▐▀απ#**
I06	COURIER BOLD	10	12	11U	**ABCDEfghij#$@[\]^`(|)˜123 íó|¦╡╢╖╕╣║╗╝╜╛┐└┴┬├─┼╞╟╚╔╩╦╠═╬╧╨╤╥╙╘╒╓╫╪┘┌█▄▌▐▀απ#**
I07	COURIER BOLD	10	12	0N	**ABCDEfghij#$@[\]^`(|)˜123 ¡¢³´¶.¹»½ÅÀÈÉÍÎÐÒÓ×ØÚÞàãë**
I08	LINE_PRINTER	16.6	8.5	8U	ABCDEfghij#$@[\]^'(|)~123 ÀÂ˚ÇÑ¡¿£§êéàèëöÄØÅæÄÜßÁÐÒ
I09	LINE_PRINTER	16.6	8.5	10U	ABCDEfghij#$@[\]^`(|)˜123 íó|¦╡╢╖╕╣║╗╝╜╛┐└┴┬├─┼απ#
I10	LINE_PRINTER	16.6	8.5	11U	ABCDEfghij#$@[\]^`(|)˜123 íó|¦╡╢╖╕╣║╗╝╜╛┐└┴┬├─┼απ#
I11	LINE_PRINTER	16.6	8.5	0N	ABCDEfghij#$@[\]^`(|)˜123 ¡¢³´¶.¹»½ÅÀÈÉÍÎÐÒÓ×ØÚÞàãë

FIGURE 30 Fonts on the Laserjet II printer

```
100:
BASIC: 10  LET T = 0
       20  FOR I = 1 TO 100
       30  LET T = T + I
       40  NEXT I
       50  PRINT T

Pascal: PROGRAM addup (output);
        VAR i, t : INTEGER;
        BEGIN
            t := 0;
            FOR i:= 1 TO 100 DO t := t + i;
            WRITELN(t)
        end.
```

Although the statements within the loop can examine the value of the loop variable, they should not attempt to change it, since the result of doing so is unpredictable.

FORMAT A format is any method of arranging information that is to be stored or displayed. The word *format* can therefore refer to many different things relating to computers. Three of its most common uses are as follows:

(1) The format of a disk or tape refers to how the information is stored on it. (See **disk**.)

(2) To format a disk is to make the computer record a pattern of reference marks on it. A brand-new disk must always be formatted before it can be used. Formatting a disk erases any information previously recorded on it.

(3) In FORTRAN, the FORMAT statement specifies the form in which data items, especially numbers, are to be read or written. Some examples of format items are:

I8   An integer occupying eight character positions.
F7.2   A floating point (REAL) number occupying seven character positions, two of which are to the right of the decimal point.
A40   A single string of 40 characters
40A1   Forty character strings, each containing only one character.
5X   Skip five blanks before printing the next item.

The following example shows how the items in a FORMAT

statement are paired up with the items in the corresponding WRITE statement:

```
WRITE (6,23)   A,        B,        K
               |         |         |
               |         |         |
               |         |         |
23   FORMAT (1X,F5.2,5X,F8.3,5X,I5)
```

The list of format items begins with 1X because, in FORTRAN, the very first character on a line of printout is not printed; it is interpreted as a code indicating whether the printer should skip a line, begin a new page, or perform some other special action. Using 1X to transmit a blank tells the printer to begin a new line in the normal manner.

FORTH The programming language FORTH was invented by Charles Moore around 1970. FORTH is noted for requiring few machine resources and giving very rapid execution.

In FORTH, the programmer defines her own statements in terms of simpler statements. FORTH is a *threaded interpretive language,* meaning that a program is represented in the computer as a list of addresses of subroutines, each of which is composed of addresses of other subroutines, and so on until the primitive operations of the language are reached. Because it has little to do except read addresses and jump to them, a FORTH interpreter can run very fast; in fact, there is little difference between an interpreter and a compiler for FORTH.

FORTH programs look very unlike programs in other languages. Most data are stored on a push-down stack (see **stack**), and some common FORTH statements include the following:

!	Store a value from the stack into a variable.
@	Push a variable onto the stack.
+	Pop two numbers off the stack, add them, and push the result onto the stack.
−	Subtract (similarly).
KEY	Read a character and place its ASCII value on the stack.
EMIT	Pop a character and display it (opposite of KEY)

Because of its stack orientation, FORTH uses Polish notation for algebraic expressions. (See **Polish notation**.) In FORTH the expression $(2 + 3) - 5$ is

2 3 + 5 −

The following line from a FORTH program defines the statement ENCRYPT as "Read a character, subtract its ASCII code from 159, and print out the resulting character":

:ENCRYPT 159 KEY - EMIT;

In other words, "Place 159 on the stack, read a character placing its ASCII code on the stack, perform the subtraction (removing two numbers from the stack and placing their difference on it), and print the characater whose ASCII code is on top of the stack."

FORTRAN FORTRAN (formula translation), developed by IBM in the late 1950s, was the first major programming language that allowed programmers to describe calculations by means of mathematical formulas. Instead of writing assembly language instructions such as

```
LOAD A
ADD B
MULTIPLY C
STORE D
```

the FORTRAN programmer writes

```
D = (A+B)*C
```

where * is the symbol for multiplication. Figure 31 shows a sample FORTRAN IV program.

FORTRAN has existed in several versions, of which the most important are FORTRAN IV (USASI Standard FORTRAN, 1966) and FORTRAN 77 (ANSI FORTRAN, 1977).

The layout of FORTRAN statements is illustrated by the following example:

```
C SAMPLE OF PART OF A FORTRAN PROGRAM
      WRITE (6,123) A, B, C,
     +D, E, F
  123    FORMAT(1X,6I5)
```

If the first column contains a C (or an asterisk in FORTRAN 77), the line is taken to be a comment, and the computer ignores it. Otherwise, the first column is blank. Columns 2 to 5 contain the statement number, if any. Ordinary statements begin column 7. If column 6 is nonblank, the line is taken to be a continuation of the statement on the preceding line.

```
C     THIS PROGRAM READS A LIST OF NUMBERS
C     AND DETERMINES WHETHER THEY ARE PRIME.
C     THIS IS IBM 360/370 FORTRAN IV.
C
      INTEGER X, HALF, DIV
      REAL    QUOT
C
C     FORMAT STATEMENTS FOR INPUT-OUTPUT
C
 100  FORMAT(I4)
 101  FORMAT(/' ',I4,' IS NOT A NATURAL NUMBER.')
 102  FORMAT(/' ',I4,' IS DIVISIBLE BY ',I4,'.')
 103  FORMAT(/' ',I4,' IS PRIME.')
C
C     THE ALGORITHM ITSELF
C
 1    READ(5,100,END=99) X
      IF (X.GT.0) GO TO 2
      WRITE(6,101) X
      GO TO 1
C
 2    IF (X.EQ.1) GO TO 3
      DIV = 2
      QUOT = FLOAT(X)/FLOAT(DIV)
      IF (QUOT.EQ.FLOAT(INT(QUOT))) GO TO 4
C            (IN FORTRAN YOU CANNOT DO DIVISION OF INTEGERS GIVING
C             NON-INTEGER QUOTIENT, NOR COMPARE INTEGERS TO REALS,
C             WITHOUT INVOKING CONVERSION FUNCTIONS EXPLICITLY.)
C
      HALF = INT(QUOT)
      DO 10 DIV=3,HALF,2
         QUOT = FLOAT(X)/FLOAT(DIV)
         IF (QUOT.EQ.FLOAT(INT(QUOT))) GO TO 4
 10      CONTINUE
C
 3    WRITE(6,103) X
      GO TO 1
C
 4    WRITE(6,102) X,DIV
      GO TO 1
C
 99   STOP
      END
```

FIGURE 31

FORTRAN variable names contain up to six letters or digits; the first character must be a letter. Variables can be declared as INTEGER, REAL (floating point), DOUBLE PRECISION (like REAL, but with more significant digits), LOGICAL (Boolean), or (in FORTRAN 77) CHARACTER. If a variable is not declared, it is assumed to be INTEGER if its name begins with I, J, K, L, M, or N, and REAL otherwise.

In FORTRAN IV, all input and output operations require references to a FORMAT statement to specify how the data are to be arranged. (See **format**.) The FORMAT statement can be located anywhere in the program and is identified by statement number. For example, the statement

```
WRITE (6,123) A, B, C
```

writes the values of A, B, and C onto device 6 (the printer) using FORMAT statement 123. The PRINT statement is equivalent to WRITE except that it always uses device 6, so that no device number need be specified; the statement

```
PRINT 123, A, B, C
```

is equivalent to the WRITE statement above. Likewise, the READ statement has two forms, one of which specifies the device number:

```
READ (5,112) A, B, C
READ 112, A, B, C
```

In FORTRAN 77, an asterisk can be used in place of the FORMAT statement number; the computer automatically chooses a format suitable for the data:

```
WRITE (6,*) A, B, C
PRINT *, A, B, C
READ (5,*) A, B, C
READ *, A, B, C
```

Comparisons are usually performed with the IF statement. For example:

```
IF (X.EQ.Y) THEN PRINT *, 'THEY ARE EQUAL'
```

Note that the comparison is written as "X.EQ.Y," not "X = Y." In FORTRAN, an equal sign, =, always indicates assignment, that is, it means that the value of an expression is to be computed and stored in a variable. Thus, it makes sense to say things like

Y = Y + 1

which means, "Compute the value of Y + 1 and store it in Y."

FORTRAN was the first major programming language to include arrays (see **array**). In addition, portions of a FORTRAN program can consist of subroutines or functions that are compiled separately from the main program (see **compiler; linkage editor**). FORTRAN assumes blindly that each subroutine or function is being called with the right number and types of parameters.

In FORTRAN, blanks within statements are ignored unless they occur within a quoted string. Thus,

X   =   A   +   BI G NUM

is exactly equivalent to

X=A+BIGNUM

This creates occasional problems. For example, the statement

DO 10 I = 1,10

marks the beginning of a DO loop in which the variable I takes on the values 1, 2, 3, 4, . . . , 10. However, if the programmer accidentally leaves out a comma and types

DO 10 I = 1 10

the computer does not generate an error message. Instead, the compiler ignores the blanks and interprets the statement as

DO10I=110

assigning the value 110 to the variable DO10I. (Remember that variables need not be declared; the computer will not complain that this is the only place in the program where DO10I is mentioned.) An early Mariner space probe was reportedly lost because of precisely this error.

Compared to FORTRAN IV, FORTRAN 77 includes more sophisticated input-output statements, especially for file handling; the ability to process character-string data; and block-structured IF-ELSE-ENDIF statements to facilitate structured programming (see **structured programming**). All standard

FORTRAN IV programs will run under FORTRAN 77, but not vice versa.

FORWARD BIASED A diode is forward biased when the voltage applied across it is in the right direction to allow current to flow. This occurs when a negative voltage is applied to the N region and a positive voltage is applied to the P region. (See **diode**.)

FOURTH-GENERATION COMPUTERS Fourth-generation computers are built around integrated circuits with large-scale integration. Some people view these computers as being advanced third-generation computers.

FRAGMENTATION A disk becomes fragmented when many files are created and erased on it over a long period of time. The space allocated to a file is not necessarily contiguous. If the file is scattered over many widely separated sectors, access to the file is relatively slow.

A disk can be defragmented by copying all the files to another disk. Programs exist for some machines that will defragment a disk "in place," by carefully rearranging the files without copying to another disk.

FRAMING ERROR A framing error occurs when an asynchronously transmitted character appears to contain the wrong number of bits. (See **asynchronous; RS-232**.) Framing errors usually result from transmitting or receiving at the wrong speed.

FREE SOFTWARE Several kinds of computer software can legally be copied and given free of charge to other users:

1 Public-domain software. This is software that is not covered by any kind of copyright. Few substantial public-domain programs exist, but the term *public domain* is often used incorrectly to refer to other kinds of free software.

2 Software that is copyrighted but is distributed free with permission of the copyright owner. One of the most famous examples is the Kermit communication program (see **Kermit**). Many UNIX utilities are also in this category.

3 Shareware. This is copyrighted software that can be distributed free to anyone, but which requests or requires a payment from satisfied users directly to the author. Shareware is often misleadingly described as "free."

FRICTION FEED PRINTER A friction feed printer relies on the pressure of the platen to move the paper. This method of feeding paper is similar to that found on a typewriter. It makes it possible to use individual sheets of ordinary paper with no sprocket holes.

FULL ADDER A full adder is a logic device that accepts three inputs (two addends and a carry input) and produces two outputs; a sum ouput and a carry output. The table characterizes the operation of a full adder. (See **binary addition.**)

Input 1	Input 2	Carry Input	Sum Output	Carry Output
0	0	0	0	0
0	0	1	1	0
0	1	0	1	0
0	1	1	0	1
1	0	0	1	0
1	0	1	0	1
1	1	0	0	1
1	1	1	1	1

FULL DUPLEX The term *full duplex* refers to the transmission of data in two directions simultaneously. (See **half duplex; modem.**)

FULL-HEIGHT DRIVE A full-height 5¼-inch disk drive is approximately 3¼ inches high, twice the height of a half-height drive.

FULL-SCREEN TERMINAL A full-screen terminal allows you to type in characters anywhere on the display screen. By way of contrast, a line-at-a-time terminal allows you to type only at the bottom line of the display.

FUNCTION A computer function is like a mathematical function: it is a set of instructions that generate a unique output value for a particular value of the independent variable (or variables). In BASIC, functions are defined using the DEF command. For example:

```
10   DEF FNR(X) = (INT(100*X + .5))/100
```

The name of the function is FNR. This function rounds a number off to the nearest hundredth. X represents the argument of the function. To use the function, type the function name followed, in parentheses, by the number you want rounded. For example, FNR(3.456) will have the value 3.46, and FRN(104.011) will have the value 104.01.

Here is an example of a simple Pascal function that doubles a number:

```
FUNCTION double(a:REAL):REAL;
   BEGIN
      double := 2*a
   END;
```

For example, double (23.4) will have the value 46.8.

Here is an example of a more complicated Pascal function that calculates the factorial of a number (see **factorial**):

```
FUNCTION fact(n:INTEGER):REAL;
VAR z :REAL; i :INTEGER;
   BEGIN
      z := 1;
      IF n>1
         THEN FOR i := 1 TO n DO
                  z := z*i;
      fact := z
   END;
```

The top line tells the computer that the name of the function is "fact," the argument is of type INTEGER, and the result is of type REAL. For example, fact (6) has the value 720.

FUNCTION KEYS Function keys (F keys) are keys labeled F1 through F12 on the IBM PC and PS/2 keyboards (F1 through F10 on earlier models). Their function depends on the software being run. See also **programmable-function key**.

g

GANTT CHART A Gantt chart is a diagram that shows the schedule for a series of tasks. (See **project manager**.)

GAS PLASMA DISPLAY A gas plasma display, which works according to the same principle as a neon light, is used for the screens for some laptop computers. Gas plasma screens are easier to read than liquid crystal display (LCD) screens, but they are more expensive and consume more power.

GATE (1) The gate is one of the three parts of a field-effect transistor. (2) Several types of logic circuits are known as gates. (See **AND gate; OR gate; NOT gate**.)

GATEWAY A gateway is a link between two or more wide-area networks.

GERMANIUM Germanium is a material used to make semiconductor devices. Each atom in a germanium crystal contains 32 protons and 32 electrons. Of the electrons 28 are bound tightly to the nucleus, while the outer 4 (valence) electrons can be dislodged easily. (See **semiconductor**.) Germanium is the second most popular material (after silicon) for making semiconductor devices.

GLITCH A glitch is an erroneous response that occurs inside a computer because signals that are supposed to be simultaneous actually arrive at slightly different times.

Software errors are occasionally called glitches. (See **bug**.)

GLOBAL VARIABLE A global variable is a variable that can be recognized anywhere in a program. For contrast, see **local variable**.

GOSUB The BASIC statement GOSUB causes the computer to jump to the subroutine that begins at the specified statement number. When the computer reaches the keyword RETURN at the end of the subroutine, it will jump back to the statement immediately following the original GOSUB statement. (See **subroutine**.)

GRAPHICS Computer graphics is the use of computer output devices, such as screens and plotters, to produce pictures. A plotter is a device that draws on paper, usually by moving a pen from point to point.

The applications of computer graphics include the following:

1 Generating graphs and charts of mathematical data. This was the earliest use to which plotters were put.

2 CAD/CAM (Computer-Aided Design and Computer-Aided Manufacturing). Using a light pen, a technician sketches the design of a piece of metalwork or a printed circuit board on the computer screen; the computer can straighten the lines, allow the technician to make changes, and then control automated factory equipment to manufacture the product.

3 Typesetting and the graphic arts. A computer can make it easy to edit a drawing by rearranging the components, changing the scale, or inserting extra space. It is possible that in a few years drawing editors (such as MacPaint on the Apple Macintosh) will be as common as word processors. Extremely elaborate computers are already being used to generate images for movie animation.

4 Education and entertainment. Graphic illustrations can enhance the value of educational computer programs, and interactive computer graphics forms the basis of all video games.

There are two basic ways to tell a computer how to draw a picture. In *vector graphics*, the computer is told to put a real or imaginary pen in a particular position and then draw a line a certain distance in a certain direction (or draw a line to another specific point). This is how most plotters work. The alternative is *raster graphics*, in which the screen or plotting area is divided into a rectangular array of points (called *pixels*, from "picture cells"), and the computer is told what color each dot should be. This is the usual technique for plotting on the screen of a microcomputer; many dot matrix printers also support it. Many computers allow the programmer to give vector-style instructions even when plotting on raster devices (e.g., all the graphics commands in the language LOGO are based on the vector concept).

The amount of fine detail that a particular graphics device can show is called the *resolution*. For vector devices, the resolution is usually given as a fraction of an inch or millimeter; for raster devices, it is given as the number of pixels in the array. For example, a 640-by-400 array of pixels will contain as much detail as the average monitor screen can reproduce; a 320-by-200 array is quite adequate for most home computers. (See also **three-dimensional graphics.**)

GRAPHICS CARD A graphics card is a video card that can display graphics as well as text. (See **video card.**)

GREEKING Greeking is the use of random letters or marks to show the overall appearance of a printed page without showing the actual text. With computers, greeking is used when the page is displayed too small for the text to be readable on the screen.

GRID In various draw programs and paint programs, a grid is a feature that allows lines to be drawn only in certain positions, as if they were drawn on the lines of graph paper. The grid makes it much easier to draw parallel and perpendicular lines, lay out diagrams, and avoid irregular breaks. However, when the grid is turned on, there are positions in which you cannot draw. (See also **draw program; paint program.**)

GRID SYSTEM The grid system is a way of standardizing the layout of many related pages, such as the pages of a multi-page document. The designer first draws a grid that will define the possible positions of columns, horizontal divisions, and pictures. Not all the possibilities of the grid are used on any single page, but the grid ensures that column positions do not vary haphazardly, and thereby makes the pages look related.

GROUNDING In any electrical device, "ground level" is the voltage level to which all other voltages are compared. In most computers, the ground level is connected to the ground pin (the third, rounded pin) of the power plug, and the power line then connects it to the earth itself, thereby assuring that the ground level for all machines is the same. This helps prevent cables from picking up noise or emitting radio frequency interference. It also reduces the danger of damage from lightning. (See **power line protection; RFI protection.**)

GW-BASIC Microsoft GW-BASIC is an interpreter for the same dialect of BASIC as is implemented in ROM on the IBM PC. However, GW-BASIC runs on machines that need not contain the IBM ROM chip. (For contrast, see **BASICA.**)

h

HACKER The word *hacker* means at least three things in relation to computer programming: (1) an exceptionally skilled computer programmer; (2) a person who programs computers for recreation or as a hobby; (3) a person who "breaks into" computers without authorization, either for malicious reasons or just to prove it can be done. (See **computer security**.)

HALF ADDER A half adder is a logic circuit that accepts two inputs and produces two outputs, as shown in the table.

Input 1	Input 2	Sum Output	Carry Output
0	0	0	0
0	1	1	0
1	0	1	0
1	1	0	1

(See **binary addition**.)

HALF DUPLEX The term *half duplex* refers to the transmission of data in only one direction at a time. (See **full duplex; modem**.)

HALF-HEIGHT DRIVE A half-height 5¼-inch disk drive is approximately 1⅝ inches high, half the height of a full-height drive.

HANDSHAKING The term *handshaking* refers to the exchange of signals between two computers to indicate that data transmission is proceeding successfully. For examples, see **X-OFF, X-ON** and **XMODEM**.

HARD CARD A hard card is a type of hard disk that is built into a card that can be plugged into a slot inside the computer.

HARD COPY A hard copy is a printout on paper of computer output.

HARD DISK A hard disk is a storage medium using rigid aluminum disks coated with iron oxide. Hard disks have much greater storage capacity than do floppy disks. Originally, 10 megabytes was a common size for microcomputer hard disks. More recently, 40-megabyte hard disks have become common, and even larger sizes are available. The read-write head travels across the disk on a thin cushion of air without ever actually touching the disk. However, hard disks have the disadvantage that they are built into the machine and cannot be removed, as can floppy disks. Hard disks are also called *winchester disks.* (See **disk; floppy disk; hard-disk management**.)

HARD-DISK MANAGEMENT Here are some tips for using a hard disk effectively:

1 Learn how to back up your hard disk, and do it frequently. *Every hard disk in use today WILL break down within just a few years!*

2 Divide the disk into subdirectories (see **directory**) and put related files in each subdirectory (e.g., all word processing files in one directory and all spreadsheet files in another). Use a further level of subdirectories where appropriate, e.g., to separate letters from reports within the word processing directory.

3 Use the MS-DOS PATH command or its equivalent so that commonly used commands will work no matter what directory you are in. You can put the PATH command in your AUTOEXEC.BAT file.

4 In MS-DOS, use the command

```
PROMPT $P$G
```

so that the command prompt will tell you what directory you are in (e.g., "C:\MYDIR>" rather than just "C>"). Again, this command can be in your AUTOEXEC.BAT file.

5 Delete files that you no longer need. Make a directory called \JUNK in which to put files that will not be needed for very long, so that they will not clutter up other directories.

6 Periodically run CHKDSK or its equivalent to check for lost clusters. (See **cluster**.)

7 If possible, run a defragmentation program every few months, or eliminate fragmentation by backing up the whole disk, erasing all files, and restoring all files from the backup. (See **fragmentation**.)

HARDWARE The hardware in a computer system consists of all the physical elements in the computer, such as integrated circuits, wires, and terminals.

HARDWARE INTERRUPT See **interrupt**.

HASHING Hashing refers to a storage mechanism where data items are stored at locations that are determined by a mathematical function of the data. For example, suppose you need to store a list of 100 numbers in memory locations whose addresses run from 1 to 100. One example of a hashing function is to calculate the remainder when the number is divided by 100 and then to store it at that location. For example, the number 538 would be stored at memory location 38. The use of hashing makes it possible to store and retrieve the data items quickly, since it is not necessary to search through the list in order to find the item. However, there is one complication: A hashing function will sometimes assign more than one data item to the same address. For example, using the rule given above, the number 638 would also be stored in location 38. To avoid that problem, a hashing system needs to be able to resolve collisions by storing the new data item in a separate place.

HAT The character "^" is sometimes called a hat.

HAYES COMPATIBILITY A modem is Hayes compatible if it responds to the same set of auto-dialing commands as the Hayes Smartmodem (made by Hayes Microcomputer Products, Inc., Norcross, Georgia).

Two modems need not be Hayes compatible in order to communicate with each other. Hayes compatibility refers only to the commands used by the computer to control the modem. A sampling of such commands is given in Table 6.

Table 6 Examples of Hayes Modem Dialing Commands.

ATDT9W555-1212	Dial 9, wait for another dial tone, and dial 555-1212 (using tone dialing).
ATDP9W555-1212	Same, but use pulse dialing.
ATH0	Hang up.
ATA	Answer an incoming call (right now) with modem.
ATO	Resume communicating (use this after you have typed "+++" to issue commands in the middle of a session). Note that this command uses the letter O, not the digit 0.
ATSO=1	Answer when the phone rings.

The modem accepts commands whenever it is not connected via phone lines to another modem. To set the modem baud rate, simply start sending commands at the baud rate you desire. To send a command to the modem while communicating to another computer, stop typing for 1 second, type "+++" (without quotes), and again stop typing for about a second. The modem will respond "OK," and you are free to give a command.

Table 7 gives the DIP switch settings for the Hayes Smartmodem 1200. Other modems use similar settings. (See also **modem; RS-232.**)

Table 7 DIP Switch Settings for Hayes Smartmodem 1200

Switch

1   *Up:* Modem uses DTR signal from computer.
     Down: Modem assumes DTR is always high (true).
     Explanation: Most computers provide a DTR signal that is high when the communications program is running, and low otherwise. When DTR is low, the modem hangs up the phone and refuses to accept commands.

2   *Up:* Modem gives English words as result codes.
     Down: Modem gives numbers as result codes.
     Explanation: Leave this switch up if you want to see messages such as "CONNECT" or "NO CARRIER".

3   *Up:* No result codes are sent.
     Down: Result codes are sent (either numbers or words as selected by switch 2).
     Explanation: See switch 2.

4   *Up:* Command characters are echoed.
     Down: Command characters are not echoed.
     Explanation: If the letters in commands are invisible on your screen, this switch should be up. If the letters appear twice, this switch should be down.

5   *Up:* Modem will answer incoming calls.
     Down: Modem will not answer incoming calls unless commanded to do so.
     Explanation: This switch should be up if your computer is going to be answering calls from another computer, and down otherwise.

6   *Up:* The CD signal will be high (true) only when a connection to another modem has been established.
     Down: The modem will always hold CD high.
     Explanation: Some computer programs refuse to transmit if CD is not high. If this prevents you from sending commands to the modem, put this switch in the down position.

7   *Up:* Single line telephone connection.
     Down: RJ12 or RJ13 telephone connection.
     Explanation: This switch should almost always be up. In the down

position, an additional relay is connected to the phone line to control an indicator light.

8   *Up:* Modem will not recognize commands.

Down: Modem recognizes commands.

Explanation: This switch should be down unless you want to disable Hayes compatibility.

9   *Up:* Modem uses Bell 103 and 212A data format.

Down: Modem uses CCITT V. 22 format.

Explanation: The Bell formats are used in the United States; the CCITT format in Europe.

10   *Up:* When DTR goes low, the modem hangs up and awaits commands.

Down: When DTR goes low, the modem hangs up and resets, canceling the effect of any commands that have been given.

Explanation: This switch should usually be up. It has no effect unless switch 1 is also up.

HEAD The head is the part of a disk drive that reads and writes information. A double-sided disk drive or multilayer hard disk has a head for each side of each layer. (See **disk.**)

HELP Many computer programs contain an on-screen help facility that a user can turn to when questions arise. For example, if you have forgotten how a particular command works, you may consult a help facility (if one is available) to refresh your memory. Different programs use different methods for obtaining help. For example, typing the F1 key will bring help if you are using Lotus 1-2-3. (See also **documentation; context-sensitive help.**)

HENRY The henry is the unit of measure of inductance. One henry is the inductance of a circuit in which an electromotive force of 1 volt is produced by a current in the circuit that varies at the rate of 1 ampere per second.

HERCULES GRAPHICS CARD The Hercules Graphics Card (HGC) provides all of the functions of the IBM Monochrome Display Adapter (MDA) with the same type of monitor, plus a high-resolution graphics mode. The Hercules Graphics Card is not an IBM product, and its graphics mode is not the same as that of any IBM product. (See **video modes [IBM PC].**)

HEURISTIC The word *heuristic* refers to a method of solving problems that involves intelligent trial and error. By contrast, an algorithmic solution method is a clearly specified procedure that is guaranteed to give the correct answer. (See **algorithm**.) For example, there is no known algorithm that tells how to play a perfect game of chess, so computer chess-playing programs must use a heuristic method of solution.

HEWLETT-PACKARD Hewlett-Packard, located in Palo Alto, California, makes a wide variety of electronics instruments and calculators, as well as the HP Vectra line of microcomputers and the LaserJet series of laser printers (see **LaserJet**).

HEXADECIMAL A hexadecimal number is a number written in base-16. A hexadecimal system consists of 16 possible digits, labeled by 0, 1, 2, 3, 4, 5, 6, 7, 8, 9, A (= 10), B (= 11), C (= 12), D (= 13), E (= 14), and F (= 15). For example, the number A4C2 in hexadecimal means

$$10 \times 16^3 + 4 \times 16^2 + 12 \times 16^1 + 2 \times 16^0 = 42{,}178$$

Hexadecimal numbers provide a good shorthand way of representing binary numbers, since binary numbers can be converted to hexadecimal numbers by looking at only four digits at a time. For example, binary 1 1 1 1 equals hexadecimal F, binary 0 1 0 0 equals hexadecimal 4, and binary 1 1 1 1 0 1 0 0 equals hexadecimal F4:

When converting a binary number to hexadecimal by this method, start by adding zeros at the left to make the number of digits a multiple of 4.

Table 8 shows the hexadecimal equivalents of the four-digit binary numbers, and Table 9 shows the decimal equivalents of the hexadecimal numbers from 00 to FF.

TABLE 8   Hexadecimal Equivalents of Binary Numbers

Binary	Hexadecimal	Binary	Hexadecimal
0 0 0 0	0	1 0 0 0	8
0 0 0 1	1	1 0 0 1	9
0 0 1 0	2	1 0 1 0	A
0 0 1 1	3	1 0 1 1	B
0 1 0 0	4	1 1 0 0	C
0 1 0 1	5	1 1 0 1	D
0 1 1 0	6	1 1 1 0	E
0 1 1 1	7	1 1 1 1	F

TABLE 9   Decimal Equivalents of Hexadecimal Numbers

00 = 0	20 = 32	40 = 64	60 = 96	80 = 128	A0 = 160	C0 = 192	E0 = 224
01 = 1	21 = 33	41 = 65	61 = 97	81 = 129	A1 = 161	C1 = 193	E1 = 225
02 = 2	22 = 34	42 = 66	62 = 98	82 = 130	A2 = 162	C2 = 194	E2 = 226
03 = 3	23 = 35	43 = 67	63 = 99	83 = 131	A3 = 163	C3 = 195	E3 = 227
04 = 4	24 = 36	44 = 68	64 = 100	84 = 132	A4 = 164	C4 = 196	E4 = 228
05 = 5	25 = 37	45 = 69	65 = 101	85 = 133	A5 = 165	C5 = 197	E5 = 229
06 = 6	26 = 38	46 = 70	66 = 102	86 = 134	A6 = 166	C6 = 198	E6 = 230
07 = 7	27 = 39	47 = 71	67 = 103	87 = 135	A7 = 167	C7 = 199	E7 = 231
08 = 8	28 = 40	48 = 72	68 = 104	88 = 136	A8 = 168	C8 = 200	E8 = 232
09 = 9	29 = 41	49 = 73	69 = 105	89 = 137	A9 = 169	C9 = 201	E9 = 233
0A = 10	2A = 42	4A = 74	6A = 106	8A = 138	AA = 170	CA = 202	EA = 234
0B = 11	2B = 43	4B = 75	6B = 107	8B = 139	AB = 171	CB = 203	EB = 235
0C = 12	2C = 44	4C = 76	6C = 108	8C = 140	AC = 172	CC = 204	EC = 236
0D = 13	2D = 45	4D = 77	6D = 109	8D = 141	AD = 173	CD = 205	ED = 237
0E = 14	2E = 46	4E = 78	6E = 110	8E = 142	AE = 174	CE = 206	EE = 238
0F = 15	2F = 47	4F = 79	6F = 111	8F = 143	AF = 175	CF = 207	EF = 239
10 = 16	30 = 48	50 = 80	70 = 112	90 = 144	B0 = 176	D0 = 208	F0 = 240
11 = 17	31 = 49	51 = 81	71 = 113	91 = 145	B1 = 177	D1 = 209	F1 = 241
12 = 18	32 = 50	52 = 82	72 = 114	92 = 146	B2 = 178	D2 = 210	F2 = 242
13 = 19	33 = 51	53 = 83	73 = 115	93 = 147	B3 = 179	D3 = 211	F3 = 243
14 = 20	34 = 52	54 = 84	74 = 116	94 = 148	B4 = 180	D4 = 212	F4 = 244
15 = 21	35 = 53	55 = 85	75 = 117	95 = 149	B5 = 181	D5 = 213	F5 = 245
16 = 22	36 = 54	56 = 86	76 = 118	96 = 150	B6 = 182	D6 = 214	F6 = 246
17 = 23	37 = 55	57 = 87	77 = 119	97 = 151	B7 = 183	D7 = 215	F7 = 247
18 = 24	38 = 56	58 = 88	78 = 120	98 = 152	B8 = 184	D8 = 216	F8 = 248
19 = 25	39 = 57	59 = 89	79 = 121	99 = 153	B9 = 185	D9 = 217	F9 = 249
1A = 26	3A = 58	5A = 90	7A = 122	9A = 154	BA = 186	DA = 218	FA = 250
1B = 27	3B = 59	5B = 91	7B = 123	9B = 155	BB = 187	DB = 219	FB = 251
1C = 28	3C = 60	5C = 92	7C = 124	9C = 156	BC = 188	DC = 220	FC = 252
1D = 29	3D = 61	5D = 93	7D = 125	9D = 157	BD = 189	DD = 221	FD = 253
1E = 30	3E = 62	5E = 94	7E = 126	9E = 158	BE = 190	DE = 222	FE = 254
1F = 31	3F = 63	5F = 95	7F = 127	9F = 159	BF = 191	DF = 223	FF = 255

HIERARCHICAL Data items have a hierarchical arrangement if a data item can be regarded as "below," or "belonging to," another data item that is at a higher level. At the very top level of the hierarchy is a data item (called the root) that is not below any other items. Hierarchical data items can be thought of as an inverted tree, with the root at the top and other locations (called nodes) branching out below. Hierarchical data structures are common both in ordinary life and when dealing with computers. For example, the executive branch of the U.S. government can be thought of as a hierarchy with the president at the top, cabinet secretaries one level down, and various bureau and office directors and their staffs below the secretaries.

The Lotus 1-2-3 menu structure is arranged hierarchically. If you are in the READY mode, then pressing the / key puts you at the top of the menu tree, with several possible choices you may branch to. If you choose the Range command, you will be presented with a new set of choices that are subcommands of the Range command. If you now choose the Name command, then you will see a new list of subcommands. This part of the command structure can be illustrated as a tree like this:

Worksheet Range Copy Move File Print Graph Data Quit

Format Label-Prefix Erase Name Justify Protect Unprotect Input

Create Delete Labels Reset

For other examples of hierarchical data structures, see **directory; outline; tree.**

HIERARCHICAL FILE SYSTEM The Hierarchical File System is a feature that gives the Macintosh the ability to store files in subdirectories (called *folders*). (See **directory.**)

HIGH-LEVEL LANGUAGE A high-level language is a computer programming language designed to allow people to write programs without having to understand the inner workings of the computer. BASIC, PL/I, FORTRAN, and Pascal are examples of high-level languages. A machine language is at the lowest level, since machine language programming requires detailed knowledge of the computer's inner workings. An assembly language is at a slightly higher level than a machine language.

HOLE A hole is a place where an electron is missing from the crystal structure of a P-type semiconductor. A hole acts as a moving positive charge. (See **semiconductor**.)

HOST COMPUTER The host computer is the computer that is in charge of the operations of a group of computers linked in a network.

HYPERCARD Hypercard is a program for data management for the Apple Macintosh. Information is arranged in stacks, which consist of collections of cards. When an individual card is displayed on the screen, the parts of the card will be visible. Each card can contain fields (which contain text), graphics, or buttons. Parts of the card are common to all cards in the stack; other parts of the card are unique to each individual card. A button will appear on the screen as a picture or text that indicates what the button will do. If a button is pressed (by using the mouse), then a specific action will occur, which may involve moving to another card in the same stack or moving to a different stack. In this way it is possible for the data items in HyperCard to be connected to each other. Users of HyperCard may work with stacks obtained from data sources, or users may author their own stacks. For example, HyperCard might be used to keep track of the organization chart for a company. Buttons could be used to move up or down the hierarchy.

i

IBM IBM (International Business Machines) is the largest computer manufacturer. IBM makes Selectric typewriters and other office equipment as well as computers, which it started manufacturing in the 1950s. A decade later, IBM had about 80% of the computer market with models such as the IBM 360 computer. The company continues to make popular mainframe computers, such as the 4300 series. In 1981 IBM introduced the IBM PC, which quickly became one of the most popular microcomputers. Now many other companies produce software or peripherals designed to be used with the IBM PC, and several companies produce computers designed to run the same programs as the IBM PC. In

1987 IBM introduced the PS/2 line of microcomputers, and in 1988 it introduced the AS line of larger computers. The headquarters of IBM is in Armonk, New York.

IBM 3270 Terminals in the IBM 3270 series are commonly used with IBM mainframe computers. They use the EBCDIC character set. An unusual aspect of 3270 series terminals is that most of the user's interaction is with a terminal cluster controller rather than with the computer itself. The cluster controller maintains the contents of the screen, and when the user presses Enter, the whole screen is sent to the computer.

See also **IBM 7171**.

IBM 7171 The IBM 7171 communications controller allows ASCII terminals such as the VT-100 (or personal computers emulating ASCII terminals) to take the place of IBM 3270 EBCDIC terminals. The 7171 performs ASCII-to-EBCDIC translation and takes the place of the 3270 cluster controller.

IBM PC AND PS/2 The IBM Personal Computer (PC), introduced in 1981, was the first of a family of very popular microcomputers, including not only IBM products but also "clones" (imitations) made by other companies. The original IBM PC used very little proprietary technology, and it was easy to build compatible machines without violating patents. (See **clone; PC compatibility**.)

IBM has maintained a high level of "upward compatibility" within the PC and PS/2 line. This means that later-model machines in this line will run virtually all software written for earlier models.

The most important machines in the PC line are shown in Table 10. IBM has built many other special-purpose PCs, including the Portable PC, the laptop PC Convertible, and the PC 3270, which is designed to emulate a mainframe terminal.

The two original machines, the PC and PC XT, are virtually identical. The XT, introduced in 1983, originally included a 10-megabyte hard disk, although later models were sold without it. Also, the XT had eight expansion slots (for plug-in cards) while the PC had only five.

The PC AT, introduced in 1984, was the first machine to use an 80286 microprocessor, enabling programs to run much faster.

The PS/2 machines were introduced in 1987. They are much more compact than comparably configured PCs or ATs, and they

Table 10 Computers in the IBM PC Family

Model	Micro processor	Bus	Video capability	Operating system
PC	8088	Conventional	Chosen by purchaser	DOS
PCjr	8088	Special PCjr	CGA	DOS
PC XT	8088	Conventional	Chosen by purchaser	DOS
XT 286	80286	Conventional	Chosen by purchaser	DOS or OS/2
PC AT	80286	Conventional	Chosen by purchaser	DOS or OS/2
PS/2 25, 30	8086	Conventional	MCGA	DOS
PS/2 30-286	80286	Conventional	VGA	DOS or OS/2
PS/2 50, 60	80286	Micro Channel	VGA	DOS or OS/2
PS/2 70, 80	80386	Micro Channel	VGA	DOS or OS/2

use the Micro Channel bus, which will make it possible in the future to use more than one CPU in a single machine. Unlike the PC, XT, and AT, the PS/2 machines have built-in video adapters.

Table 11 IBM PC Family Diskette Formats.

Size	Capacity	Used by
5¼" single-sided double-density	160K	Earliest PCs (DOS 1.0)
5¼" double-sided double-density	360K	Most PCs
5¼" high density	1.2 MB	PC AT, XT 286 (These drives can also read, write, and format conventional double-density disks. There is a small chance that after being written on by a high-density drive, such a disk will not be readable in a double-density drive.)
3½" conventional	720K	PS/2 25 and 30
3½" high density	1.4 MB	PS/2 50 and up (Can also read, write, and format 3½"conventional diskettes)

Table 12 Versions of DOS Recommended for Computers in the IBM PC Family.

Machine	DOS version
PC	1.0 and up (2.1 and up for present-day software)
PC XT	2.0 and up
PCjr	2.1 only
PC AT	3.0 and up
XT 286	3.2 and up
All PS/2s	3.3 and up

All the machines in the PC and PS/2 line can run appropriate versions of DOS (PC-DOS, also known as MS-DOS). Two other operating systems, CP/M-86 and the UCSD P-System, were originally offered for the same machines but are seldom used today. The machines with 80286 or 80386 processors can run OS/2, Microsoft's new multitasking operating system (see **OS/2**).

Table 11 shows the diskette formats used by machines in the PC line. Table 12 shows recommended versions of DOS.

FIGURE 32.   IBM PC Special Characters, Grouped by Function

These computers use the ASCII character set (see **ASCII**). In addition, they define printed representations for all character codes from 0 to 255, even those that are not defined by the ASCII standard. Some of these characters can never be printed because they are equivalent to codes such as Return or Line Feed.

Figure 32 shows special characters that can be printed on most IBM printers, along with their numeric codes. These characters are typed by holding down the Alt key and typing the appropriate number on the numeric keypad at the right side of the keyboard. For example, to type a shaded block, hold down Alt, type 1 7 8, and then release Alt.

An unusual characteristic of all IBM PCs, ATs, and PS/2s, but not of clones, is that if the machine is unable to load an operating system from disk, it calls up a BASIC interpreter that is stored on a ROM chip. This BASIC interpreter ("Cassette BASIC") was originally implemented so that low-budget computer hobbyists could use IBM PCs without disk drives, storing their programs on cassette tape. The same ROM code was included in later machines because it is used by the BASIC interpreter that runs under DOS. (See **BASICA; GWBASIC.**)

IC See **integrated circuit.**

ICON An icon on a computer screen is a picture that represents a particular object or command. For example, on a Macintosh computer, the picture of a trash can stands for "delete." Use the mouse to move a file to the trash can, and it will be deleted. (See **mouse.**)

IDENTIFIER An identifier is a symbolic name used in a program and defined by the programmer. Most identifiers stand for variables (see **variable**); however, some languages allow the use of identifiers to represent constants, so that the value of a particular constant, wherever it occurs in the program, can be changed by changing the statement that defines the identifier. (See **constant.**)

IF In many programming languages the keyword IF is used to specify an action that is to be executed only if a specified condition is true. Here is an example of an IF statement in BASIC:

```
100  PRINT "INPUT PRICE"
110  INPUT P
```

```
120  IF P< 0 THEN PRINT "PRICE CAN'T BE < 0!":
     GOTO 100
```

If the condition "P<0" is true, then the two commands:

```
PRINT "PRICE  CAN'T BE < 0!"
GOTO 100
```

will be executed.

Here is an example of an IF command in Pascal:

```
IF hours <= 40
    THEN BEGIN
        pay := hours * wage;
        WRITELN('No overtime hours')
    END
ELSE  BEGIN
        pay := wage * 40 + 1.5 * wage * (hours - 40);
        WRITELN('Overtime wages paid')
    END;
```

If the condition "hours <= 40" is true, then the two statements between the first BEGIN/END pair will be executed. If the condition is false, then the two statements between the BEGIN/END pair following the word ELSE will be executed.

IMPEDANCE The impedance of an electrical circuit is a measure of how easily an alternating current can pass through it. The impedance of a resistor is the same as its resistance. Capacitors and inductors also affect impedance.

The characteristic impedance of coaxial cable results from the interaction of its inductance and capacitance. It is not a resistance and cannot be measured with an ohmmeter. (See **coaxial cable.**)

INCREMENTAL BACKUP An incremental backup is one that only copies files that have not already been backed up. (See **backup.**)

INCREMENTAL COMPILER An incremental compiler compiles the lines of a program as they are typed into the computer, rather than compiling the whole program at once. (See **compiler.**)

INDUCTANCE The inductance of an inductor, or coil, is a measure of the strength of the magnetic field that is generated when a current is passed through that inductor. (See **inductor**.)

INDUCTOR An inductor is a coil of wire that can store energy in the form of a magnetic field. When a current flows in a wire, a magnetic field forms around the wire. When the current is turned off, the magnetic field collapses. A moving magnetic field generates an electric current, so as the magnetic field collapses it will briefly cause a current to flow in the direction opposite the original current flow. The magnetic field of a single wire will be very small, but the field can be made much stronger by wrapping the wire around an iron core many times. The symbol for an inductor is a little coil (see Figure 33). The strength of the magnetic field that an inductor will generate is measured in a unit called the *henry*.

In a direct-current circuit, the inductor acts like a resistor. The amount by which the inductor resists current flow in an alternating-current circuit increases as the frequency increases. Each time the current changes direction, the collapsing magnetic field generates a reverse current.

FIGURE 33 Inductor

INFERENCE ENGINE See **expert system.**

INFORMATION HIDING See **structured programming**.

INK-JET PRINTER An ink jet printer forms characters by firing tiny dots of ink at the paper.

INPUT The input to a computer is the data that are fed into the computer for it to process. (Note that the terms *input* and *output* are always used from the computer's point of view.) The input data may be either numbers or character strings (e.g., a list of names). The computer receives input through an input device, such as a keyboard, or from a storage device, such as a disk drive.

INSERTION POINT The insertion point in a full-screen editor or drawing program is the place where characters will appear if you start typing. The insertion point is usually indicated with a cursor or a thin vertical bar.

INSERTION SORT The insertion sort algorithm is a way of placing the elements of an array in ascending or descending order. Suppose we wish to sort the following list of numbers:

2404   8653   1354   5781

To perform an insertion sort, we examine every item in the list except the first. Whenever we find an item whose immediate neighbor on the left should be to the right of it, we pick up the current item, shift its neighbor on the left one space to the right, and see whether we can put the current item in the space thus vacated. If not, we shift that item to the right and try again. Here is an example, using ascending order:

Step 1.   Examine 8653. Its neighbor on the left is 2404, which should indeed be to the left of 8653, so all is well; proceed to the next item.

Step 2.   Examine 1354, Its neighbor on the left is 8653, which should be to the right of it. Pick up 1354:

2404   8653   ...   5781

Shift 8653 one space to the right:

2404   8653   5781

Can 1354 be put into the empty space? No; its neighbor on the left would be 2404, a larger number. Therefore we shift 2404 one space to the right:

....   2404   8653   5781

Now we can put 1354 into the empty space:

1354   2404   8653   5781

Step 3.   Examine 5781. Its neighbor on the left, 8653, should be to the right of it. We pick up 8653 and shift it one space to the right then put 5781 into the empty space:

1354   2404   8653   ....

1354   2404   8653

1354   2404   5781   8653

Now all the elements are in order, and the process is complete. Here is a Pascal program to perform an insertion sort:

```
PROGRAM insertionsort;
VAR
   a: ARRAY [1..10] of INTEGER;
   i, value, position: INTEGER;
BEGIN
   { Read in the data }
      FOR i := 1 to 10 DO
         BEGIN
            WRITE('Enter item ',i:2,':');
            READLN(a[i])
         END;
   { Perform the insertion sort }
      FOR i := 2 to 10 DO
         BEGIN
            value := a[i];
            position := 1;
            WHILE a [position-1] > value DO
               BEGIN
                  a[position] :=
                     a[position - 1];
                  position := position - 1
               END;
            a[position] := value
         END;
      { Print the results }
      FOR i := 1 to 10 DO WRITE(a[i]:5);
      WRITELN
END.
```

INSULATOR An insulator is a material in which all the electrons are tightly bound to their atoms, so electric current cannot flow through an insulator. A material in which current can flow is called a *conductor*.

INTEGER An integer is whole number or the negative of a whole number, such as 1, 2, 3, 0 , –10, –26, 157, 567, or –2.397. An integer does not contain a fractional part.

INTEGRATED CIRCUIT An integrated circuit is an electronic device consisting of many miniature transistors and other circuit elements on a single silicon chip. The first integrated circuits were developed in the late 1950s, and since then there has been continued improvement. The number of components that can be placed on a single chip has been steadily rising.

The advantages of integrated circuits include the fact that they are very small (less than $\frac{1}{4}$ inch square), their internal connections are more reliable, they consume much less power, they generate much less heat, and they cost less than similar circuits made with separate components.

Integrated circuits are classified by their level of complexity. "Small-scale integration" refers to circuits containing fewer than 10 logic gates; "medium-scale integration," to circuits containing 10 to 100 gates; and "large-scale integration," to circuits with more than 100 gates.

The pattern of components to be placed in an integrated circuit is first mapped out by a computer. It is necesary to add impurities to the silicon-crystal to create either P-type or N-type regions. (See **semiconductor**.) An evaporated metal is engraved on the circuit by photographic techniques in the places where electrical conducting paths are needed. Integrated circuits are mass produced by making many identical circuits at the same time from a single wafer of silicon. Each circuit must be individually tested, however, because a single defect in the crystal can compeletely ruin the circuit.

The ultimate integrated circuit is the microprocessor, which is a single chip that contains the complete arithmetic and logic unit of a computer.

INTEGRATED SOFTWARE An integrated software package is a program that combines several functions in one program. For example, Lotus 1-2-3 is an integrated program that combines spreadsheet calculations, data management operations, and graphics. The advantage of an integrated program stems from the fact that the transfer of information from one application to another is easier than it would be if a separate program was used for each application.

INTEL Intel produces the 8088 microprocessor that is used in the IBM PC and other computers. The 8088 processor has 16-bit internal registers.

INTERACTIVE SYSTEM In an interactive computer system the user communicates with the computer through a keyboard and a CRT screen. The computer presents the results almost immediately after an instruction has been entered, and the user can type in new instructions after seeing the results of the previous ones. See, for contrast, **batch processing**.

INTERBLOCK GAP An interblock gap is a blank space on a magnetic tape between two adjacent blocks. The presence of the gap makes it easier to keep track of the locations of the blocks when the tape is started and stopped.

INTERNAL STORAGE The internal storage of a computer is the memory that is built in (see **memory**). For contrast, see **auxiliary storage**.

INTERNATIONAL BUSINESS MACHINES See **IBM**.

INTERPRETER An interpreter is a program that executes a source program by reading it one line at a time and doing the specified operations immediately. Most BASIC systems are interpreters. For contrast, see **compiler**.

INTERRUPT An interrupt is an instruction that tells a microprocessor to put aside what it is doing and call a specified routine. The processor resumes its original work when the *interrupt service routine* finishes.
Interrupts are used for two main purposes:

1 To deal with hardware events such as a key being pressed or a character arriving through a serial port. These events cannot be ignored; the incoming data must be either processed immediately or stored in a buffer.
2 To call subroutines that are provided by the hardware or operating system. On the IBM PC, most DOS and BIOS services are called through interrupts rather than through the ordinary instruction for calling a subroutine. OS/2 services, on the other hand, are called as ordinary subroutines.

These correspond to the two main ways of causing an interrupt: by receiving a signal from outside the microprocessor (a *hardware interrupt*) or by executing a machine instruction (a *software interrupt*).

INTERRUPT SERVICE ROUTINE See **interrupt**.

INVERTER (1) A NOT gate is often called an inverter. (See **NOT gate**.)

(2) A device that converts direct current to alternating current for power supply purposes (e.g., to power a computer from a car battery) is called an inverter.

ISDN An ISDN (Integrated Services Digital Network) telephone line is an all-digital line that offers the ability to transmit digital data as well as voice, without a modem. ISDN service began in the U.S. in 1988 and will eventually replace conventional telephone serivce. (See **modem.**)

ISO ISO stands for International Standards Organization. There are ISO standards for many industries.

The most important ISO standard related to computers is the official standard version of the Pascal language, ISO Pascal. Most actual implementations of Pascal contain all of the features of ISO Pascal plus some others added by the implementor. However, the most popular implementation, Turbo Pascal, lacks some ISO features and therefore will not run all ISO Pascal programs. (See **Turbo Pascal.**)

ITERATION Iteration is the process of repeating a particular action. A definite iteration occurs when the specified action will be repeated a fixed number of times. For example, you can find the sum of all the integers from 1 to 100 with the following BASIC program, which uses iteration:

```
10   T = 0
20   FOR I = 1 TO 100
30   T = T + I
40   NEXT I
```

(See **loop.**) An indefinite iteration occurs if the repetitions stop when a particular condition is met, but you don't know in advance how many repetitions will take place before the condition is met. An example of an indefinite iteration is a binary search routine. (See **binary search.**) In that case the iteration will continue until the item you're looking for has been found, or you establish that it is not in the list.

j _____

JACKET A floppy disk is encased in a stiff plastic jacket which contains holes giving the disk drive access to the information on the disk. The disk should never be removed from the jacket.

JCL The Job Control Language of a computer is the command language used in batch jobs to tell the computer what to do. (See **batch processing**.) The acronym JCL usually refers to the job control language used on large IBM computers, but sometimes designates very different languages used for the same purpose on other computers.

The following is an example of JCL for an IBM 360; the language is the same for all IBM mainframe computers running operating systems derived from OS/360, such as OS/VS2 and MVS:

```
//JONES JOB 123456,TIME=5
// EXEC PLIXCG
//PLI.SYSIN DD DSN=JONES.SAMPL.PLI,DISP=SHR
//GO.SYSIN DD *
 1 2 3 4
/*
//
```

The first statement is the JOB card, which gives the job a name, specifies the user's account number, and establishes a CPU time limit of 5 minutes for the whole job. The EXEC PLIXCG statements calls up the procedure to compile and execute a PL/I program; its operation happens to consist of two steps, PLI (compile) and GO (execute). The SYSIN (standard system input) file for the PLI step is defined as a catalogued disk data set named JONES.SAMPL.PLI; the SYSIN for the GO step is given in the job itself, beginning after DD * and ending with /*. The // card marks the end of the job.

In IBM JCL, each statement has up to four fields, as in this example:

//GO.SYSIN DD * INPUT FILE

Here GO.SYSIN is the name field, DD is the operation field, * is the operand field, and INPUT FILE is the comment field. The rules for coding the fields are as follows:

1 The fields are separated by at least one blank. Only the first 71 characters of every line (not 72, as you might expect) are significant.

2 The name field is immediately adjacent to the two slashes at the beginning of the line. Often the EXEC statement has no name field; when this is the case, be sure to type

```
// EXEC
```

and not

```
//EXEC
```

The name field cannot contain any blanks.

3 The next field after the name field is the operation field, usually JOB, EXEC, or DD. The operation field also cannot contain any blanks.

4 The next field after the operation field is the operand field; this too cannot contain any blanks unless they are in quotation marks.

   If the operand field will not fit on one line, it can be continued to a second line, as in this example:

```
//GO.SYSIN DD DSN=JONES.OLD.DATA,
//             DISP=SHR,
//             DCB=(LRECL=80,BLKSIZE=3120)
```

   Here every line except the last ends with a comma. Every line except the first begins with two slashes followed by from 1 to 13 blanks. (A common error is to include too many blanks.)

5 Anything after the operand field is considered to be a comment and is ignored by the computer.

   JCL also includes a null statement (consisting of // by itself), which marks the end of a job, and a comment statement, which begins with //*. Comment statements are ignored by the operating system itself but are often used to convey information to utilities that have been added onto the operating system for various purposes (e.g., automatic allocation of tape drives).

   The details of JCL vary considerably from installation to installation; consult local manuals for more information.

JOB See **batch processing**.

JOB CONTROL LANGUAGE See **JCL**.

JOYSTICK A joystick is a computer input device especially helpful when playing computer games. The joystick consists of a handle that can be pointed in different directions. Because the computer can sense in which direction the joystick is pointed, the joystick can be used to control the movements of objects displayed on the computer screen.

JUNCTION The junction is the part of a diode or transistor where two opposite types of semiconductor material meet. (See **diode; transistor**.)

JUSTIFICATION Justification is the insertion of extra space between words in lines of type so that both the left and right margins are even, smooth. Most of the type in this book is justified.

On a typewriter, the only way to justify is to insert extra spaces equal to the width of whole characters, thereby lengthening most lines. This makes the text harder to read because of the large, irregular spaces between words.

A better way to justify is to use *microspacing*, i.e., to insert small, equal amounts of space between all the words. Some printers will do this. But with fixed-pitch type, the results can still be hard to read (see **pitch**).

The best justification is obtained with microspacing and proportional-pitch type. Even then, justification is only practical when the columns are wide enough that the extra space does not look awkward or conspicuous.

See also **river**.

k

K K is the symbol for the unit used to measure the size of a computer's memory; a computer with memory of 1K can store 1,024 characters. The number 1,024 is significant because $2^{10} = 1,024$. K is short for *kilobyte*, which is approximately 1,000 bytes. The maximum memory size (without bank switching) is 64K for older 8-bit systems and 640K for the IBM PC. Some more recent microcomputers have several megabytes of memory.

KAYPRO Kaypro Corporation of Solona Beach, California, manufactures the Kaypro 286 and Kaypro 386 microcomputers, which contain 80286 and 80386 microprocessors, respectively, and come with word processing and other software. In the early 1980s, Kaypro manufactured 8-bit computers using the CP/M operating system (the Kaypro 2, Kaypro 4, and Kaypro 10).

KERMIT Kermit is the name of a protocol for transferring files from one computer to another. It is also the name of a program (distributed free by Columbia University) that implements this protocol. (Other communications programs also implement part or all of the Kermit protocol.)

Like XMODEM, Kermit makes an exact copy of the original file even when transmitting over a noisy line. All data packets are error-checked and erroneous packets are retransmitted.

Kermit is slightly slower than XMODEM. Its advantages include the following:

1 The file name is sent along with the file.
2 A group of files can be sent by using wild card characters in file names (see **wild card**).
3 Eight-bit communication is not required. Kermit can be implemented on mainframe computers that transmit only 7 bits per byte. (See **RS-232**.)
4 Kermit is implemented on a very wide variety of machines, including many that have no other file-transfer protocol.

KERNING Kerning is a reduction in the amount of space between certain combinations of letters in proportional-pitch type. If the combination "To" is typeset with the same letter spacing as "Th," the letters seem to be too widely spaced. "To" looks better if the top of the "T" is allowed to overhang the "o" slightly. See Figure 34.

KEY (1) The buttons on a keyboard are called keys.

(2) The item by which a data file is sorted or searched is called the key. For instance, if a file of names and addresses is sorted by ZIP codes, then the ZIP code is the key.

(3) The password or other secret information needed to decode an encrypted message is called the key. (See **encryption**.)

KEY DISK Some copy protection systems require that a particular noncopyable disk be inserted in the computer to start a program, even if the program is not actually on that disk. Such a disk is called a key disk.

Equally Spaced

Kerned

FIGURE 34 Kerning

FIGURE 35

KEYWORD A keyword is a word that has special meaning in a particular programming language. For example, GOSUB is a keyword in BASIC, and BEGIN is a keyword in Pascal.

KILOBYTE See **K**.

KIRCHHOFF'S LAW Kirchhoff's law states that the sum of the voltages across the devices in a series circuit is equal to the total voltage applied to that circuit. (see Figure 35).

KLUDGE A kludge (pronounced "klooge") is an improvised, jury-rigged, poorly thought out solution to a problem, usually intended only for temporary use. The word may be derived from German *klug*, "clever."

KNOWLEDGE BASE See **expert system.**

l _____

LABEL (1) In some programming languages a *statement label* is a name that represents a particular statement. For example, in PL/I a statement label (which is optional) is written before the statement it labels, separated from it by a colon:

```
START: GET EDIT (X) (F(10));
```

The label can then be used in a GOTO statement, such as

```
GOTO START;
```

(2) A file stored on tape is preceded by an *identifying label*, containing information about the file.

(3) In MS-DOS (PC-DOS) and OS/2, disks have identifying names ("volume labels") recorded on them.

LAN See **local-area network.**

LANDSCAPE Landscape orientation refers to paper oriented so that it is wider than it is high, like a landscape painting. This results from turning the paper sideways relative to the way it is most commonly used ("portrait orientation"). Laser printers typically offer a choice of portrait or landscape orientation.

LAP-B LAP-B (Link Access Procedure—Balanced) is a method for detecting and correcting errors in data transmission. (For a description of another method in detail, see **XMODEM**.) LAP-B error correction is built into some high-speed modems so that erroneous data are never sent to the computer.

LAPTOP A laptop computer is a small, lightweight computer (under 8 pounds) with a flip-up screen that can be powered by batteries and is easily portable. Laptops are especially valuable for people who travel frequently and need to be able to work on a computer while on the road.

LARGE-SCALE INTEGRATION The term *large-scale integration* refers to integrated circuits that contain more than 100 logic gates. (See **integrated circuit**.)

LASER PRINTER A laser printer uses a laser beam to generate an image, then transfers it to paper electrostatically. (See **electrostatic printer**.) Laser printers provide letter-quality output for text. They also can print graphics and are quieter and faster than printers that mechanically strike the paper (see **dot-matrix printer** and **daisywheel printer**.) Laser printers are often used in desktop publishing. However, they are more expensive than other printers that are commonly used on microcomputers. For specific examples, see **Laserwriter** and **LaserJet**.

LASERJET The LaserJet is a popular laser printer produced by Hewlett-Packard. The LaserJet has space for plug-in font cartridges; it is also possible to use software-provided fonts loaded into the printer directly from the computer. Commands to the LaserJet can be sent with escape sequences (that is, a sequence of ASCII codes beginning with code 27). Table 13 shows some of the common sequences. (Note that a software program that is LaserJet-compatible will send these codes automatically to the printer.)

Table 13 Some LaserJet Command Codes

ASCII code numbers	Action
27 38 108 ## 80	set page length to ## lines per page
27 38 108 ## 69	set top margin to ## lines
27 38　97 ## 76	set left margin to column ##
27 38　97 ## 77	set right margin to column ##
27 38 108 54 68	set vertical spacing to 6 lines per inch
27 61	half line feed

27 38 97 ## 82	position cursor at row ##
27 38 97 ## 67	position cursor at column ##
27 38 108 48 79	switch orientation to portrait
27 38 108 49 79	switch orientation to landscape
27 40 56 85	switch font to internal Roman-8
27 40 115 ## 72	set primary pitch to ## characters per inch
27 40 115 ## 86	set primary point size to ##
27 40 115 48 83	set primary style to upright
27 40 115 49 83	set primary style to italics
27 40 ## 88	set primary font to number ##

LASERWRITER The Apple Laserwriter is a laser printer commonly used with the Macintosh computer. It uses the Postscript command language. (See **Macintosh; Postscript**.)

LCD LCD (Liquid Crystal Display) is the type of display found on many portable computers and digital watches.

LEADING Leading (pronounced "ledding") is the insertion of extra space between lines of type. On old printing presses, this was originally done by inserting strips of lead between rows of type cast in lead. (See **typeface**.)

LED The acronym LED stands for Light-Emitting Diode. An LED device will light up when the proper current is passed through it. The display on many calculators is made of LEDs.

LETTER QUALITY A letter-quality printer produces print equal in quality to that of the best typewriters. All laser printers and daisywheel printers are letter quality; so are some ink-jet printers and dot-matrix printers.

LIBRARY A library is a collection of files, computer programs, or subroutines. A loader library is a file containing subroutines that can be link-edited into a machine language program.

LIGHT-EMITTING DIODE See **LED**.

LIGHT PEN A light pen consists of a light-sensitive detector and is used to control pictures on a computer terminal. By using the light pen the operator can change the appearance of the lines on the screen.

LIM-EMS See **expanded memory**.

LIMITS OF COMPUTER POWER Computers can perform only tasks that can be reduced to mechanical procedures (algorithms).

They are therefore inapplicable to tasks that cannot or should not be reduced to mechanical form, such as judging the greatness of a work of art or administering psychotherapy.

Rather suprisingly, however, there are some tasks that are mathematically precise but that present-day computers cannot perform. These fall into two major types: (1) problems with no known algorithmic solution, and (2) problems whose best known algorithmic solutions require unreasonable amounts of time. (Some mathematical problems can be proved to have no algorithmic solution, but they seldom turn up in practical work.)

An example of a problem of the first type (i.e., one with no presently known algorithmic solution) is how to get a computer to recognize the structures of sentences in a human language such as English. Obviously, this is something computers will have to be able to do if we are ever to be able to communicate with them in English, and there is no reason to think it impossible. The difficulty is simply that English (and all other human languages) are so complicated that complete algorithms for processing them have not yet been discovered.

A good example of the second type of problem, one that takes an unreasonable amount of time to solve, is the so-called *traveling salesman problem*. The task is to find the shortest route by which a salesman can visit a particular set of cities (in any order). The only known way to solve this problem is to try all possible routes. A few shortcuts are possible—for instance, the testing of each route can be abandoned as soon as its length exceeds the shortest length already found, without pursuing it to the end—but the number of steps is never substanially fewer than N factorial, where N is the number of cities (see **factorial**).

Suppose the fastest imaginable computer could perform one step in this algorithm by moving an electric charge a distance of 1 millimeter at the speed of light. This would mean that it could perform 3×10^{11} steps per second. Then the times required to solve the traveling salesman problem (in N! steps) would work out as follows:

Number of Cities	Number of Steps	Time Required
5	120	0.36 picosecond
10	3,628,800	12 microseconds
15	1.3×10^{12}	4.4 seconds

20	2.4×10^{18}	94 days
25	1.6×10^{25}	1.6 milliom years
30	2.7×10^{32}	2.8×10^{13} years

And this is with a computer millions of times faster than any that presently exist! Obviously, it will never be feasible to solve the traveling salesman problem for more than a few cities unless a much better algorithm is found.

Another interesting class of computational problems, known as *NP-complete problems*, has been proved to be equivalent to the traveling salesman problem; if a better algorithm is found for any NP-complete problem, it will be applicable to all of them.

LINE PRINTER A line printer is a high-speed printer for computer output. A line printer consists of a separate chain of type elements for each column, so it is capable of printing an entire line of output at one time. Fast line printers are capable of printing output at rates of up to 1,400 lines per minute.

LINKAGE EDITOR A linkage editor, also known as a *linker*, is a program, supplied with the operating system, that puts together machine-language programs from several sources (e.g., the output of a compiler plus a predefined subroutine library supplied with the compiler) to yield a complete, executable program, called a *load module*.

LINKED LIST A linked list is a way of organizing data items in the computer so that they are retrievable in a particular order that is not necessarily the same order of the physical locations in which they are stored. Each data item consists of two parts: the data itself, and a number giving the location of the next item, Figure 36 shows how this is usually diagrammed. To read the items in order, you need only know which item is the beginning (the *head*) of the list; having located it, you go next to the item whose address was stored with it; and so on.

Linked lists allow items to be added or removed without requiring that other items be moved to make room. For instance, the list A-D-E of Figure 36 can be changed into A-B-C-D-E by adding two items. As Figure 37 shows, the newly added items B and C can be placed in the unused area after the E, and "inserted" into the list by changing the address associated with item A. Figure 38 shows that an item can be "deleted" by changing the addresses so that there is no longer a path to that item. In either

FIGURE 36

FIGURE 37

case, using linked lists can eliminate the need to move hundreds or thousands of data items when an insertion or deletion takes place.

Figure 39 shows a way to construct a linked list in an ordinary two-dimensional array; this can be done in practically any programming language. Each row of the array contains a data item and an integer indicating which row the next item is on (or zero, to indicate that there are no more items). In the example, it is assumed that the first item in the list will always be in row 1; if you wish to be able to delete the first item, you can use a separate

(deleted)

FIGURE 38

item no.	data item	address of next item
1	A	4
2	D	3
3	E	0
4	B	5
5	C	2

FIGURE 39

integer, outside the array, to keep track of where the list starts. See also **data structure**.

LINKER See linkage editor.

LIQUID CRYSTAL DISPLAY See LCD.

LISP The programming language LISP (List Processor) was developed in the early 1960s at MIT under the direction of John McCarthy. Because of the ease with which it can handle complex data structures, LISP is used for artificial intelligence research and for writing programs whose complexity would render them intractable in other languages.

A LISP program is easy to recognize because of the accumulation of closing parentheses at the end of the program. All LISP statements and data structures are linked lists, written as lists of elements in parentheses (see **linked list**). The programmer builds a complex program by defining her own statements (actually functions) in terms of those previously defined: For example, a function that computes the factorial of X is:

```
(DEFUN FACTORIAL (X)
    (COND ((= X 0) 1)
          (T      (* X (FACTORIAL (- X 1)))))))
```

Translating into English, we have the following: "This is the definition of a function called FACTORIAL whose parameter is X. If X is zero, its factorial is 1; otherwise, its factorial is equal to X times the factorial of X–1." Here COND introduces a series of lists to be tried in succession until one beginning with a true predicate is found, and T means "true" (thereby introducing a clause that executes if (= X 0) is false). This function calls itself recursively; recursion is the normal way of expressing repetition in LISP.

LISP varies from implementation to implementation even more than BASIC; it is almost impossible to transfer a LISP program from one computer to another without making some changes in it. A standard language called *Common LISP* has been proposed, but it has so many features that complete implementations of it are rare.

LIST A list is a set of data items that are to be accessed in a particular order; for instance, a list of the students in a class might be accessed in alphabetical order. Lists are stored in arrays or linked lists. (See **array; linked list.**)

LITERAL A literal is a symbol in a computer program that stands for a particular value and is not progammer-defined (i.e., cannot possibly stand for any other value). For example, in the following BASIC program:

```
10    LET A = 2.4
20    LET B$ = "THE ANSWER IS"
30    PRINT B$, A
```

the literals are "THE ANSWER IS" and 2.4.

LN The function LN(X) in Pascal and some other languages calculates the natural logarithm of X. (See **logarithm.**)

LOAD To load is to transfer information from an auxiliary storage device into a computer.

LOAD In many implementations of BASIC the LOAD command causes a program that is stored on a disk to be loaded into the computer's memory. For example, the command LOAD "GAME" will load the program GAME into the computer's memory. Then you can execute the program by typing RUN.

In TSO and other operating systems the LOAD command causes a machine language program (object module) to be placed into memory and executed.

LOCAL-AREA NETWORK A local-area network connects together several machines that are located nearby (in the same room or building) allowing them to share files and devices such as printers. For example, see **Ethernet; token ring.**

A local-area network can be very valuable if several people must constantly enter data into a single data base. Some data base programs, such as Paradox, have network versions designed specifically for this purpose. For example, several workers might work on the same inventory-control system, one of them logging new merchandise as it comes in, the other logging sales as they take place.

The value of local-area networks for printer sharing is more questionable. It is often cheaper to buy several printers or to buy a simple accessory for the printer that allows it to take input from more than one machine. Also consider the possibility of carrying a diskette from one machine to another.

There has been serious criticism of the use of local-area networks merely to "manage" groups of machines. If there is no real need to share data, the network can be a needless expense. Networks do not save on the cost of software because it is usually necessary to license the software separately for each machine (see **software license; copyright**).

LOCAL VARIABLE A local variable has meaning only within a particular function or subroutine. The name of a local variable can be used in another subroutine elsewhere in the program, where it will mean something totally different.

Most programming languages contain provisions to make a particular variable a local variable. In Pascal, a variable is local to a particular procedure if it is declared within that procedure. Here is an example of a Pascal program where *a* is a global variable, c is a local variable inside procedure pl, and the name *b* represents two variables; a global variable and a local variable inside procedures pl.

```
PROGRAM example (INPUT, OUTPUT);
   {This program demonstrates local and global
   variables.}
VAR
   a, b : INTEGER;
PROCEDURE pl;
   VAR
      b, c : INTEGER;
   BEGIN
      a := 500;
      b := 100;
      c := 200;
```

```
      WRITELN ('We are now in procedure pl.');
      WRITELN ('a= ',a,' b= ',b,' c= ',c)
   END;
BEGIN {Main program }
   a := 10;
   b := 20;
   WRITELN ('We are in the main program block.');
   WRITELN ('a= ',a,' b= ',b);
   pl;
   WRITELN ('We are back in the main program
      block.');
   WRITELN ('a= ',a,' b= ',b):
END.
```

Here is the output:

```
We are in the main program block.
a = 10 b = 20
 We are now in procedure pl.
a = 500 b = 100 c= 200
We are back in the main program block.
a = 500 b = 20
```

Note that, when we change the value of a in procedure pl, the change affects the global variable a. Changing the value of b in procedure pl changes only the local variable, and so does not affect the value of b in the main block. We could not include the statement WRITELN(c) in the main block because c is a local variable that will be recognized only inside procedure pl.

The advantage of using local variables is not obvious in short programs. However, it is a good idea when writing a long program to make as many variables as possible into local variables, because then there will be no problem if you wish to use the same name to mean something else at another point in the program. This rule is even more important if several different people are writing subroutines that will be combined into one main program. (See also **side effect**.)

LOG In many verisons of BASIC and other languages, the function LOG(X) calculates the natural logarithm of X. However, in some versions, LOG(X) is the common logarithm and LN(X) is the natural logarithm. (See **logarithm**.)

LOGARITHM If $y = a^x$, then x is the logarithm of y to the base a

(written as $x = \log_a y$). The most common bases for logarithm functions are 10 and e. Base-10 logarithms are called *common logarithms*; base-e logarithms, *natural logarithms*. For example, the common logarithm of 10,000 is 4 ($\log_{10} 10,000 = 4$) because $10^4 = 10,000$.

LOGIC GATE A logic gate is a device that accepts binary digits (bits) as inputs and produces an output bit according to a specified rule. For examples, see **AND gate; OR gate; NOT gate.**

LOGO LOGO is a programming language developed by Seymour Papert of MIT for use in teaching programming to children. Papert's funadmental insight was that computer-aided instruction is of little use unless the pupil can control the computer, rather than the other way around. To experiment with this idea, he designed a language that is markedly easier to use than BASIC and does not share BASIC's preoccupation with numerical calculation.

Although LOGO offers a full range of computer functions, most elementary LOGO exercises revolve around the "turtle," originally a robot that rolled around on a sheet of paper making marks with a pen. (The present-day turtle is more often a triangle that moves around the screen, drawing a line if told to do so.) Drawing shapes with the turtle appeals to children who would not be attracted to mathematical calculation or verbal input-output; at the same time, it serves as a good medium for teaching geometry and logical problem solving.

LOGO is an extensible language; that is, programs are constructed by defining statements in terms of previously defined statements. For example, the following procedure draws a square:

```
TO SQUARE
   CLEARSCREEN
   FORWARD 50
   RIGHT 90
   FORWARD 50
   RIGHT 90
   FORWARD 50
   RIGHT 90
   FORWARD 50
END
```

In other words, "Clear the screen (and put the turtle in the center), go forward (up) 50 units, do a 90-degree right turn, go forward 50 units, do a 90-degree right turn," and so forth.

Since LOGO procedures can call themselves recursively, complicated snowflake-like patterns are relatively easy to generate.

LOG ON To log on to a computer is to establish a connection from your terminal to the computer and to identify yourself as an authorized user.

LOOP A loop in a computer program is a set of statements that are to be executed repeatedly. For example, the BASIC program

```
10  FOR I = 1 TO 5
20      PRINT I,I∧2
30  NEXT I
```

contains a loop. Statement 20 will be executed five times, first with I equal to 1, then with I equal to 2, and so on. The output from the program will look like this:

```
1       1
2       4
3       9
4       16
5       25
```

The program above contains a loop that will always be executed the same number of times. It is also possible to establish a loop that will be executed until a particular condition occurs. For example, these Pascal statements:

```
i := 1;
REPEAT
    WRITELN(i);
    i := 2 * i;
UNTIL i > 1000;
```

produce this output:

```
1
2
4
8
16
```

```
 32
 64
128
256
512
```

LOST CLUSTER In MS-DOS (PC-DOS) and other operating systems, a lost cluster is a group of disk sectors that are not marked as free but are not allocated to a file. Lost clusters result when the operation of creating a file is interrupted. They waste space and should be cleaned up periodically; this is done with the CHKDSK /F command.

LOTUS 1-2-3 Lotus 1-2-3, an integrated software package produced by Lotus Development Corp., has become one of the best selling business decision-making tools. Lotus 1-2-3 combines the functions of a spreadsheet program with data management capabilities and graphics. See **spreadsheet; data base management,** and **graphics** for information on these topics.

   Work in 1-2-3 is based on a worksheet of rows and columns that appears on the screen. The rows are numbered, and the columns are identified with letters. Each individual cell can be identified by specifying its row and column; for example, C4 is the cell in the third column and the fourth row. Numbers, text, or formulas can be entered into cells. The arrow keys on the keyboard are used to move the cell pointer to new locations. The start of a 1-2-3 command is signaled by typing "/," which causes a command list menu to appear on the top of the screen.

   Here is an example of a 1-2-3 spreadsheet. We will enter information on the personal finances of an individual with money in four places; a checking account, a savings account, an Individual Retirement Account (IRA), and cash. We will use the first row to display a label that identifies the table, and we will enter the labels for each category in column A. The numbers themselves will go in column B.

   Figure 40 shows what the spreadsheet looks like. The symbol B3: at the upper left corner indicates that the cell pointer is currently pointing at cell B3, and this cell currently holds the value 450.53. You can tell that we have just pressed the "/" key in this case because the command menu has appeared in the second and third lines of the screen.

   The value of the spreadsheets stems from their ability to store formulas in cells and then automatically calculate the values

```
B3: 450.53                                                              MENU
Worksheet  Range  Copy  Move  File  Print  Graph  Data  Quit
Global, Insert, Delete, Column-Width, Erase, Titles, Window, Status
       A        B        C        D        E        F        G        H
1    Personal Financial Data
2             Today
3    Checking    450.53
4    Saving      832.52
5    IRA        3040.11
6    Cash        83.43
7
8
9
10
11
12
13
14
15
16
17
18
19
20
```

FIGURE 40

given by these formulas. We would like to calculate the total
amount of money in the four places. To do that we will enter the
formula @SUM(B3..B6) into cell B7. The @ symbol is put in
front of all 1-2-3 functions. The SUM function automatically
calculates the sum of all cells in the indicated range. The notation
B3..B6 means to take all cells from B3 to B6. Figure 41 shows
the result.

   If we change one of the numbers in cells B3 to B6, then 1-2-
3 will automatically calculate the new total and display that value

```
B7: @SUM(B3..B6)                                                       READY

       A        B        C        D        E        F        G        H
1    Personal Financial Data
2             Today
3    Checking    450.53
4    Saving      832.52
5    IRA        3040.11
6    Cash        83.43
7    Total      4406.59
8
9
10
11
12
13
14
15
16
17
18
19
20
```

FIGURE 41

in cell B7. (Note that we included a label for the total in cell A7.)

It is often helpful to enter a formula in one cell and then copy that formula into several other cells. For example, if you wish to compare your financial position today with your position in 1972, you need to divide each amount by the price level (which measures the amount that prices have risen because of inflation since 1972). Enter the value 2.23 for the price level into cell E3. Then enter this formula into cell C3: (B3/$E$3); the "/" is used to represent division. The dollar signs in the cell address $E$3 indicate that this is an absolute address, that is, this address will always refer to cell E3 even if we copy this formula into a cell at a different location in the worksheet. The B3 in the formula does not contain dollar signs, so this is a relative address. Since B3 is one cell to the left of C3 (where we put the formula), the computer treats B3 as meaning "the cell that is one cell to the left." If we then copy the same formula to cell C4, the computer will automatically change the B3 to B4, since B4 is the cell that is one cell to the left of C4.

To copy a formula, type /C; 1-2-3 will then ask you for the range to copy to. We would like to copy the formula in cell C3 into cells C4 to C7. After we have copied the formulas, 1-2-3 will automatically calculate the values in column D. The result is shown in Figure 42.

If we now move the pointer to cell C4, the top of the screen will display the formula stored in cell C4, which is (B4/$E$3). Note that $E$3 is the same as it was in the formula for cell C3, but the

C4: (B4/$E$3)   READY

```
       A         B         C         D      E        F       G      H
 1  Personal Financial Data
 2            Today      1972 $            Price Level
 3  Checking   450.53  202.0313              2.23
 4  Saving     832.52  373.3273
 5  IRA       3040.11  1363.278
 6  Cash        83.43  37.41255
 7  Total     4406.59  1976.049
 8
 9
10
11
12
13
14
15
16
17
18
19
20
```

FIGURE 42

first part of the formula is now B4, since B4 is the cell that is one cell to the left of C4. If we change the value in cell E3, then 1-2-3 will automatically recalculate all of the values in column C.

A big advantage of 1-2-3 is its ability to draw graphs representing the information contained in the worksheet. There are several types of graphs that can be drawn: line diagrams, bar graphs, *x-y* scatter diagrams, and pie charts. Let's draw a pie chart showing the fraction of the total in each category. Type /G to enter the graphics menu; a list of graphics commands will appear at the top of the screen. Type T to indicate that you wish to select the type of graph, type P to indicate that you will draw a pie chart, and type A to indicate that you are defining which cells will be part of the data range that 1-2-3 calls the "A" range. Then 1-2-3 will ask you to enter the range of cells, which will be B3..B6 in the present case. (For some types of graphs you will have more than one data range. The other data ranges are indicated by the letters B to F.) In a pie chart the data are contained in the A range, and the labels for the sector data are contained in the X range. Type X and then respond to the question by entering the cells A3..A6 for the X range. Now type V (for view), and the graph will appear on the screen. (See Figure 43.)

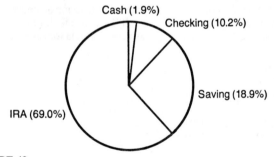

FIGURE 43

LOTUS DEVELOPMENT CORP. Lotus, a software company located in Cambridge, Massachusetts, produces Lotus 1-2-3, the integrated programs Jazz and Symphony, and the information-management program Agenda.

m

MACDRAW See **draw program**.

MACHINE-DEPENDENT PROGRAM A machine-dependent program works on only one particular type of computer.

MACHINE-INDEPENDENT PROGRAM A machine-independent program can be used on many different types of computers.

MACHINE LANGUAGE A machine language contains instructions that a computer can execute directly. Machine language statements are written in a binary code, and each statement corresponds to one machine action.

An assembly language is a language in which each statement corresponds to one machine language statement, but the statements themselves are written in a symbolic code that is easier for people to read. (See **assembly language**.) A single statement in a high-level language such as BASIC may contain many machine instructions.

MACHINE-READABLE DATA Machine-readable data are data in any form that can be fed into a computer through an input device. Examples of machine-readable data include data stored on magnetic tape or punched cards, and data on forms that can be read by an optical scanner. A table of numbers in a book is not machine readable because somebody needs to type the numbers on a terminal before a computer can use them.

MACINTOSH The Macintosh computer, introduced by Apple in 1984, was the first personal computer to use a graphical user interface with a mouse. Users copy files and activate software by pointing to symbols (icons) on the screen rather than by typing commands. The screen is always in graphics mode; it is divided into windows and can display all the typefaces that the printer can print. The Macintosh user interface was derived from that of Xerox workstations; it has been imitated by a number of other operating systems, including Microsoft Windows and OS/2 Presentation Manager.

Most importantly, the mechanisms for using windows, icons, and mouse menus are provided by the operating system, which means they look virtually the same in all programs. Thus, anyone who knows how to use any Macintosh software package will also know how to perform similar operations in any other software package.

The original Macintosh used a 7.8-MHz Motorola 68000 microprocessor with 128K of RAM (see **microprocessor**). This machine drew some criticism because its memory and processing speed were somewhat inadequate and because, in an attempt to make the machine seem simple, some on-screen messages left out vital technical information.

The Macintosh 512, Macintosh 512KE, Macintosh Plus, and Macintosh SE resemble the original Macintosh but have 512K of RAM. The Macintosh II, introduced in 1986, is a completely different machine. It has a 15.6-MHz Motorola 68020 processor and runs about five times as fast as the original Macintosh. Further, it supports a color display, an IBM PC-like keyboard, and the ability to add additional CPUs on plug-in cards.

For serial port pinouts, see **RS-232**.

MACPAINT See **paint program**.

MACRO A macro is an instruction that stands for a sequence of simpler instructions.

(1) In assembly language, a macro is a user-defined abbreviation for one or more lines of code.

(2) A macro is also a group of keystrokes that have been combined so that they can be easily accessed. Many software packages make it possible to define macros for commonly used keystroke combinations. For example, in Lotus 1-2-3, a macro is defined by entering characters into a cell (or range of cells) and then giving that cell a name. Suppose we frequently wish to format a group of cells to have currency format with two decimal places. The commands to do this are / Range Format Currency. To spare yourself from typing these characters each time, enter the expression ' /RFC2~ into a convenient cell. The quotation mark at the beginning indicates that this is a label; the 2 indicates that two decimal places are to be taken, and the ~ symbol represents the return key. Use the /Range Name Create command to give this cell a name, consisting of a backslash followed by a letter. We could give the macro the name \F, since F stands for format. The macro has now been defined. In order to execute the macro, press the ALT key and then the letter that names the macro (in this case F). The result will be the same as if we had pressed

each of the keys / R F C 2 (RETURN) individually.

Macros can become much more complicated. For example, it is possible to create a macro that pauses at some point to obtain input from the user.

MACRO ASSEMBLER The Microsoft Macro Assembler is the most widely used assembler for the IBM PC family of computers. An assembler translates assembly language programs into machine code (see **assembly language**). A macro assembler is one that allows the programmer to define macro instructions (see **macro**).

MAGNETIC BUBBLE MEMORY Magnetic bubble memory can be used in the same way as RAM but does not go blank when power to it is turned off. At present, bubble memories are more expensive than disks; they are used in very lightweight, portable computers when a disk drive would be too bulky or too fragile.

MAINFRAME COMPUTER A mainframe computer is a large computer occupying a specially air-conditioned room and supporting typically 100–500 users at a time. The IBM 370 and IBM 3081 are examples of mainframe computers.

MARK I The MARK I was an early computer developed at Harvard University.

MATH COPROCESSOR See **coprocessor.**

MATRIX See **array; table.**

MATRIX PRINTER A matrix printer forms letters and other symbols by patterns of dots. (See **dot-matrix printer**.)

MB MB stands for megabyte, which refers to a memory size of 2^{20} = 1,048,576 bytes. One megabyte can store more than 1 million characters. One megabyte equals 1024 kilobytes. Some computers come with hard disks that are capable of storing 40 MB (or more).

MCGA The IBM Monochrome/Color Graphics Adapter (MCGA) is built into the PS/2 Model 25 and 30. It offers all the features of the MDA and CGA, plus some additional video modes of its own. However, it lacks some of the modes supported by the EGA and VGA. (See **video modes [IBM PC]**.)

MDA The IBM PC Monochrome Display Adapter (MDA) provides very sharp, readable text, but no graphics, on a monochrome screen. (See **video modes [IBM PC].**)

MEDIUM-SCALE INTEGRATION The term *medium-scale integration* refers to an integrated circuit that contains from 10 to 100 logic gates. (See **integrated circuit.**)

MEGABYTE See **MB.**

MEGAHERTZ Megahertz means "million hertz" or "million cycles per second." (See **clock.**)

MEMORY The memory, formerly called the *core*, is the space within a computer where information is stored while being actively worked on. Most microcomputers have a small amount of read-only memory (ROM), containing the built-in programs that start the operation of the computer when it is turned on, and a large amount of random-access memory (RAM) for user's programs and data. Except for ROM, memory goes blank when the computer is turned off; any data in it must be copied to disk or tape if they are to be saved.

The memory requirements of a computer are dictated by the software that is to be run on it. General-purpose microcomputers usually have 64 to 640K of RAM (see **K**). Computers that run only small BASIC programs can get by with as little as 1K of RAM, while some large software packages require as much as 640K.

MEMORY CHIPS memory is often added to a computer simply by plugging RAM chips into sockets. This entails checking the following things:

1 The type of memory chips required. Each chip holds a particular number of bits (e.g., 64K, 256K, or 1 megabyte). Some computers allow use of different types of chips (e.g., 64K or 256K) by setting a switch to indicate which kind are installed. Check that you actually have space to install additional chips; you may need to buy an additional board to hold them.

2 The number of chips needed. A byte is 8 bits (even on a 16- or 32-bit processor), so if you are adding 64K bytes of memory, you will need eight 64K chips to hold the data, plus (on most computers) a ninth 64K chip for parity checking.

3 The speed rating of the chips, typically 120 or 150 nano-seconds. This is a measure of how quickly the chip can return valid data to the CPU. If you install chips that are too slow, you will get memory errors; if your chips are faster than needed, you may be wasting money, because the CPU controls the speed at which the chips actually run.

4 How to tell the computer that additional memory has been installed. This usually involves setting switches or running a configuration program.

MEMORY-MAPPED VIDEO The video display of a computer is memory-mapped if the contents of the screen are controlled by storing appropriate value in a block of memory that is directly accessible to the CPU. (See **video memory**.) For example, the IBM PC has memory-mapped video; the DEC Rainbow does not.

MEMORY RESIDENT A memory resident program is one that remains in memory after being run, so that it can be called up later. Memory resident programs are often called TSRs ("terminate-and-stay-resident").

Memory resident programs extend the capabilities of the operating system or provide "pop-up" functions, such as a calendar or calculator, that can be called up in the middle of another program without disturbing it. You can then return to the original program as if nothing had happened.

MENU A menu is a list of choices that appears on the screen while a particular program is being executed. By typing the number or letter that corresponds to a particular command operation, you can cause the command to be executed. The presence of menus in a program makes it easy for people to use the program because they don't need to memorize all the commands. By looking at the menu, they can see all their options.

MERGE To merge two ordered lists or files means to combine them into one list or file that is also in order. Below is an example of a BASIC program to merge two lists. Array A contains N elements; array B contains M elements; so the merged array C will contain $P = M + N$ elements. (This program assumes that arrays A and B have already been read into the computer.)

```
10    REM MERGE PROGRAM
20    REM C IS THE RESULT OF MERGING
```

```
 21    REM ARRAYS A AND B
 25    P = M + N
 30    J = 1
 40    K = 1
 50    FOR I = 1 TO P
 60       IF J>N GOTO 90
 70       IF K>M GOTO 120
 80       IF A(J)<B(K) GOTO 120
 90       C(I) = B(K)
100       K = K + 1
110       GOTO 140
120       C(I) = A(J)
130       J = J + 1
140    NEXT I
150    END
```

MERGE SORT The merge sort is a procedure for sorting an array. The process begins by first dividing the array into a collection of two-element lists and then putting each of these small lists in order. Next, each two-element list is merged with another two-element list, so the large array now consists of a group of ordered four-element lists. (See **merge.**) Then the four-element lists are merged to form eight-element lists, and the process is continued until the entire list has been sorted.

Below is an example of a BASIC program to perform a merge sort on an array A. It is assumed that the values for A have already been read into the computer, and that A contains 2^k values, where k is some integer. (In other words, the number of elements in A is either 2, 4, 8, 16, 32, etc.) If you need to sort a list that contains an arbitrary number of elements, you can add enough zero elements to the end of the list to make the total number of elements a power of 2.

```
 1    REM MERGE SORT PROGRAM
 2    REM N IS THE NUMBER OF ELEMENTS IN A
10    DIM D(128) : REM D IS A TEMPORARY
11                   REM STORAGE ARRRAY
20    M = 1 : REM M IS THE NUMBER OF ELEMENTS
21            REM IN EACH SMALL LIST
30    L = N/M : REM L IS THE NUMBER OF
31              REM SMALL LISTS
40    FOR H = 1 TO L/2
```

```
50      B = 2 * M * H - 2 * M + 1 : B1 = B
60      C = 2 * M * H - M + 1      : C1 = C
70      FOR I = 1 TO 2 * M
80          IF B>= (B1 + M) GOTO 140
90          IF C>= (C1 + M) GOTO 110
100         IF A(B)>(A(C) GOTO 140
105     REM
110         D(I) = A(B)
120         B = B+ 1
130         GOTO 160
135     REM
140         D(I) = A(C)
150         C = C + 1
160     NEXT I
170     FOR J = 1 TO 2 * M
180         A(B1 - 1 + J) = D(J)
190     NEXT J
200     NEXT H
210     M = 2 * M
220     IF M<N GOTO 30
230     END
```

MHz See **megahertz.**

MICRO The prefix *micro-* means one millionth (10^{-6}). For example, a microsecond is one millionth of a second (0.000001 second), and a microfarad is one millionth of a farad.

MICRO CHANNEL The Micro Channel is the bus design used in the IBM PS/2 computers, model 50 and higher (see **bus**). It contrasts with the bus design of the IBM PC, XT, and AT, which is also used in the lowest PS/2 models. Plug-in cards designed for one bus cannot be used with the other.

Unlike the original bus, the Micro Channel is designed to allow use of more than one CPU in a single computer.

MICROCOMPUTER A microcomputer is a computer whose CPU consists of a single integrated circuit known as the *microprocessor.* Ordinarily, a microcomputer is used by only one person at a time. All home computers are microcomputers. (See **integrated circuit; microprocessor.**)

MICROFLOPPY DISK A microfloppy disk is a 3½-inch disk

encased in a hard protective shell. Even though these disks are smaller than standard 5¼-inch floppy disks, they have comparable or greater storage capacities. Microfloppy disk drives are standard equipment on machines such as the Apple Macintosh and the HP-150.

MICROPRO Micropro is a software company located in San Rafael, California; it produces the popular word processing program WordStar. (See **WordStar**.)

MICROPROCESSOR A microprocessor is an integrated circuit containing the entire CPU of a computer, all on one chip, so that only the memory and input-output devices need to be added. The first popular microprocessor, the Intel 8080, came out in 1973 and cost approximately $400; it now sell for about $1.

Microprocessors are commonly described as "8-bit," "16-bit," or the like. The number can refer either to the number of bits in each internal data register, or to the number of bits on the data bus (see **bus**); these two numbers are often, but not always, the same. Other things being equal, larger registers and a larger bus enable the processor to do its work faster.

Clock speed is also important. The *clock* is the oscillator that causes the microprocessor to proceed from one step to the next in executing instructions. (Each machine instruction takes several clock cycles.) Clock speed is measured in megahertz (MHz); 1 MHz is 1 million cycles per second. Higher clock speeds result in faster computation—but only if exactly the same machine instructions are being executed; this is why it is misleading to compare the clock speeds of processors of different types. It is even possible for two microprocessors with the same instruction set and clock speed to perform computations at different rates because of differences in internal design. An 8-MHz 80286, for example, is much faster than an 8-MHz 8086.

Table 14 describes a number of popular microprocessors. The processors in each group (e.g., the Z80, Z80A, and Z80(B) use the same machine language and run the same programs.

MICROSOFT Microsoft, one of the leading software-producing companies, was founded by William Gates and Paul Allen in 1975, when they wrote a version of BASIC. Microsoft BASIC, sold with the IBM PC as PC BASIC, is one of the most commonly used versions of BASIC. (See **BASICA; GW-BASIC.**)

TABLE 14 Commonly Used Microprocessors

Manufac-turer	Type	No. of Register Bits	No. of Data Bus Bits	Clock Frequency (MHz)	Comments
Intel	8080	8	8	2	1973 classic, still used
Zilog	Z80	8	8	2	Improved 8080, popular
	Z80A	8	8	4	
	Z80B	8	8	6	
MOS	6502	8	8	1	Used in Apple II
Technology	6502A	8	8	2	Used in Commodore VIC-20
	6502B	8	8	3	
Intel	8088	16	8	5	Used in IBM PC
	8086	16	16	5	8088-compatible, faster
	8086-2	16	16	8	Faster 8086
	80186	16	16	8	
	80286	16	16	8	Used in IBM PC AT
	80386	32	32	*	Used in Compaq 386
	386SX	32	16	*	For putting 386 in 286 machine
Motorola	68000	32	16	8	Used in Apple Macintosh; very fast
	68010	32	16	*	Supports virtual memory
	68020	32	32	*	
National Semi-conductor	32032	32	32	6	True 32-bit processor

*These processors are manufactured for a variety of clock speeds in the range 16–25 MHz. The manufacturers offer faster speeds as the design is refined.

Microsoft's most widespread product is the operating system MS-DOS, sold with the IBM PC as PC-DOS and also used on many other computers based on the 8088 microprocessor. In 1987 Microsoft introduced OS/2, which is designed to be downward compatible with MS-DOS while at the same time taking advantage of the multitasking features available on microcomputers based on the 80386 or 80286 microprocessors (such as the IBM PS/2 line). Microsoft also produces many other products, including QuickBasic, compilers for several other programming languages, the word processing program Microsoft Word, the spreadsheets Multiplan and Excel, and Microsoft Windows. The company is located in Redmond, Washington.

MICROSOFT WORD Microsoft Word is a word processing program produced by Microsoft, Inc. It can be used with a mouse that allows you to move the cursor around the screen while editing (see mouse). It also allows you to work on more than one area of text at a time by dividing the screen into different windows.

MICROSPACING Microspacing is the insertion of extra space in a printed document in units smaller than the size of one character. (See **justification**.)

MIDI MIDI stands for <u>M</u>usical <u>I</u>nstrument <u>D</u>igital <u>I</u>nterface, which is a standard way for communicating information about music between different electronic devices, such as computers and sound synthesizers. A device with a MIDI out port can be connected to a device with a MIDI in port, and the music can be transmitted between the devices by using a standardized system of codes.

MILLI- The prefix *milli-* means one-thousandth (10^{-3}). For example, a millisecond is one-thousandth of a second (0.001 second), and a millimeter is one-thousandth of a meter.

MINICOMPUTER A minicomputer is a computer intermediate in size between a mainframe computer and a microcomputer; two examples are the Digital Equipment Corporation VAX and the IBM System/3. A minicomputer typically occupies a large area within a room and supports 10 to 100 users at a time. Minicomputers are typically used by medium-sized businesses and academic institutions.

MINIFINDER On the Macintosh, the MiniFinder is a menu of commonly used pieces of software. By configuring the MiniFinder appropriately, the user can find commonly used pieces of software without searching through all the files on the disk.

MNEMONIC A mnemonic is a device that helps you remember something. For example, the expression "Spring forward, fall back" helps you remember which way to adjust your clocks in the spring and the fall for daylight saving time.

A *mnemonic variable name* is a variable name that helps the programmer remember what the variable means. For example, in a PL/I payroll program the variable to represent the hours worked could be named X312W17HK, but it would be much better to give the variable a mnemonic name such as HOURS.

MNP MNP (<u>M</u>icrocom <u>N</u>etworking <u>P</u>rotocol) is a method for detecting and correcting errors in data transmission. (For a description of another method in detail, see **XMODEM**.) MNP error correction is built into some high-speed modems so that erroneous data is never sent to the computer.

MODEM A modem (short for <u>mo</u>dulator-<u>dem</u>odulator) is a device that encodes data for transmission over a particular medium, such as telephone lines, coaxial cables, fiber optics, or microwaves.

The modems commonly used with computer terminals and microcomputers transmit RS-232 serial data over telephone lines. (See **RS-232; serial**.) Since the RS-232 interface is standard, practically any modem can be used with any terminal or computer. (An exception is an *internal modem*, which mounts inside the computer and contains its own RS-232 port.)

To be used with a modem, a microcomputer must run a program that makes it act like ("emulate") a communications terminal.

Some important features of modems include the following:

1 Baud rate. The original Bell 103 method for transmitting data on telephone lines works only for transmission rates of 300 baud (30 characters per second) and slower. At 1,200 baud (120 cps), a different system, known as Bell 212A, is used. Most 1,200 baud modems support both kinds of transmission; less expensive modems can be used only at 300 baud and below. At higher baud rates, the applicable standards are CCITT V.22 bis (2400 baud) and V.32 (4800 and 9600 baud).

2 Originate and answer modes. When two modems are linked together, they transmit at different frequencies so that each one receives signals from the other, rather than from itself. The two sets of frequencies are known as *originate mode* and *answer mode*. Normally, terminals and microcomputers use originate mode, and the mainframe computer that they are calling uses answer mode. Inexpensive modems support only originate mode, since it is usually the only one needed. However, if two microcomputers are to be linked together by telephone, one of the modems must be in originate mode and the other in answer mode (it doesn't matter which is which).

3 Auto-answer capability. An auto-answer modem can be set up to answer incoming telephone calls. This is necessary if it is to be used with a computer that will receive calls from outside, rather than just making calls under the control of the user.

4 Auto-dial feature. With most modems, the user must dial a telephone number on an ordinary telephone, and then turn on the modem once the other computer answers. An auto-dial modem, however, can do its own dialing in response to special commands transmitted to it by the computer or terminal.

5 Full- and half-duplex modes. This is normally a switch setting on the modem, the computer terminal, or both. In full-duplex mode, characters typed by the user do not appear on the screen until the other computer receives them and transmits them back. This provides visible proof that they are being received correctly. In half-duplex mode, characters appear on the screen when typed and are not repeated by the computer on the receiving end.

If what you are typing does not appear on the screen, switch to half-duplex. If each character appear twice, switch to full-duplex. If there are half-/full-duplex switches on both the terminal and the modem, at least one of them should always be set to full-duplex.

MODEM ELIMINATOR An RS-232 cablethat interchanges conductors 2 and 3 is known as a modem eliminator. (See **DCE**; for diagram, see **RS-232**.)

MODEM, NULL See **null modem; modem eliminator**.

MODULA-2 The programming language Modula-2 was developed by Niklaus Wirth in the late 1970s as a replacement for Pascal, which Wirth had developed some 10 years earlier. Modula-2 replaces an earlier version, called simply Modula. As its name suggests, Modula-2 is designed to encourage modularity (see **structured programming**).

Modula-2 is very similar to Pascal, especially the extended versions of Pascal that most compilers now implement. The main differences are the following:

1 In Modula-2, routines can be compiled separately and linked together at load time. Compiled units are called MODULES.

2 The IMPORT and EXPORT declarations control recognition of names. IMPORT means "Recognize names here that are declared in another module;" EXPORT means "Allow other modules to IMPORT names that are declared here."

3 Modula-2 allows the programmer to divide the program into concurrent tasks that run simultaneously. (See **timesharing**.)

4 The BEGIN and END statements are used only to mark the beginning and end of the program. Within the program, each IF, WHILE, or FOR construct is terminated with an END. (As in Pascal, REPEAT is terminated with UNTIL.)

5 Each standard input-output statement handles only one item of a specific type. For instance, the Pascal statement

```
WRITELN('The answer is ',A)
```

is replaced by the sequence:

```
WriteString('The answer is');
WriteReal(A);
WriteLn
```

This feature makes it easier for users to write their own replacements for input-output routines.

6 As in PL/I, procedures can determine, at run time, the size of arrays passed to them as parameters. This makes it practicable to handle variable-length character strings.

7 The CASE statement has an ELSE clause (as it already has in most implementations of Pascal).

8 Upper and lower case are distinguished throughout the program; reserved words must be entirely in upper case, and names differing only in case (e.g., WRITELN vs. WriteLn) are not equivalent. An entire name is significant, not just its first eight characters.

Here is a sample program in Modula-2:

```
MODULE Demo;
FROM InOut IMPORT WriteInt;
VAR k : INTEGER;
BEGIN
   k := 1;
   REPEAT
     WriteInt(k,4);
```

```
        k := k * 2
      UNTIL k>1000
    END.
```

MODULE A module is a part of a larger system. For example, a Lunar Module is a part of the Apollo rocket system. A module in a computer program is a part of the program that is written and tested separately and then is combined with other modules to form the complete program. (See **top-down programming**.)

MONADIC OPERATION A monadic operation requires only one operand. For example, negation (finding the negative of a number) is an operation that requires only one operand and is therefore monadic.

MONITOR (1) A monitor is a computer program that supervises the activity of other programs.

(2) A device similar to a television set that accepts video signals from a computer and displays information on its screen is known as a monitor. The monitor itself does no computing at all.

The first generation of personal computers used TV-type *composite video* monitors. The sharpness of the image on the screen depended on the *bandwidth*, or frequency response, of the monitor. Users were quick to note that color-TV monitors had much poorer bandwidth than black-and-white (monochrome) monitors.

The IBM PC popularized two new types of monitors. The IBM Monochrome Display, a *TTL monochrome monitor*, provides very sharp images and accepts the same input voltages as TTL integrated circuits.

The IBM Color Display, an *RGB color monitor*, produces a color image by accepting separate signals for red, green, and blue on separate wires. The result is much sharper than a color TV picture but still not really adequate for prolonged reading of text. A higher-resolution RGB monitor was introduced with the Enhanced Graphics Adapter (EGA). It offered the important ability to scan the screen at different rates in different modes. (See **video modes [IBM PC]**.)

Newer computers use *analog* color monitors that provide crisp text with an unlimited range of colors. Many present-day monitors have "multiscan" or "multisync" capability, which means that they automatically detect the scan frequencies used by the computer to which they are attached.

MONOCHROME MONITOR A monochrome monitor is a computer monitor that can display only one color. Monochrome monitors generally are better when working with text because they provide sharper resolution for numbers and letters than do color monitors. However, a color monitor is needed if you would like your computer to do color graphics. A monochrome monitor usually displays white, green, or amber characters on a black background. Different people have different preferences as to which arrangement is easiest on the eyes.

MONTE CARLO Monte Carlo is a type of simulation method that uses random numbers to determine the evolution of a system. Suppose that you know the probability that a particular event will happen, but it is too difficult to calculate the probability that a complicated combination of events will occur. In the Monte Carlo method you use a random number generator to calculate a random number between 0 and 1, and then compare that number with the probability of the event. For example, if the probability of the event is .62, and the random number generated is .58, then the program will simulate that the event has occurred. The name Monte Carlo comes from the fact that this method is a bit like a game of chance.

Below is an example of a BASIC baseball simulation program using the Monte Carlo method. Suppose you know the batting averages of the nine members of a baseball team. The batting average can be treated as the probability that the player will get a hit during a particular time at bat. Then you can use the Monte Carlo method to estimate the number of runs that this team is likely to get in a nine-inning game. This program also considers the probability that a player will get a home run, but it makes some other simplifications. It does not allow for walks, errors, doubles, or triples, and it assumes that, in the event of a single, runners on second and third will always score and a runner on first will always advance to second.

```
1      REM    MONTE CARLO BASEBALL PROGRAM
5      DIM H1(9), H4(9)
10     FOR P = 1 TO 9
20     PRINT "INPUT BATTING AV/HOME RUN PROB"
30     PRINT "FOR PLAYER";P
40     INPUT H1(P),H4(P)
50     NEXT P
100    I = 0 : REM I IS THE INNING NUMBER
```

```
110     P = 0 : REM P IS THE PLAYER NUMBER
120     R = 0 : REM R IS THE NUMBER OF RUNS
130     I = I + 1 : REM START NEW INNING
135     PRINT "INNING";I
140     IF I>9 GOTO 360 : REM END OF GAME
150     A = 0:B = 0:C= 0
155     REM A = 1 IF RUNNER ON 1ST
156     REM B = 1 IF RUNNER ON 2ND
157     REM C = 1 IF RUNNER ON 3RD
160     O = 0: REM O IS THE NUMBER OF OUTS
170     P = P + 1
180     IF P>9 LET P = 1
190     D = A + B + C : REM NUMBER OF
191     REM BASE RUNNERS
195     X = RND
200     IF X<H4(P) GOTO 340 : REM HOME RUN
210     IF X<H1(P) GOTO 250 : REM SINGLE
220     O = O + 1 : REM BATTER IS OUT
230     IF O=3 GOTO 130 : REM START NEW INNING
240     GOTO 170 : REM NEXT BATTER IS UP
250     IF D=0 LET Z = 0 : GOSUB 420 : GOTO 320
260     IF D=3 LET Z = 2 : GOSUB 430 : GOTO 320
270     IF D=2 GOTO 300
280     IF A=0 LET Z = 1 : GOSUB 420 : GOTO 320
290     Z = 0 : GOSUB 430 : GOTO 320
300     IF A=0 LET Z = 2 : GOSUB 420 : GOTO 320
310     Z = 1 : GOSUB 430
320     REM*****Z IS NUMBER OF RUNS
321     REM                    SCORED*****
325     R = R + Z
330     GOTO 170 : REM NEXT BATTER IS UP
340     REM HOMERUN
345     R = R + 1 + D:A = 0:B = 0:C = 0
350     GOTO 170 : REM NEXT BATTER IS UP
360     REM*****END OF GAME**********
370     PRINT "RUN:";R : END
420     C = 0:B = 0:A = 1 : RETURN
430     C = 0:B = 1:A = 1 : RETURN
```

MOTOROLA 68000 See **microprocessor.**

MOUSE A mouse is a special computer input device, connected by a wire to the computer. The mouse has a roller on its bottom designed to roll along the desk top beside your computer. When you move the mouse with one hand, the cursor will move along the screen in the same direction in which the mouse is being moved. A mouse can be useful when working with word processing editing programs, graphics programs, or spreadsheet programs, where it is helpful to be able to move the cursor quickly around the screen.

The basic command structure of Apple's Macintosh computer is built around its mouse. A menu of commands appears on the screen. Then, using the mouse, you move the screen pointer until it points to the command you want to select. When you press the button on the mouse, the chosen command is executed.

MS ms is an abbreviation for millisecond, which is one-thousandth of a second. (See **access time.**)

MS-DOS MS-DOS, the M̲icrosoft D̲isk O̲perating S̲ystem, is an operating system for computers that use the 8086 or 8088 microprocessor. MS-DOS is marketed by IBM as PC-DOS for the IBM PC. (See **OS/2.**)

Versions 1.0, 1.1, and 1.25 of MS-DOS are very similar to CP/M but slightly more user-friendly. (See **CP/M; user-friendly.**) As in CP/M, file names consist of up to eight letters or digits, optionally followed by a period and a one-to-three-character *extension.* (Some nonalphanumeric characters are allowed, but the exact set varies from version to version.) A file name can be prefixed with a letter and a colon to indicate what disk drive the file resides on; if this is not done, it is assumed to reside on the default (logged) drive. Here are some examples:

> ALPHA   (assumed to be on the default drive)
> BETA.COM   (assumed to be on the default drive)
> B:GAMMA.TXT   (on drive B)

MS-DOS signals its readiness for a command with a prompt such as

> **A>**   or   **A:**

where the A indicates that drive A is the default. Some common MS-DOS commands are as follows:

> B: Change the default drive to B.
> DIR A: Display a list of the files on
>   drive A.

COPY A:ALPHA.EXE B: Copy the file ALPHA.EXE
                                           from drive A to drive B.

TYPE C:INVNTRY.TXT   Display on the screen the
                                           contents of file
                                         INVNTRY.TXT, which is
                                         on drive C.

These are "resident" commands, meaning that they can be executed at any time. Most commands, however, are "transient"; that is, in order to execute them, the computer must refer to a file whose name is the same as the command, with the extension EXE, COM, or BAT. In such a case, if the command file is not on the default disk, the computer must be told where it is. To do this, type the disk drive letter and a colon in front of the name:

A:BASIC

This gets you into Microsoft BASIC using the file BASIC.COM, which is on drive A, even though the default drive may be something else.

Unlike CP/M, MS-DOS does not keep the current disk directory in memory; it examines the disk every time a file is opened. Therefore the user is free to change disks at any time unless a file is actually in the process of being read or written. In MS-DOS, unlike CP/M, a copy of the operating system is not needed on every disk; it is seldom necessary to reboot during a session, and the operating system files are fairly bulky.

Versions 2.0 and higher of MS-DOS are fully compatible with verisons 1.0, 1.1, and 1.25, but the file-handling system has been remodeled to resemble the tree-structured directory system of UNIX (see **UNIX**). The MKDIR command creates a directory; the CHDIR command changes the current default directory; and the PATH command specifies alternative places to look for commands not found in the current directory. In addition, pipelining and input-output redirection are supported, though they work correctly only for programs specially written to support them (including all the system commands). For example,

DIR A: > B:DIRECTRY

performs the DIR A: command but writes the output on the file B:DIRECTORY, and

DIR A: | SORT | MORE

does a DIR A:, writing its output on a temporary file that is passed as input to SORT; this in turn passes its output as input to MORE, which displays it on the screen one screenful at a time.

MULTIPROCESSING Multiprocessing is the use of more than one CPU in a single computer system.

MULTIPROGRAMMING Multiprogramming is the apparently simultaneous execution of more than one program on a single computer through timesharing.

MULTISCAN, MULTISYNC See **monitor.**

MULTITASKING Multitasking is the execution of more than one program apparently at the same time on the same computer. In reality, the CPU rapidly switches its attention among the various programs (see **timesharing**). Multitasking makes it possible to print one document while editing another, or to perform lengthy computations "in the background" while working on something else on the screen. (See **OS/2.**)

A more primitive form of multitasking allows you to switch from one program to another, but only one program at a time actually runs; the others are frozen until you return to them.

MVS MVS (Multiple Virtual Storage) is an operating system for IBM mainframe computers; from the user's point of view, it is almost completely compatible with OS/360. (See **OS/360; JCL; TSO.**)

n ———————————————————————————

N-TYPE An N-type semiconductor region is formed by doping a silicon crystal with an impurity that contains five outer-level electrons. (See **semiconductor.**)

NAK In XMODEM and some other protocols, ASCII code 21 (CTRL-U) stands for "not acknowledged" (abbreviated "NAK"); it is sent when a data packet is received incorrectly or is not received when expected.

NAND GATE A NAND gate (Figure 44) is a logic gate whose output is 0 if both of the inputs are 1, and is 1 otherwise, as shown in the table.

FIGURE 44

Input 1	Input 2	Output 3
0	0	1
0	1	1
1	0	1
1	1	0

A NAND gate is equivalent to an AND gate followed by a NOT gate (Figure 45).

Figure 46 shows how other gates can be contructed from combinations of NAND gates. This is commonly done in designing TTL and CMOS digital integrated circuits.

FIGURE 45

NANO- The prefix nano- means one billionth (10^{-9}). For example, 1 nanosecond is one billionth of a second.

NATURAL LANGUAGE PROCESSING At present, all human communication with computers is done in artificial languages such as BASIC and Pascal. Computers would be much more useful if they could understand instructions in ordinary human languages (natural languages) such as English and French. In the early days of computers, it was assumed that successful natural language processing programs would be easy to construct, given sufficient computing power. However, progress has been slow.

NOT gate

OR gate

AND gate

NOR gate

FIGURE 46 Other Gates Constructed from NAND Gates

There are three main problem areas:

1 Syntax. No one has yet produced a complete, mathematically precise description of the possible sentence structures of any human language. There are a number of promising approaches (all derived, directly or indirectly, from the work of Noam Chomsky in the 1950s), but all of them run into difficulties with some types of sentences. The correct interpretation of pronouns such as *himself* and *each other* is especially problematic; human beings seem to know intuitively how to use such words in a sentence as soon as they learn what they mean, but no one has ever captured this knowledge in a completely satisfactory set of explicit rules. Facts such as this have led Chomsky and his followers to suspect that the human brain is genetically "preprogrammed" in quite specific ways for certain features of human language.

2 Semantics. If the computer is to understand sentences, it must have some kind of internal representation of their meanings. The most straightforward way to represent meanings in a computer is to decompose them into a finite set of primitive elements; for example, *grandfather* can be rendered as MALE PARENT OF PARENT OF SELF, where MALE, PARENT, OF, and SELF are part of a small "built-in" vocabulary.

There are, however, many words whose meanings defy representation in this form.   For example, as Geoffrey Sampson has pointed out, the word *picturesque* cannot be broken up into simpler elements; but one would hardly want to say that the human brain acquired a new "built-in" primitive concept, PICTURESQUE, just a couple of centuries ago when the word first came into use. Many meanings seem to consist of mental images or sets of associated ideas that admit of considerable vagueness.

3 Phonetics. Although computers can now produce reasonably intelligible synthetic speech, it is difficult to get them to recognize human speech.   The problem is that, although speech seems to consist of strings of distinct sounds (*m, a*, and *n* for *man*), in reality the sounds are merged together, even in the clearest radio-announcer speech. (The *a* and *n* in *man*, for instance, are almost completely simultaneous.)   In addition, variations betwen speakers often lead to ambiguity; for instance, many New Yorkers pronounce *man* almost exactly the way Southerners pronouce *men*.   There are even substantial differences between the sound waves produced when the same person pronounces the same word twice.   The best speech-recognition systems available today recognize only a few hundred words and usually have to be "tuned" to the speech of a particular person.

There are many approaches to natural language processing. Some programs attempt to model processes in the human brain, while others use any available procedure to obtain practical results, even if it is something human speakers could not possibly do (e.g., processing the words of each sentence in reverse order). There is some controversy over whether it is better to try to determine the sentence structure first, and then the meaning, or whether the computer should construct a representation of the meaning of a sentence in one step; the latter approach results in programs that are less neatly organized, but that can use information about meaning to help make decisions about sentence structure.

The best currently available natural language processors often perform impressively (e.g., Yale University has developed one that reads incoming news stories from a teletype line and prepares summaries of them), but none of them is highly reliable; each program misinterprets certain types of sentences, often producing ludicrously incorrect results. Natural conversations between human beings and computers are still several years away. (See also **parsing**.)

NATURAL LOGARITHM See **logarithm**.

NEAR LETTER QUALITY A near-letter-quality printer produces output that resembles the print of an old cloth-ribbon typewriter. Near-letter-quality printing is completely satisfactory for student papers, magazine articles, and book manuscripts, but not for dissertations or correspondence on corporate letterheads.

NEST A nest occurs when one program structure is placed inside another structure of the same type. For example, a loop can be contained in another loop, or in some languages a procedure definition can be contained in another procedure definition.

Figure 47 shows a BASIC program that demonstrates nested loops. Note that loop 3 is nested inside loop 2, and loop 2 is itself nested inside loop 1.

```
10 FOR I=1 TO 2 :REM LOOP 1
20    PRINT "******":I:"**********"
30    FOR J=1 TO 3 :REM LOOP 2
40       PRINT " <":J:">"
50       FOR K=1 TO 3 :REM LOOP 3
60          PRINT "(":I:J:K:")"
70       NEXT K  :REM END OF LOOP 3
80    NEXT J  :REM END OF LOOP 2
```

212

```
90 NEXT I  :REM END OF LOOP 1
****** 1 *********
      < 1 >
(   1   1   1   )
(   1   1   2   )
(   1   1   3   )
      < 2 >
(   1   2   1   )
(   1   2   2   )
(   1   2   3   )
      < 3 >
(   1   3   1   )
(   1   3   2   )
(   1   3   3   )
****** 2 *********
      < 1 >
(   2   1   1   )
(   2   1   2   )
(   2   1   3   )
      < 2 >
(   2   2   1   )
(   2   2   2   )
(   2   2   3   )
      < 3 >
(   2   3   1   )
(   2   3   2   )
(   2   3   3   )
```

FIGURE 47

NETWORK A network is a set of computers connected together. (See **local-area network; wide-area network**.)

NIBBLE A nibble consists of 4 bits, or half of 1 byte.

NODE (1) A node is an individual computer (or occasionally another type of machine) in a network. (See **local-area network; wide-area network**.)

(2) A node is a location in a tree where branches connect. (See **tree**.)

NONDESTRUCTIVE READ A nondestructive read occurs when

information is transferred from a memory location without erasing the information that is stored in that memory location. For the opposite, see **destructive read.**

NONDOCUMENT MODE In WordStar and other word processors, the nondocument mode is used for typing files that are to be used for some purpose other than printing—for example, computer programs. Nondocument mode procedures plain-text files with no special codes for hyphenation, page breaks, or the like. (See **document modes; text file.**)

NOR GATE A NOR gate (Figure 48) is a logic gate whose output is 0 when either or both of the two inputs are 1, as shown in the table.

FIGURE 48

Input 1	Input 2	Output 3
0	0	1
0	1	0
1	0	0
1	1	0

A NOR gate is equivalent to an OR gate followed by a NOT gate (Figure 49), but its circuit is no more complex than that of a single OR gate (Figure 50). In fact, the circuit shown here is more reliable than the circuits illustrated in the articles on AND and OR gates, since the emitters of both transistors are grounded, and their input impedances therefore do not vary with changes in the state of the rest of the circuit. For this reason, it is common to construct all the other gate circuits from combinations of NOR gates (Figure 51). (This type of circuitry, known as RTL (Resistor-Transistor Logic) is now obsolete for everything except demonstration circuits. TTL and CMOS logic circuits are often built up in an analogous way from combinations and NAND gates.)

FIGURE 49

FIGURE 50

NORTON UTILITIES The Norton Utilities, by Peter Norton, are a set of programs for the IBM PC. Their most important function is to recover erased files and correct other problems with disks. (See **recovering erased files**.)

NOT GATE A NOT gate (Figure 52) is a logic gate whose output is 1 if the input is 0, and vice versa, as shown in the table.

Input	Output
0	1
1	0

A NOT gate can be constructed with a switch (see Figure 53). If the switch is closed, representing 1, then the output voltage will be the same as the ground voltage (0 volt). If the switch is open,

FIGURE 51 Other Gates Constructed from NOR Gates

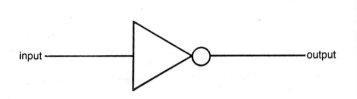

FIGURE 52

then the output voltage is the same as the power supply voltage (which represents 1).

The same idea can be used to build a NOT gate with a transistor (see Figure 54). If the input is at O, the transistor does not conduct, and the output is 5 volts (representing 1). But if the input is 5 volts, the transistor conducts, and the output voltage is zero.

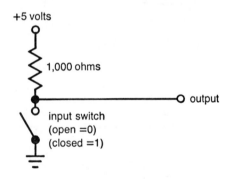

FIGURE 53

NP-COMPLETE PROBLEM See **limits of computer power.**

NULL MODEM A null modem is a cable for connecting two computers together without a modem. (See **modem eliminator.**)

NUMBER CRUNCHER A number cruncher is a computer designed to perform massive amounts of complex scientific calculations.

NUMERIC KEYPAD A numeric keypad is a separate set of keys

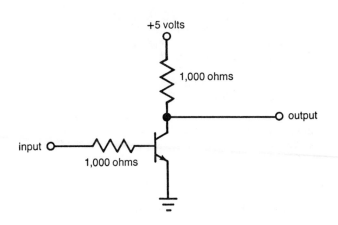

FIGURE 54

beside the main alphabetic keypad that contains the digits 0 to 9 and a decimal point key. The digits are arranged in the same way as they are on an adding machine. If you have to type large quantities of numeric data, a numeric keypad is quicker to use than the number keys on the regular keypad.

NUMERICAL INTEGRATION Numerical integration is the process of finding the area under a particular curve by dividing the area into many tiny rectangles, adding up the heights of individual rectangles, and then multiplying the sum by their common width. Numerical integration is the kind of task that is best left to a computer.

For example, in probability it is important to find the area under the curve

$$y = \frac{1}{\sqrt{2\pi}} e^{-1/2 x^2} \text{ from } x = -\infty \text{ to } x = b$$

This area can be found with the following BASIC program, which uses a loop to perform a numerical integration:

```
10      INPUT B
20      A = 0
25      P = SQR(2 * 3.14159)
```

```
30      FOR I = 1 TO INT(100 * B)
35      X = I / 100 - .005
40      Y = EXP(-X * X/2)
45      A = A + Y
50      NEXT I
55      PRINT .5 + A/(100 * P)
60      END
```

As you might imagine, it would take a long time to perform this calculation with a calculator, since you would have to retype all the instructions each time.

O

OBJECT-ORIENTED GRAPHICS See **draw program**.

OBJECT-ORIENTED PROGRAMMING Object-oriented programming is a technique often used in Lisp and other highly abstract programming languages. An "object" is a data item of a particular type, plus a set of procedures for handling items of that type (e.g., printing them or comparing them). These procedures are activated by sending "messages" to the object.

For instance, if you wanted to do vector arithmetic, you would create a class of object called "vector" that included both a data structure for representing the vector and a set of procedures for adding, multiplying, and displaying vectors. You could then create individual vectors and send messages to them to perform these operations.

OBJECT PROGRAM An object program is a program that has been translated into machine language and is ready to be run. (See **compiler**.)

OCTAL An octal numbers system is a base-8 number system. Octal numbers use only the digits 0, 1, 2, 3, 4, 5, 6, and 7.

OFFSET (1) On a microprocessor such as the 8088, each memory address is given as two numbers, a segment and an offset. To find the actual address, the segment is shifted one hexadecimal digit to the left and the offset is added to it. For instance, the address F123:1114 (segment F123, offset 0004) means:

```
        F123
   +    1114
```
```
        F2344
```

where F2344 is the *absolute address*. Note that F000:2344 refers to exactly the same address; so does F200:0344, and so on. See also **segment**.

(2) Offset printing is printing on paper by means of ink transferred by a rubber roller from another surface. Most print shops use offset printing to produce large numbers of high-quality copies from camera-ready art. (See **camera-ready**.)

OHM The ohm is the unit of measure of electric resistance. If an object has a resistance of 1 ohm, then an applied voltage of 1 volt will cause a current of 1 ampere to flow through the device. (See **Ohm's law**.)

Impedance is also measured in ohms. Impedance is similar to resistance but is defined in terms of alternating current rather than direct current. (See **impedance**.)

OHM'S LAW Ohm's law states that the current that will flow through a circuit element is equal to the voltage applied across that element divided by the resistance of that element: $I = V/R$, where I = current, in amperes; V = voltage, in volts: and R = resistance, in ohms.

ON-LINE SYSTEM In an on-line system, data are entered into a device, such as a terminal, that is connected directly to a computer.

OPEN (1) In some editing, word processing, and drawing programs, to open a file or document means to call it up from disk in order to work with it.

(2) In several programming languages, a file is said to be open when it is ready to have data transferred into or out of it.

(3) A switch is open when it is turned off so that no current can flow (Figure 55).

FIGURE 55 Open Switch. Current cannot flow.

OPEN SYSTEMS INTERCONNECTION See **data communication**.

OPERANDS The items on which a mathematical operation is performed are called its *operands*. For example, in the expression

$$2 + 3$$

the plus sign is the operator, and 2 and 3 are the operands.

OPERATING SYSTEM An operating system is a program that controls a computer and makes it possible for users to enter and run their own programs.

A completely unprogrammed computer is incapable of recognizing keystrokes on its keyboard or displaying messages on its screen. Most computers are therefore set up so that, when first turned on, they automatically begin running a small program supplied in read-only memory (ROM), or occasionally in another form (see **boot**). This program in turn enables the computer to load its operating system from disk or tape, though some microcomputers have complete operating systems in ROM.

Under the control of the operating system, the computer recognizes and obeys commands typed by the user. In addition, the operating system provides built-in routines that allow the user's program to perform input-output operations without specifying the exact hardware configuration of the computer. A computer running under one operating system cannot run programs designed to be run under another operating system, even on the same computer.

For articles on specific operating systems, see **CP/M, MS-DOS, UNIX, DOS, MVS, OS/2**.

OPERATIONS RESEARCH Operations research is concerned with the development of mathematical models of repetitive human activities, such as those involved in traffic flow, assembly lines, and military campaigns. Operations research makes extensive use of computer simulation.

OPTICAL CHARACTER READER An optical character reader is a device that can recognize typed or handwritten characters on paper. Reliable optical character readers usually require that their input be typed with a specific kind of typewriter.

OPTICAL DISK An optical disk is a high-density storage device that uses lasers to create patterns to represent the information. (See **CD ROM; WORM.**)

OR GATE An OR gate (see Figure 56) is a logic gate whose output is 1 when either or both of the inputs are 1, as shown in the table.

FIGURE 56

Input 1	Input 2	Output 3
0	0	0
0	1	1
1	0	1
1	1	1

An OR gate can be constructed by using two switches in parallel (see Figure 57). The output signal will be present (nonzero) if either switch 1 or switch 2 is closed.

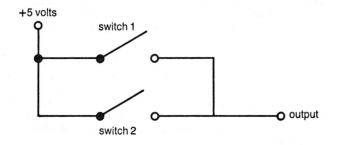

FIGURE 57

The same concept can be used to construct an OR gate with transistors (see Figure 58). In this circuit, logic level 0 is represented by 0 volts, and logic level 1 is represented by 5 volts.

FIGURE 58

A positive voltage at the input of either transistor causes it to conduct; the output voltage is approximately 5 volts if either or both of the transistors are conducting.

ORPHAN The last line of a paragraph is called an orphan if it appears by itself as the first line of a page. Some word processors automatically adjust page breaks so that there are no orphans. See also **widow**.

OS/2 The OS/2 operating system was developed by Microsoft for the IBM PC AT and PS/2 computers. It runs only on machines with 80286 or 80386 microprocessors. Version 1.0 of OS/2 uses a command language almost identical to that of MS-DOS (PC-DOS); version 1.1 uses Presentation Manager, a mouse-and-window-oriented user interface similar to that of Microsoft Windows.

OS/2 is a multitasking operating system. That is, it enables the computer to shift its attention rapidly back and forth between several processes, seemingly running several programs at the same time. This has several advantages:

1 A user can have more than one program active at the same time (e.g., a word processor and a spreadsheet), switching back and forth between them. It is not necessary to save and quit in one program before starting another.

2 Slow computations and data transfers can be done "in the background" while the user works with another program.

3 Multitasking can lead to better performance with complex programs such as word processors. The manufacturer can divide the word processor into tasks that are managed by the operating system, such as a task that checks for keyboard input, a task that updates the screen, and a task that sends output to the printer. The user need never know that multitasking is going on.

OS/2 uses the same disk formats as DOS, except that every disk should have a label (labels are permitted but not required under DOS). OS/2 can run most DOS software in real mode as well as running OS/2 software in protected mode. (See **real mode; protected mode.**)

Unlike DOS or CP/M, OS/2 can swap to disk, using extra disk space as a substitute for RAM. Thus, although OS/2 requires about 4 megabytes of RAM for good performance, there is no fixed amount of RAM needed to run a particular program.

OS/360 OS/360, the operating system released with the IBM 360 in the early 1960s, formed the basis of many subsequent operating systems (OS/VS2, MVT, MVS, etc.) See also **TSO; JCL.**

OSI See **data communication.**

OUTLINE An outline program makes it possible to organize your ideas into a hierarchical outline. People generally need to arrange large amounts of information into hierarchies. For example, a long book is divided into chapters, and each chapter may be further divided into sections. Outlining programs are available that allow you to organize information you write in this form. When working with an outline, you will sometimes want to see only the broadest points—say, the top two or three levels of the outline. At other times you will want to look at all of the specific information for part of the outline.

For example, suppose you are writing a book about different types of animals. It would help to enter the information about the classification of animals as an outline. If you start at the top level and display four levels down, here is what part of the outline will look like:

Animals
    Invertebrates
    Arthropods
    Vertebrates
        Fishes
            Teleostei (bony fishes)
            Holostei
            Chondrostei
        Amphibians
            Urodela (salamanders and sirens)
            Anura (frogs and toads)
        Reptiles
            Chelonia (turtles)
            Sauria (lizards)
            Crocodilia (crocodiles)
            Serpents (snakes)
        Birds
            Sphenisciformes (penguins)
            Anseriformes (waterfowl)
            Falconiformes
        Mammals
            Carnivora (dogs, cats, others)
            Artiodactyla (cattle, pigs, others)
            Rodentia (rats, mice, others)
            Chiroptera (bats)
            Lagomorpha (rabbits, hares)
            Insectivora (shrews, moles, others)
            Perissodactyla (horses and others)
            Cetacea (whales, dolphins, porpoises)
            Proboscidea (elephants)
            Primates

(Note that not all categories of animals have been included in this outline.) Now, suppose you want to focus on Cetacea. if you move to the Cetacea location and display four levels down from there, the outline looks like this:

        Cetacea (whales, dolphins, porpoises)
            Odontoceti (toothed)
                Physeteridae
                    Sperm whale
                Monodontidae
                    Narwhal
                    Beluga

Phocoenidae
  Porpoise
Delphinidae
  Dolphin
  Killer whale
Mysticeti (baleen)
  Eschrichtiidae
    Gray whale
  Balaenidae
    Right whale
  Balaenoteridae
    Humpbackwhale

The outline is structured as a tree (see **tree**). Each data item (node) is displayed below the item above it, and lower levels are indented more than upper levels. Recursion can be used in the program to display the outline. The part of the outline below each data item can be displayed as if it were a complete outline on its own. (See **recursion**).

OUTPUT The output of a computer is the information that the computer generates as a result of its calculations. Computer output may be either printed on paper, displayed on a terminal, punched on cards, or stored on magnetic tapes or disks.

OVERFLOW An overflow error condition arises when the result of a calculation is a number too big to be represented on the computer.

OVERLAID WINDOWS Overlaid windows can overlap; when they do, one window hides the parts of others that are behind it. To bring another window to the front, move the mouse pointer into it and click the button. (See **windows.**)

P

P-TYPE A P-type semiconductor region is formed by doping a silicon crystal with an impurity that contains three outer-level electrons. (See **semiconductor.**)

PACKET A packet is a group of consecutive characters sent from one computer to another over a network. For an example, see **XMODEM**. On many local-area networks, all communications are in the form of packets that begin with labels indicating the machine to which they are addressed.

PACKET RADIO Packet radio is the transmission of data (in packets) by radio. It is a fast-growing hobby among radio amateurs ("hams") and also has commercial applications as a way of linking computers without wires.

A typical amateur packet system consists of a computer linked by a terminal-node controller (TNC) to a radio transmitter and receiver. The TNC constructs and recognizes packets. The packet radio protocol effectively prevents two systems from transmitting at the same time, and all data are error-checked. Packet systems are often used to run bulletin boards (see **BBS**). Unlike telephone-line BBSs, packet BBSs are inherently multiuser systems, because each packet contains a label indicating its sender and receiver. Thus, the computer can keep track of many users concurrently.

Commercial packet systems involve portable computer terminals carried by delivery or service personnel. The terminals are linked by radio to a main computer many miles away.

PAGE See **virtual storage.**

PAGE FAULT See **virtual storage.**

PAGEMAKER PageMaker, produced by Aldus Corporation, was one of the pioneering programs used for desktop publishing when it was introduced for the Apple Macintosh in 1984. An updated version (PageMaker 3.0) was introduced in 1988 for both the Macintosh and the IBM PC. Its capabilities include the ability to move text or graphics around the page and to use style sheets so that all subheads will have the same form automatically. (See **desktop publishing.**)

PAINT PROGRAM A paint program is one type of program for drawing pictures on a personal computer. The user draws with the mouse pointer (see **mouse; pointer**), and commands are provided for drawing circles, lines, rectangles, and other shapes, as well as for drawing freehand and creating shaded areas.

Paint programs treat the picture as a grid of pixels (see **pixel**). Shadings are easy to produce simply by making individual pixels black or white, but the pixel grid puts a fundamental limit on the sharpness of the picture. By contrast, see **draw program**.

Some popular paint programs include MacPaint (supplied with the Apple Macintosh) and Microsoft Windows Paint (supplied with Microsoft Windows).

PALETTE A palette is a set of colors chosen from a much larger set. For instance, the IBM VGA can display more than 250,000 different colors, but the programmer or user must choose a palette of no more than 256 to use at a time.

The whole set of displayable colors is also sometimes called a palette.

PARALLEL (1) Two electronic circuit elements are connected in parallel if the electric current will reach the same destination by flowing through either element. Figure 59 shows two resistors connected in parallel.

(2) Parallel data transmission is the transmission of several bits at the same time over different wires; it is usually faster than serial transmission (see **serial**). In connecting a printer to a microcomputer, it is important to know whether the printer requires parallel or serial (RS-232) data.

FIGURE 59

PARALLEL PROCESSING Parallel processing is what a computer does when it carries out more than one computation at the same time on different CPUs. By contrast, most multitasking is accomplished by making a single CPU switch its attention among several tasks. This is called **concurrent processing** or **timesharing**.

PARAMETER A parameter in a procedure is a symbol that will be replaced by a supplied value when the procedure is called. The use of parameters allows you to make your instructions much more general. For example, here is a set of cooking instructions that uses parameters:

1. Put the object in the oven.
2. Set the temperature to the temperature listed in the recipe.
3. Set the timer to the time listed in the recipe.
4. Wait until the timer goes off.
5. Take the object out of the oven.
6. Turn the oven off.

There are three parameters here: "object," "the temperature listed in the recipe," and "the time listed in the recipe." Before you can actually execute the instructions, you must be given specific values for these three items. Here is how the instructions look once you have some specific values:

1. Put the tuna casserole in the oven.
2. Set the temperature to 375 degrees.
3. Set the timer to 30 minutes.
4. Wait until the timer goes off.
5. Take the tuna casserole out of the oven.
6. Turn the oven off.

Here is a Pascal program containing a procedure called swap. The procedure uses two parameters: *x* and *y*. The first time the procedure is called, the variables *a* and *b* are substituted for the parameters. The next time *b* and *c* are used.

```
PROGRAM swapnum (INPUT, OUTPUT);
  VAR
    a, b, c : INTEGER;
    PROCEDURE swap(VAR x, y : INTEGER);
    VAR temp : INTEGER;
    BEGIN
```

```
   temp := x;
   x  := y;
   y := temp
  END;
 BEGIN {Main program}
  READLN(a, b, c,);
  WRITELN('a=',a,' b=',b,' c=',c);
  swap(a,b);
  WRITELN('a=',a,' b=',b,' c=',c);
  swap(b,c)
  WRITELN('a=',a,' b=',b,' c=',c)
 END.
```

Here is a sample run of this program with the numbers 239, 535, and 66 as input:

```
a=239 b=535 c=66
a=535 b=239 c=66
a=535 b=66 c=239
```

The names that are used for the parameters in the procedure declaration (*x* and *y* in this case) are known as the *formal parameters*. The names used when the procedure is called (*a, b,* and *c* in this case) are the *actual parameters*.

PARITY (1) The parity of a number is its quality of being odd or even. Often, when groups of bits (1's and 0's) are being transmitted or stored, an extra bit is added so that the total number of 1's is always odd (or, alternatively, always even). This is called the parity of the data. An error in transmission has a 50 percent chance of changing the parity, so that if errors are frequent, the recipient of the information will have some warning that they are present.

If you are setting up a computer terminal and do not know how to set the parity and related parameters, try the following, which is the most popular combination:

Baud rate:	300
Parity:	Even
Data bits:	7
Stop bits	1
Duplex:	Full (FDX) (Change to half duplex if you cannot see what you type.)

A terminal set to the wrong parity can often be recognized because about half of the characters are incorrect, while the rest are received normally.

(2) The memory of the IBM PC and PS/2 is parity checked. The message PARITY ERROR 1 or PARITY ERROR 2 means that a memory chip is defective.

PARK To park the head of a hard disk drive means to disengage it so that the disk will be protected from possible damage if the computer is moved.

PARSING Parsing is the analysis, by computer, of the structure of statements in a human or artificial language. For instance, MS-DOS (PC-DOS) has to parse the command

```
dir b: /p
```

to determine that "dir" is the name of the command, that "b:" specifies the files to be shown, and that "/p" is another parameter (in this case, it means "pause when the screen is full"). Compilers and interpreters have to parse statements in programming languages. (See **compiler; interpreter**.) Programs that accept natural-language input have to parse sentences in human languages.

Parsing is done by comparing the string to be parsed to a *grammar*, which defines possible structures. For example, Figure 60 shows the structure of the sentence "The dog chased the black cat." Figure 61 shows a small part of a grammar of English.

Parsing can be done either *top-down* or *bottom-up*. In top-down parsing, the computer starts by looking for a particular con-

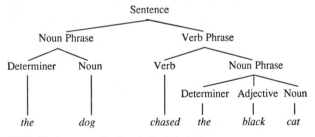

FIGURE 60. Structure of a Simple English Sentence.

(1)	Sentence	→	Noun Phrase + Verb Phrase
(2)	Noun Phrase	→	Determiner + Noun
(3)	Noun Phrase	→	Determiner + Adjective + Noun
(4)	Verb Phrase	→	Verb + Noun Phrase
(5)	Determiner	→	*the*
(6)	Noun	→	*dog*
(7)	Noun	→	*cat*
(8)	Adjective	→	*black*
(9)	Verb	→	*chased*

FIGURE 61. A Small Part of a Grammar of English. Each rule states that the constituent named on the left can consist of the constituents named on the right, in the specified order.

stituent. It consults the grammar to determine what this constitutent consists of, then looks for those constituents instead, thus:

```
Look for Sentence
Rule 1:Sentence consists of Noun Phrase + Verb Phrase
      Look for Noun Phrase
      Rule 2:Noun Phrase consists of Determiner + Noun
          Look for Determiner
              Accept Determiner the from input string
          Look for Noun
              Accept Noun dog from input string
      Look for Verb Phrase
```
(etc.)

The process is complete when the input string is empty and all of the elements of a sentence have been found.

In bottom-up parsing, the computer accepts elements from the input string and tries to put them together, thus:

```
Accept the, which is a Determiner
Accept dog, which is a Noun
Determiner + Noun make a Noun Phrase
Accept chased, which is a Verb
Accept the, which is a Determiner
Accept black, which is an Adjective
Accept cat, which is a Noun
Determiner + Adjective + Noun make a Noun Phrase
Verb + Noun Phrase make a Verb Phrase
Noun Phrase + Verb Phrase make a Sentence
```

Parsing algorithms must be able to *backtrack* (back up and try alternatives) because the grammar provides alternatives. For example, a noun phrase may or may not contain an adjective; and a word like *leaves* may be a verb or a noun. Further, parsing algorithms usually use *recursion* to handle the recursive structure of human languages. For example, a noun phrase can contain a noun phrase, which can contain another noun phrase, as in *the discoverer of the solution to the problem*. (See **recursion; backtracking; natural language processing**.)

PASCAL Pascal, a programming language developed by Niklaus Wirth, is designed to encourage programmers to write modular and well-structured programs. Pascal has become one of the most popular languages for microcomputers, and there are several common versions. Here are some of its features:

1. The first word in a Pascal program is PROGRAM, followed by the program name. The first line also normally includes the words (INPUT,OUTPUT). The first part of the program is a declaration section for constants, variables, procedures, and functions. Every variable used in a Pascal program must be declared. The action part of the program starts with the word BEGIN, and the program concludes with the word END, followed by a period. Statements are separated from each other by semicolons.

2. Pascal provides four standard data types: real, integer, Boolean, and char. *Integer* variables can take on only values that are whole numbers or the negatives of whole numbers. *Real* variables can take on numerical values that include fractional parts, such as 23.432. *Boolean* variables are logic variables that can only have two possible values: true or false. *Char* variables can take on single character values.

   Here is an example of a declaration section:

   ```
   VAR
     count, total : INTEGER;
     average : REAL;
     error : BOOLEAN;
     c : CHAR;
   ```

3. An assignment statement in Pascal looks like this:

   ```
   x : = 3;
   ```

   Note that a colon followed by an equal sign is the symbol used for assignment. This statement will cause the variable *x* to take on the value 3. For integers and real numbers, + means

addition, – means subtraction, * means multiplication, and **
means exponentiation (although exponentiation is not available on all Pascal versions). Division for real numbers is
represented by /. There are two separate division commands
for integers. The expression a DIV b will be the quotient of *a*
divided by *b*, ignoring the remainder. The expression a MOD
b will be the remainder when *a* is divided by *b*. For example,
14 DIV 5 is 2, and 14 MOD 5 is 4.

4 The two input commands are READ and READLN. If you are
using Pascal interactively, the statement READ(x) will cause
the computer to stop and wait for you to type a value for *x* at
the keyboard. READLN (which stands for "read line") works
the same way except that after a READLN is executed the
computer will start looking at the next data line when it
reaches the next input statement.

The two output commands are WRITE and WRITELN.
The command WRITE(x); causes the value of the variable *x*
to be displayed. The command WRITE ('Hello'); causes the
word *Hello* to be displayed. The command WRITE (x:6)
causes the value of *x* to be displayed in a field that is six
characters wide, and the command WRITE(x:7:3) causes the
value of *x* to be displayed in a field that is seven characters
wide and three characters to the right of the decimal point
displayed. After a WRITE command is executed, the output
for subsequent output statements will be displayed on the
same line. After a WRITELN statement, the output from
subsequent output statements will be displayed on a new line.

5 The IF/THEN/ELSE statement can be used to control the
actions of a program. For example:

```
IF x > 0 THEN WRITELN ('x is positive')
ELSE WRITELN ('x is negative');
```

If you would like more than one action to be executed if the
condition is true, you may form a compound statement that
starts with the word BEGIN and concludes with the word
END. For example:

```
IF x > 0 THEN
  BEGIN
    WRITELN ('The value of x is a positive');
    WRITELN ('The square root of x is',SQRT(x))
  END;
```

Pascal provides for three types of loops: REPEAT, WHILE and FOR loops. Each of the following program segments causes the numbers from 1 to 10 to be printed:

```
number := 0;
REPEAT
  number := number + 1;
  WRITELN(number);
UNTIL number >= 10;
. . .
number := 1;
WHILE number <= 10 DO
  BEGIN
    WRITELN(number);
    number := number + 1
  END;
. . .
FOR number := 1 TO 10 DO WRITELN(number)
```

6 Arrays are declared by listing the highest and lowest allowable values for their subscripts. For example, the declaration

```
VAR officenum : ARRAY [1 .. 20] OF INTEGER;
```

defines officenum as being a 20-element one-dimensional array, and the declaration

```
VAR table: ARRAY [0 .. 10, 0 .. 15] OF REAL;
```

defines tables as being a two-dimensional array with 11 rows (labeled 0 to 10) and 16 columns (labeled 0 to 15).

7 One of the most valuable features of Pascal is the capability it provides for writing modular programs. A procedure is a mini Pascal program defined in the declaration section of the main program. The procedure can be executed from the main program simply by listing its name. A procedure may have parameters, and any variables that are declared within the procedure are local to that procedure. (See **procedure**.) Pascal also provides for functions that return values to the calling program. (See **function**.)

8 A special feature of Pascal is that it provides the capability for the programmer to define new data types that can be used in addition to the four standard types. Pascal also allows the programmer to define sets, and then perform a set operation

such as union or intersection. By using a structured data type called a *record*, it is possible to organize related data of different types. (See **record**.)

9 Comments in Pascal begin with a left brace. {, and end with a right brace, }. On some system comments begin with (* and end with *). A Pascal program can be very readable if it consists of several procedures that all have meaningful mnemonic names.

Here is a sample program written in Pascal:

```
PROGRAM primecheck (INPUT,OUTPUT);
   {*This program reads in an integer n and then
   n determines whether or not it is prime.*}
VAR n,i,max : INTEGER:
   continue : BOOLEAN:
   status : CHAR:
BEGIN
   READLN (n);
   status := 'Y':
   continue := TRUE:
   i := 1:
   max := TRUNC(SQRT(n)):
WHILE continue
   DO BEGIN
      i := i + 1:
      continue := (i < max);
      IF (n MOD i) =0 THEN BEGIN
          status := 'n';
      continue := FALSE
      END
   END;
WRITELN (n);
WRITELN ('PRIME: YES(Y) OR NO (N):'):
WRITELN (status)
END.
```

PASCAL, BLAISE Pascal was a French mathematician who built in 1642 a mechanical adding machine that was one of the early forerunners of calculators and computers.

PASSWORD A password is a secret character string that is required to log onto a computer system, thus preventing unauthorized persons from obtaining access to the computer.

PASTE To "paste" material is to transfer it from a holding area into the document you are editing. (See **cut; copy**.)

PATENT A patent gives legal protection for the design of a machine or mechanical process, preventing others from using the same idea without the inventor's permission. Unlike a copyright, a patent protects an idea itself, not just the expression of the idea. In the U.S., a patent remains in force for 17 years.

Computer programs usually cannot be patented, but patents have been issued for a few programs having to do with the automatic control of machines.

Integrated circuits are often protected by both patents (for the circuit design) and copyrights (for the artwork from which the tiny etch pattern is made, or for data recorded on the chip).

See also **copyright**.

PATH (1) A path specifies how to find a file on a disk that has more than one directory. In MS-DOS (PC-DOS), paths have either of two forms. For example,

\AAA\BBB\CCC

means, "In the root directory there is a directory called AAA. In AAA there is a directory called BBB. In BBB there is a directory or file called CCC."

If the initial backslash is left out, the path starts at the directory currently in use rather than at the root directory. For example, the path

AAA\BBB\CCC

means, "In the current directory there is a directory called AAA. In AAA is a directory called BBB. In BBB is a directory or file called CCC."

Paths in UNIX are written the same way but with forward slashes ("/" rather than "\").

(2) The PATH command in MS-DOS (PC-DOS) specifies directories where DOS can search for command files (.BAT, .COM, and .EXE files) if they are not found in the current directory.

See also **directory**.

PC COMPATIBILITY The original IBM Personal Computer (PC) was designed quickly by IBM and used little new technology; hence few patents protect it, and it is easy for other companies to make compatible machines (see **clone**).

Clones available today are almost perfect imitations of the IBM PC, XT, or AT; programs that will run on an IBM but not on a clone are extremely rare. Earlier MS-DOS machines, such as the DEC Rainbow or Texas Instruments Professional Computer, were PC-compatible only to a limited extent; they could read the same disks, but they ran only a subset of IBM software because they did not emulate the IBM BIOS (see **BIOS**).

If a computer merely needs to exchange data with an IBM PC, it need not be IBM-compatible at all; all it needs is a suitable communications medium (such as phone lines or a local-area network) with suitable software.

PDP See **Digital Equipment Corporation.**

PEEK PEEK is an instruction or function in BASIC that allows the programmer to read the contents of a particular memory location, identified by its address. The uses of the PEEK function depend on the exact type of computer and even the accesories installed. See also **POKE.**

PERIPHERAL A peripheral is a device connected to a computer. Three examples of a peripheral are *terminals, card readers,* and *disk drives.*

PERSONAL COMPUTER A personal computer is designed to be used by only one person, either at home or in a business setting. The term *personal computer* includes some microcomputers that are too large and expensive to be referred to as home computers. One of the first personal computers was the Digital Equipment Corporation PDP-8, a minicomputer often used in scientific laboratories in the early 1970s.

PI The greek letter π (pi) is the symbol for a special number that is approximately equal to 3.14159. If the radius of a circle is r, then the circumference is $2\pi r$, and the area is πr^2.

PICA (1) A pica typewriter prints 10 characters per inch. So do most fixed-pitch computer printers.

(2) In typesetting, a pica is ⅙ inch, or 12 points.

PICO- The prefix *pico-* means one trillionth (10^{-12}). One picosecond is one trillionth of a second.

PILOT PILOT is a programming language especially suited for writing programs for computer-assisted instruction. PILOT makes it easy for teachers to write conversational instructional programs without needing to know much about the details of programming.

PIN The pins in a dot-matrix printer press on the ribbon to make dots on the paper. A 9-pin printer produces readable but inelegant type. Some 9-pin printers have a near-letter-quality mode in which they simulate 18 pins by making two passes across each line; the result resembles the type from a cloth-ribbon typewriter. Printers with 24 pins produce very sharp letter-quality text.

PIPELINE In UNIX, MS-DOS, and similar operating systems, a pipeline (or *pipe*) is a way of stringing two or more programs together so that the output of one of them is fed to the other as input. For example, the MS-DOS command

        A> DIR | SORT | MORE

invokes DIR (which lists the names of the files on a disk), feeds its output to SORT (which puts the items in alphabetical order), and feeds that output to MORE (which displays it one screenful at a time).

PIRACY Piracy is the unauthorized copying of software, which is forbidden by law. (See **software license; copyright.**)

PITCH The pitch of a printer is the number of characters per inch (most commonly 10). Fixed-pitch type has every character the same width; proportional-pitch type has some characters wider than others (e.g., "M" wider than "I"), and the pitch can only be measured approximately as the average of many different letters.

PIXEL A picture on a CRT screen is made up of tiny elements called pixels. For example, a color screen for a DEC Rainbow in high-resolution mode consists of an 800-by-240 pixel array. You can draw pictures on the screen by controlling the color of each pixel. (See **graphics.**)

PL/I (PL/1) PL/1 is a very powerful programming language developed by IBM in the early 1960s to accompany its System/360 computer. The name stands for Programming Language One (1) and is also written as PL/1.

PL/I can be described as a combination of ALGOL 60 block

structure, FORTRAN arithmetic, and COBOL data structuring. PL/I is the language of choice for writing complex programs on IBM mainframe computers, but it has received little use on other types of machines.

Some of the main features of PL/I are the following:

1 Many data types are available, including floating-point numbers, fixed-point binary numbers, and fixed-point decimal numbers (all of these with any number of significant digits, up to hardware-imposed limits); character strings (of fixed or varying length); bit strings; and several more exotic types such as variables whose values are statement labels. Undeclared variables are taken to be fixed-point binary numbers if their names begin with I, J, K, L, M, or N, and floating-point numbers otherwise.

2 Values of any type can be assigned to variables of practically any other type: conversions are done automatically. For example, if the fixed-point number 2.45 is assigned to a character string, the result is the string '2.45'. A subroutine can determine, at execution time, the size of an array or character string passed to it as a parameter.

3 Each statement ends with a semicolon. The beginning of a comment is maked with /* and the end of a comment with */.

4 The arithmetic operators are + (addition), – (subtraction), * (multiplication), / (division), and ** (raising to a power). The equals sign, =, is used both in assignment statements and in comparisons.

5 There are many ways of doing input and output. For example,

GET LIST (A, B, C);

instructs the computer to read A, B, and C from the standard input file; the values of A,B, and C can be written in any reasonable format (as with Pascal's READ and READLN). The corresponding output statement is PUT LIST (A, B, C,);

The statement

GET EDIT (A, B, C) ((3)(F(4,2)));

tells the computer that A, B, and C are each represented as four digits, two of which are to the right of the decimal point (as in FORTRAN's FORMAT statement; see **format**). A complete record of a file can be read in one step with the READ INTO statement.

6   There are several types of loops. The equivalent of a FOR-NEXT loop in BASIC is of the form

```
ALPHA: DO I=10 TO 20 BY 2;
  /* statements in middle go here */
END ALPHA;
```

There are also DO WHILE and DO UNTIL loops, corresponding to Pascal's WHILE and REPEAT constructs.

7   Subroutines and functions are defined by the word PROCE-DURE, as in the following:

```
IC: PROCEDURE(A, B, C);
  /* statements */
END IC;
```

Procedures are invoked with a CALL statement, as in FOR-TRAN:

```
CALL IC (-2, 3, ZZZ);
```

The main program is a procedure with the option MAIN.
   Here is a program written in PL/I:

```
PRMCHK: PROCEDURE OPTIONS(MAIN);
  /* THIS PROGRAM READS A SEQUENCE OF
  NUMBERS AND IDENTIFIES WHICH ONES ARE
  PRIME.*/
    DECLARE   (N, I) FLOAT;
              ON ENDFILE GO TO STOP;
    START:    GET LIST(N)
    LOOP:     DO I = 2 TO (TRUNC(SQRT(N))+1);
                IF N/I = TRUNC(N/I) THEN
                  GO TO NPRIME;
              END LOOP;
              PUT SKIP(2) LIST(N, 'IS PRIME');
              GO TO START;
    NPRIME:PUT SKIP(2) LIST(N,'IS NOT PRIME');
              PUT SKIP LIST('IT IS DIVISIBLE BY',I);
              GO TO START;
    STOP:  END PRMCHK;
```

PLATEN A platen is the roller in a typewriter or printer against which the keys strike. Some printers use the pressure of the platen to pull the paper forward.

PLATO PLATO is a system of computer-based education developed by Control Data Corporation. PLATO software packages are available that include courses in many different subjects, such as foreign languages, mathematics, science, and computers.

PLOTTER A plotter is a device that draws pictures on paper by moving pens according to directions from a computer. (See **graphics**.)

POINT In typesetting, a point is $\frac{1}{72}$ inch. The height of type is usually expressed in points. However, this is not a measurement of the size of the letters, but rather of the metal blocks on which the letters were originally cast for printing presses. Therefore, different typefaces of the same point size may be somewhat different sizes.

In a typical book-sized line of type, about 25 picas wide, readability is greatest with 10-point type with 2 points of leading. Greater width calls for larger type, lesser width (as a newspaper column) calls for smaller type. This works out to 6 lines to the inch. (See **leading; typeface; typesetting mistakes**.)

POINTER (1) A pointer is a data item consisting of an address that tells where to find a desired item. For examples, see **linked list; tree**.

Pascal provides a specific data type called a pointer variable that can be used to keep track of data structures that vary in size as the program is executed.

(2) The pointer is a symbol that moves around a computer screen under the control of the user. For example, to execute a command on an Apple Macintosh, use the mouse to move the pointer to the icon representing that command, and then press the button on the mouse.

POKE POKE is a BASIC instruction that allows you to put a specific value in a specific memory location. To use the POKE command, you must specify two numbers: an address and the value you want poked into that address. (Fortunately, you may give these values as decimal numbers or expressions.) The effects of the POKE statement depend on the exact type of computer and even the accesories installed. For example, in a Commodore-64 computer, memory location 53281 controls the color of the screen, and 2 is the code for the color red. Therefore, the command

```
POKE 53281,2
```

causes the screen to turn red. See also **PEEK**.

POLISH NOTATION Polish notation is a way of writing algebraic expressions that does not require parentheses to state which operations are done first. It is named in honor of its inventor, Jan Lukasiewicz (1878-1956), whose name most English-speaking mathematicians cannot pronounce.

The ordinary algebraic expression

$$4 + (5 - 3) + 2$$

translates into Polish notation as

$$4\ 5\ 3\ -\ +\ 2\ +$$

To evaluate the expression, work through it from left to right until you encounter an operation (a plus or minus), then perform that operation using an appropriate number of numbers immediately to the left of the operator. Replace the numbers and the operator with the result of the operation, and keep going in the same manner. For the expression above, this works out as follows:

This is technically known as *reverse Polish notation (RPN)*; the expression can also be written in the other direction and worked through from right to left.

Many calculators and programming language interpreters translate expressions into Polish notation in order to evaluate them. Also, Hewlett-Packard calculators use Polish notation rather than parentheses on the ground that Polish notation is easier to work with once the user becomes accustomed to it.

POP See **stack**.

POP-UP UTILITY See **memory resident.**

PORT A port is a connection between the CPU and another device that provides a means for information to enter or leave the computer.

PORTABLE (1) A portable computer is a computer small enough and light enough (under 12 pounds) so that it can be carried around more easily than can a desktop microcomputer. A portable computer is more powerful than a laptop computer, but a laptop computer is easier to carry.

(2) A *portable program* is a program that is machine independent; that is, it can be used on more than one type of machine.

PORTRAIT Portrait orientation refers to paper oriented so that it is higher than it is wide, like a portrait painting. Most printers print with the paper in portrait orientation. If the paper can be turned sideways, the result is called *landscape orientation.* Laser printers typically offer a choice of portrait or landscape orientation.

POSTSCRIPT Postscript, developed by Adobe Systems of Palo Alto, California, is a graphical command language for laser printers (and, potentially, other graphics devices). It is used in the Apple Laserwriter but not in the lower-priced Hewlett-Packard LaserJet.

A Postscript printer accepts not only characters to be printed but also commands to change the size of type fonts or to draw lines or circles in specific positions.

POWER LINE PROTECTION Several things can go wrong with the AC power supplied to a computer from the wall outlet.

1 Brief bursts ("spikes") of excessive voltage can damage the computer. These spikes come from lightning or from large electric motors switching off. They are easily absorbed by a surge protector (see **surge protector**).

2 Power failures cause the computer to shut down or restart suddenly, losing the data that you were working on. A surge protector cannot prevent this; if the problem is frequent, you may want to invest in an uninterruptable power supply (UPS).

3 The computer can emit radio or TV interference through the power line. (See **RFI protection**.)

PRECEDENCE The precedence rules of a programming language determine in what order the computer will perform the operations if a single expression contains more than one operation. For example, in BASIC, as in many other languages, exponentiations are done first, then multiplications and divisions, and finally additions and subtractions. For example, the BASIC expression

2 + 3 * 4 ↑ 2

means 2 + 3 * 16 = 2 + 48 = 50.

You can use parentheses to change the order of the operations when you need to, since any operation in parentheses will be done first.

Not all languages have the same precedence rules. For example, APL has no precedence rules at all. All APL operations are done in order from right to left.

PRECISION The precision of a quantity refers to how exactly it is specified. For numbers the precision is the number of significant digits that the computer keeps track of when it carries out arithmetic operations.

PRESENTATION MANAGER In OS/2 1.1 and higher, the Presentation Manager is a user interface similar to Microsoft Windows. It enables the user to control files and software graphically by using a mouse. (See **Windows, Microsoft; OS/2.**)

PRESS To press a mouse button is to depress it and hold it down for about half a second. By contrast, see **click**.

PRIMITIVE A primitive is a basic element or concept in terms of which larger elements or concepts are formed. For example, in programming languages such as FORTH and LISP, it is common for the programmer to create his own statements by defining them in terms of primitives provided by the langauge.

PRINT SPOOLER A print spooler is a program that stores computer output in memory so that the user's program can finish creating the output without waiting for the printer to print it. The spooler then sends the stored output to the printer at the proper speed. See also **spooling; buffer**.

PRINTER A printer is a device for putting computer output on paper. (See **line printer; daisywheel printer; dot-matrix**

printer; electrostatic printer; ink-jet printer; laser printer; thermal printer.)

PROCEDURE A procedure is a miniature program that is part of a main program. The procedure is executed when the main program calls for it. Here is an example of a Turbo Pascal program with a procedure:

```
PROGRAM divide (INPUT,OUTPUT);
   {This program reads in two integers and then per-
   forms the division, giving both the quotient and the
   remainder.}
TYPE strin=STRING[50];
VAR a,b:INTEGER;
   PROCEDURE readint(VAR z:INTEGER);
      {This prodcedure reads in an integer from the
      keyboard.In the case of invalid input, the com-
      puter will ask the user to reenter the data.}
   VAR x:STRIN; code,z2:INTEGER;
   BEGIN
      WRITE('Enter value:');
      READLN(x)
      val(x,z2, code);
      WHILE code <>0 DO
      BEGIN
         WRITE('|',x,'| is invalid; enter integer value:');
         READLN(x);
         val(x,z2,code)
      END;
      z:=z2
   END;
BEGIN {Main program block}
   readint(a); {The procedure is called in each of these}
   readint(b); {two lines.}
   WRITELN('Quotient: ', (a DIV b));
   WRITELN('Remainder: ', (a MOD b))
END.
```

There are two main advantages to using procedures when writing programs:

1 Often there will be a set of instructions that must be executed at more than one place in a program or in several different programs. Defining those instructions as a procedure saves work and memory space. In the example program, the procedure readint is called twice. This procedure can be included in any program where you need to read in a value that must be an integer.

2 A large program is easier to understand if it consists of procedures. Each procedure should have a well-understood purpose. (See **top-down programming**.)

For another example of a Pascal procedure, see **parameter**. For an example of the equivalent concept in BASIC, see **subroutine**.

PROCESSOR See **microprocessor; coprocessor; CPU.**

PROGRAM A program is a set of instructions for a computer to execute. A program can be written in a programming language, such as BASIC or Pascal, or in an assembly language. You may write your own programs if you know a programming language, or you may buy prewritten programs that perform standard tasks, such as word processing or financial calculations. The programs that direct a computer are called *software*.

PROGRAMMABLE FUNCTION KEY A programmable function key is a key on a computer keyboard whose function depends on the software being run. In many cases, programmable function (PF) keys can be defined as equivalent to combinations or sequences of other keys. For example, in IBM PC BASIC, the command

```
KEY 1,"CLS"+CHR$(13)
```

defines function key 1 as equivalent to typing CLS followed by a carriage return [represented by CHR$(13)].

PROGRAMMER A programmer is a person who prepares instructions for computers.

PROGRAMMING Programming is the process of writing instructions for a computer to carry out. A programmer needs to develop a well-defined concept of how to solve a problem. (See **algorithm**.) Then this concept must be translated into a computer language. (See **programming language**.) Finally, the program needs to be turned into machine-readable form and fed into the computer through an input device.

PROGRAMMING LANGUAGE The following is a classification
of commonly used programming languages according to their
main applications. Several languages fit into more than one
category; most are dealt with in separate articles in this book. See
also **machine language** and **assembly language.**

1 General purpose for large, complex programs: PL/I, C,
   Pascal, Modula-2, Ada.
2 General purpose for smaller programs, especially on microcomputers: BASIC, Pascal.
3 Computer-based education: BASIC, PILOT, LOGO.
4 Mathematical calculation, science, and engineering: FOR-
   TRAN, APL, and the general-purpose languages named
   above.
5 Business data processing: COBOL, RPG. Where microcomputers are involved, BASIC, Pascal, and C are coming into
   use.
6 Artificial intelligence and programs of extreme logical
   complexity: LISP and its derivatives.

   Another useful classification is based on the way the
   program is organized.

1 Sequential languages treat the program as a series of steps,
   with an occasional GOTO statement as a way of breaking out
   of the sequence. In this category are FORTRAN, BASIC, and
   COBOL (though COBOL also allows programs to be written
   in a style more like a block-structured language).
2 Block-structured languages encourage structured programming by allowing the programmer to group statements into
   functional units. (See **structured programming.**) In this
   category are ALGOL 60 and 68, PL/I, C, Pascal, Modula, and
   Ada.
3 Extensible languages build up complex programs by allowing
   the programmer to define her statements in terms of previously defined statements. This category includes FORTH,
   LISP, and LOGO.

PROJECT MANAGER A project-manager program is a program
designed to help plan the scheduling of a complex project involving many different tasks. A typical task requires some resources
and a certain amount of time; it also requires that certain other
tasks have already been finished. You may sometimes schedule

two tasks to be performed simultaneously if they don't overtax the supply of available resources, but when the tasks are sequential, you must schedule them in the proper order. For example, the engines on the wings of an airplane cannot be installed until the wings have been built. A project-manager program takes the information the user enters for each task and then determines how to schedule the tasks. The results are often presented in the form of a diagram called a Gantt chart (see Figure 62).

Task	Weeks						
	1	2	3	4	5	6	7
visit houses	■						
make decision		■					
loan application			■	■			
shop for furniture			■	■			
send notices of address change				■	■		
sign closing papers						■	
order phone						■	
move							■

FIGURE 62 Gantt Chart. This sample shows the scheduling of activities that need to be done when a family moves to a new home. The blocked-out sections show when each task is scheduled.

PROLOG The programming language Prolog (Programming in Logic) was developed in the early 1970s by Alain Colmerauer at the University of Marseilles. Prolog is used for writing computer programs that model human thinking. It exemplifies logic programming, a kind of programming developed by Robert Kowalski of the University of London.

In ordinary programming, a program describes the steps that a computer is to work through in order to solve a problem. In *logic programming*, the program gives the computer facts about the problem, plus rules by means of which other facts can be inferred. The computer then applies a fixed procedure to solve the problem automatically.

Suppose, for example, we want to know whether Atlanta is in North America. We have the following information to work from:

1. X is in North America if X is in the United States.
2. X is in North America if X is in Canada.
3. X is in the United States if X is in Georgia.
4. X is in the United States if X is in Florida.
5. Atlanta is in Georgia.

As Kowalski has pointed out, this can be described equally well in terms of reasoning procedures as follows:

1. To show that X is in North America, show that X is in the United States.
2. To show that X is in North America, show that X is in Canada.
3. To show that X is in the United States, show that X is in Georgia.
4. To show that X is in the United States, show that X is in Florida.
5. To show that Atlanta is in Georgia, do nothing.

It is then obvious that our problem can be solved by chaining statements 1, 3, and 5 together.

We would express the available information in Prolog as follows:

```
/* Rule 1 */ north_america(X) :- united_states(X).
/* Rule 2 */ north_america(X) :- canada(X).
/* Rule 3 */ united _states(X) :- georgia(X).
/* Rule 4 */ united_states(X) :- florida(X).
/* Rule 5 */ georgia(atlanta).
```

The symbol /* indicates the beginning of a comment, and */ indicates the end of the comment. All of these statements are rules, X is a variable that can be matched with any constant, and : – means "if." Rule 1 means "If X is in the United States, then X is in North America." Rule 5 is a special kind of rule called a *fact* because it does not contain an "if."

To find out whether Atlanta is in North America, we then give Prolog the following query:

```
?- north_america(atlanta).
```

To solve the query, Prolog looks for a rule the first part of which will match the query. Rule 1 will work, provided that variable X is given the value "atlanta." Then the second part of the rule becomes the new query:

?- united_states(atlanta).

Again, we look for a rule that will match the query. Rule 3 will work, and the new query becomes

?- georgia(atlanta).

When we look for a rule that matches this query, we find that rule 5 matches it exactly and does not contain an "if"—hence it does not introduce a new query, the process is complete, and the question can be answered "yes." If the process had ended with a query that no rule would match, the question would be answered "no."

One of the most important properties of Prolog is its ability to *backtrack*, that is, to back up and try alternative solutions. This is necessary whenever the search starts pursuing a chain of rules that do not lead to a solution. For example, rules 2 and 4 do not lead to a solution in our example; if the computer tried either of them, it would need to back up and try alternatives.

The Prolog example shown above uses the syntax implemented by W.F. Clocksin and C.S. Mellish at the University of Edinburgh. Some implementations use a more LISP-like syntax in which the preceeding example would look like this:

```
((NORTH_AMERICA X) (UNITED_STATES X))
((NORTH_AMERICA X) (CANADA X))
((UNITED _STATES X) (GEORGIA X))
((GEORGIA ATLANTA))
```

See also **expert system.**

PROM PROM is an acronym for <u>P</u>rogrammable <u>R</u>ead-<u>O</u>nly <u>M</u>emory, which is a computer memory that can be programmed once, but not reprogrammed.

PROMPT The prompt is a symbol that appears on a computer terminal screen to signal to the user that the computer is ready to receive input. Different programs use different prompts. For example, under CP/M and IBM PC DOS, the prompt looks like A> or B>, depending on whether A or B is the default drive. The PROMPT command can be used to change the appearance of the prompt in MS-DOS. For an example, see **hard-disk management.**

PROPORTIONAL PITCH In proportional-pitch type, different letters are of different widths (e.g., "M" is wider than "I"). Compared to an ordinary typewriter or printer, this improves the appearance of the type and makes it more readable. Most books and newpapers are set in proportional type. (See **type; typeface.**)

Because the letters are of different widths, it is not possible to count letter spaces in proportional-pitch type the way one does on a typewriter. (See **typesetting mistakes.**)

PROPRIETARY "Proprietary to" means "owned by." A feature of a computer is proprietary if one company has exclusive rights to it.

PROPRINTER The IBM Proprinter is a dot-matrix printer that recognizes Epson control codes and supports Epson-compatible graphics modes. (See **Epson.**)

PROTECT(ED) MODE Protected mode (also called protect mode) is the mode in which an 80286 or 80386 microprocessor can access the largest possible amount of memory. In this mode, these processors can only run programs designed for protected mode, not programs designed for earlier processors such as the 8088. In OS/2, the user can switch between protected mode (for running OS/2 programs) and real mode (for running DOS programs).

In protected mode, different parts of memory are allocated to different programs, and memory is "protected" in the sense that a program can only write to the memory allocated to it. By contrast, see **real mode.**

PROTOCOL A protocol is a standard way of regulating data transmission between computers. (See **handshaking; X-OFF; X-ON; XMODEM; Kermit.**)

PS/2 See **IBM PS/2.**

PSEUDOCODE One of the best ways to plan a computer program is to make an outline of it, using a mixture of a programming language and a human language. This mixed language is called pseudocode.

For example, here is a pseudocode outline of a Pascal program to find the largest of a set of 10 numbers:

```
begin
  repeat
    read a number;
```

```
      test whether it is the largest found so far
   until 10 numbers have been read;
   print the largest
end.
```

Here is the program that results from translating all of the pseudocode into genuine Pascal:

```
PROGRAM findthelargest (INPUT, OUTPUT);
VAR
   num, largest, count : INTEGER;
BEGIN
   count := 0;
   largest := 0;
   REPEAT
      count := count + 1;
      READ(num);
      IF num> largest THEN largest := num
   UNTIL count = 10;
   WRITELN('The largest number was',largest)
END.
```

(This program assumes that the largest number will be greater than zero.)

The advantage of pseudocode is that it allows the programmer to concentrate on how the program works while ignoring the details of the language. By reducing the number of things the programmer must think about at once, this technique effectively amplifies the programmer's intelligence.

PUBLIC DOMAIN A computer program is in the public domain if it is not covered by any kind of copyright. Few substantial public-domain programs exist, but the term "public domain" is often used incorrectly to describe other kinds of freely copyable software (see **free software**).

PUNCHED CARD A punched card is a carboard card on which holes can be punched according to a particular pattern that can be read by a computer. Standard punched cards are $7\frac{3}{8}$ inches long and $3\frac{1}{4}$ inches high. Each card contains 80 columns and 12 rows. Each column represents one letter, number, or other symbol, depending on the pattern of holes in that column. Figure 63 shows a standard way for coding symbols on the card.

253

FIGURE 63

The holes are usually punched on the cards by a keypunch machine, which has a keyboard like a typewriter. Since most people have trouble reading punched-card hole langugage, most keypunch machines print the symbol stored in each column at the top of the column.

The computer reads the cards when they are passed through a card reader, which can flip through cards at a rate of up to 1,000 card per minute. Each card passes between a light source and a row of solar cells, which detect the location of the holes in the card. The pattern of holes is thus transformed into a pattern of electric signals. The card reader sends these signals to the computer, where they are translated into machine instructions.

The use of punched cards for data processing actually preceded the invention of the computer by more than 50 years. Herman Hollerith realized that it took several years to process data from the 1880 census. He figured that, unless a faster method was found, the U.S. Census Bureau would still be working on the results from the 1890 census when it came time to start the 1900 census. Hollerith developed a system in which census data were punched on cards, and machines were used to sort and tabulate the cards. Even earlier, in 1801, a system of punched cards was used to direct the weaving pattern on the automatic Jacquard loom in France.

In the 1960s, punched cards were the dominant way of feeding programs into computers. As interactive terminals became more readily available, punched cards became less popular. It can be nuisance to carry a deck of punched cards around, and the cards cannot be read by the card reader if they are folded, spindled, mutilated, or wet.

PUSH See **stack**.

PUSHDOWN STACK See **stack**.

PUSHDOWN STORE See **stack**.

q

QUERY LANGUAGE When you are communicating with a data base system, you type commands to the computer using the query language that is part of that system.

QUEUE A queue is a data structure from which items are removed in the same order in which they were entered. By way of contrast, see **stack**.

QUICKBASIC Microsoft QuickBASIC is a high performance compiler for BASIC. It accepts programs written for BASICA or GWBASIC, but it also adds many new kinds of statements and allows the programmer to leave out line numbers. Beginning with version 4.0, QuickBASIC has two unusual technical features. First, it is an incremental compiler, meaning that lines are compiled as soon as they are typed in. Second, it compiles into threaded code, a special kind of machine language that corresponds line-by-line to the original program. Thus, compilation is very fast and can be undone to reconstruct the BASIC program that was compiled.

QUICKSORT Quicksort is a sorting algorithm invented by C.A.R. Hoare and first published in 1962. Quicksort is faster than any other sorting algorithm available unless the items are already in nearly the correct order, in which case it is relatively inefficient.

Quicksort is a recursive procedure (See **recursion**.) On each iteration, it rearranges the list of items so that one item (the "pivot") is in its final position, all the items that should come before it are before it, and all the items that should come after it are after it. Then the lists of items preceding and following the pivot are treated as sublists and sorted in the same way.

Figure 62 shows how this works.

(a) Choose the last item in the list, 41, as the pivot. It is excluded from the searching and swapping that follow.

(b), (c) Identify the leftmost item greater than 41 and the rightmost item less than 41. Swap them.

(d), (e), (f), (g) Repeat steps (b) and (c) until the leftmost and rightmost markers meet in the middle.

(h), (i) Now that the markers have met and crossed, swap the pivot with the item pointed to by the leftmost marker.

(a)	40	43	54	86	53	25	30	28	96	41
(b)	40	43	54	86	53	25	30	28	96	41
(c)	40	28	54	86	53	25	30	43	96	41
(d)	40	28	54	86	53	25	30	43	96	41
(e)	40	28	30	86	53	25	54	43	96	41
(f)	40	28	30	86	53	25	54	43	96	41
(g)	40	28	30	25	53	86	54	43	96	41
(h)	40	28	30	25	53	86	54	43	96	41
(i)	40	28	30	25	41	86	54	43	96	53
(j)	40	28	30	25	41	86	54	43	96	53

FIGURE 64 Quicksort in Action

(j) Now that the pivot is in its final position, sort each of the two sublists to the left and in right of it.

Quicksort is difficult to express in languages, such as BASIC, that do not allow recursion. The amount of memory required by Quicksort increases exponentially with the depth of the recursion. One way to limit memory requirements is to switch to another type of sort, such as selection sort, after a certain depth is reached. (See **selection sort**.)

The following program shows the Quicksort algorithm expressed in Pascal:

```
PROCEDURE quicksort (a,b: INTEGER);
   { C.A.R. Hoare's QUICKSORT algorithm in Pascal. }
   { See R. Sedgewick, ALGORITHMS (Addison-Wesley,
   1983), ch. 9 }
   { X is assumed to be an array of type XTYPE. }
   { the sort goes from X[A] to X[B]. }
VAR left, right : INTEGER;
    save,temp : xtype;
LABEL 1;
BEGIN
   IF b>a THEN
```

```
      BEGIN
        { Define starting point }
        save  := x[b]:
        left  := a-1:
        right := b:
        { Scan until left and right markers cross }
        REPEAT
          { Scan from left }
          REPEAT left := left + 1
          UNTIL x[left] >= save:
            { Scan from right }
          REPEAT right := right-1
          UNTIL x[right] <= save:
          IF right <= left THEN GOTO 1;
            { Swap conflicting items }
          temp  := x[left];
          x[left]  := x[right]
          x[right] := temp
        UNTIL right <= left:
          {This test always bypassed by GOTO}
          {Swap x[left] with original rightmost element}
1:        temp := x[left]:
          x[left] := x[b]:
          x[b] := temp:
          { Call QUICKSORT recursively }
        quicksort (a,left-1):
        quicksort (left+1,b)
      END
    END:
```

QUIETWRITER The IBM Quietwriter printers are extremely-high-resolution dot-matrix printers whose output looks like the output of a daisywheel printer.

The Quietwriter II and III recognize Epson control codes and support Epson-compatible graphics modes. (See **Epson.**)

r

RACAL-VADIC Racal-Vadic is a company that manufactures modems and other electronic equipment. The Racal-Vadic 3400 format is a method of sending 1200-baud serial data over phone lines; it is similar but not identical to the Bell 212A format. (See **Bell 212A.**)

RADIAN MEASURE Radian measure is a way of measuring the size of angles in which a complete rotation measures 2p radians. (See **angle.**)

RADIO SHACK Radio Shack is a division of Tandy Corporation, of Fort Worth, Texas, which makes Tandy computers. Radio Shack operates one of the most widespread chains of retail computer stores. The TRS-80 line of computers was one of the earliest lines of home computers in the late 1970s and early '80s.

RADIX The radix of a number system is the same as the base of the number system. Binary numbers have a radix of 2π, and decimal numbers have a radix of 10.

RADIX SORT The radix-sort algorithm takes advantage of the fact that data are actually represented as a sequence of characters. For example, suppose you needed to alphabetize a batch of papers. You would likely put all the names that start with A in one stack, the Bs in another stack, and so on. Then you could alphabetize each stack by looking at the second letter of the name. By repeating this process, the papers would eventually be alphabetized.

Here is a Pascal program to perform a radix sort on a list of names. The program actually starts by sorting the items according to the last letter of the name, then the second to the last letter, and so on. The last step is to sort according to the first letter. This program assumes that the values have been read into memory, but it could work just as well if the data items were in a random access file.

```
PROGRAM radixsort (INPUT,OUTPUT);
   { This Turbo Pascal program performs a radix
   sort of a list of names, assuming that the input
   consists of no characters other than upper and
   lower-case letters and blacks, and that no name is
   longer than 12 characters. }
```

```
CONST maxbins = 27; maxitems = 500;
       maxlength = 12;
TYPE stringtype = STRING[maxlength];
VAR
   Inorder : BOOLEAN; f : TEXT;
   fname : STRING[20]
   charnum,i,n,longestlength : INTEGER;
   a : ARRAY[1..maxitems] OF stringtype;
   ind1,ind2 : ARRAY[1..maxitems] OF INTEGER;
     {The array ind1 contains an index telling where to
     find the item that belongs in a specific position;
     for example, ind1[6] is equal to 10, meaning that
     the 10th item of the list belongs in place 6 when
     the list is ordered. The array ind2 contains an
     index telling where to put a particular data item.
     For the example given, ind2[10] would be 6. Note
     that the data items in the array themselves are
     never actually moved. }
PROCEDURE binplace(charnum:INTEGER);
   { We can imagine that each item is placed in a
   "bin" according to the letter in the position that
   is being sorted. }
VAR i,j,k,binnumber:INTEGER;
     keyword : stringtype;
     bincount, binstartloc : ARRAY[1..maxbins] OF
                                  INTEGER;
     binlist : ARRAY[1..maxitems] OF INTEGER;
   FUNCTION bincalc (keyword : stringtype ;
                     charnum : INTEGER) : INTEGER;
   VAR binnumber: INTEGER;
   BEGIN
     IF charnum>LENGTH(keyword) THEN
        binnumber :=1
     ELSE BEGIN
        binnumber := ORD(keyword[charnum])- 95;
        {Note: 97 is the ASCII code of "a", and the
        a's are placed in bin 2. }
        IF binnumber<0 THEN
          IF binnumber=-63 THEN
             binnumber:=1       {blank}
          ELSE binnumber := binnumber + 32
          {This statement handles capital letters }
```

```
      END;
      bincalc :=binnumber
   END;
BEGIN  { procedure binplace }
   FOR k := 1 TO maxbins DO bincount[k] :=0;
   FOR i := 1 TO n DO
      BEGIN
      {This loop counts how many items go in each bin }
         j := ind1[i];
         binnumber := bincalc(a[j],charnum);
         binlist[j] := binnumber;
         bincount[binnumber]
               := bincount[binnumber]+1;
      END;
   binstartloc[1] :=1;
   FOR k := 2 TO maxbins DO
      binstartloc[k] := binstartloc[k-1]+bincount[k-1];
   FOR i := 1 TO n DO
      {This loop determines the new position }
      { that a data item should have after it }
      {has been placed in its imaginary bin.}
      BEGIN
         j := ind1[i];
         bin number := binlist[j];
         ind2[j] := binstartloc[binnumber];
         binstartloc[binnumber]
               := binstartloc[binnumber] + 1
      END
END;
BEGIN  { main program block }
   { **** Input section **** }
   WRITE('Enter number of items:'); READLN(n);
   FOR i:= 1 TO n DO READLN(a[i]);
   FOR i := 1 TO n DO ind1[i] := i;
   charnum := maxlength;
   ( **** Perform the sorting operation **** )
   REPEAT
      binplace(charnum);
      FOR i := 1 TO n DO ind1 [ind2[i] ] :=i;
      charnum := charnum -1;
   UNTIL charnum=0;
```

```
{ **** Output section **** }
  FOR i := 1 TO n DO WRITELN(i:3,' ',a[indl[i])
END.
```

The radix-sort method can be used effectively with binary numbers, since there are only two possible bins for the items to be placed.

If the names are long, it would take too long to start with the last character. Instead, the program could be redesigned so that it would sort on only the first 4 or 5 characters. Then the program could complete the sort by switching to another method that is efficient with an almost-sorted list, such as insertion sort.

RAGGED A ragged margin is one that has not been evened out by justification. For an example, see **flush left**.

RAM RAM is an acronym for Random-Access Memory, which is a memory device whereby any location in memory can be found, on average, as quickly as any other location. A computer's RAM is its main memory where it can store data, so the size of the RAM (measured in kilobytes) is an important indicator of the capacity of the computer. (See **memory**.)

RAM DISK A RAM disk, also called a *virtual disk*, is an area of RAM (random-access memory) that is used to simulate an additional disk drive (see **disk**). Data can be written and read much more quickly on a RAM disk than on a real disk. Naturally, a RAM disk goes blank whenever the computer is turned off; its contents must be copied onto it from a real disk whenever the computer is turned on. RAM disks are ordinarily employed to store frequently used programs or temporary working files.

RAM disks are especially popular under the MS-DOS operating system (see **MS-DOS**). A RAM disk is created by modifying the operating system so that an area of RAM is treated in a special way; no modification to the machine is required.

RANDOM-ACCESS DEVICE A random-access device is a memory device in which it is possible to find any particular record as quickly, on average, as any other record. The computer's internal RAM and disk storage devices are examples of random-access devices. For contrast, see **sequential-access device.**

RANDOM-ACCESS MEMORY See **RAM**.

RANDOM-NUMBER GENERATOR A random-number generator is a computer program that calculates numbers that seem to have been chosen randomly. In reality, a computer cannot generate numbers that are truly random, since it always generates the numbers according to a deterministic rule. However, certain generating rules produce numbers whose behavior is unpredictable enough that they can be treated as random numbers for practical purposes. The RND function in BASIC is an example of a random-number generator contained in a computer programming language. Randon-number generators are useful in writing programs involving games of chance, and they are also used in an important simulation technique called **Monte Carlo simulation.**

RASTER A raster is a scan pattern that fills the screen of a CRT. Like television sets, present-day computers scan the entire screen continuously with an electron beam. Earlier graphics terminals worked more like oscilloscopes—they directed the electron beam only at places where lines were to be drawn. (See **bit-mapped graphics; vector graphics.**)

RBBS RBBS is a popular program for implementing bulletin-board systems. (See **BBS.**)

READ A computer is said to read information when it transfers it from one location, such as a floppy disk, to its memory.

READ (1) The READ command in BASIC causes the computer to take the top item in the data stack and assign its value to a specified variable name. A data stack is created with the DATA statement. For example, after executing statement 100 in this sequence:

```
100 READ X, Y, Z
110 DATA 10, 105, 50
```

X will have the value 10, Y will have the value 105, and Z will have the value 50.

(2) The READ command in Pascal causes the computer to read in a value from the terminal or input file. For example, the command READ(amount) causes the computer to wait for the user to type in a value that it then assigns to the variable "amount." See also **READLN.**

READ-ONLY MEMORY See **ROM.**

READLN The READLN command is one of the Pascal input commands. READLN is similar to READ except that, after executing a READLN command, the computer will look for the data for the next input statement on the next input line.

REAL MODE Real mode is the operating mode in which an 80286 or 80386 microprocessor acts like an 8086 or 8088, with a maximum of 1 megabyte of memory of which only 640K is available to user programs. The PC AT and PS/2 run DOS in real mode. By contrast, they run OS/2 in protected mode, allowing access to much larger amounts of memory. In OS/2, the user can switch between protected mode and real mode.

In real mode, the segment and offset registers contain the true addresses of memory locations, while in protected mode, segment registers point to entries in a lookup table. (See **protected mode**.)

REAL NUMBER The set of real numbers consists of all of the numbers that can be represented either as integers, decimal fractions with a finite number of digits, decimal fractions with an infinite number of digits that endlessly repeat the same pattern, or decimal fractions with an infinite number of digits that do not repeat a pattern. Each real number can be represented by a point on a number line and vice versa.

REAL TIME The term *real time* refers to the actual amount of time consumed by an operation, rather than just the amount of computer time. (On a timesharing computer, programs do not consume computer time when the computer is working on something else. See **timesharing**.)

Real-time programming is programming in which the proper functioning of the program depends on the amount of real time consumed. For instance, computers that control automatic machinery must often both detect and introduce time delays of accurately determined lengths.

REBOOT To reboot is to restart a computer, that is, turn it off and then on again. (See **boot**.)

RECOGNIZER A recognizer for a particular programming language is a program that reads in a program written in that language and then determines whether the program is valid according to the rules of the language.

RECORD A record is a collection of related data items. A collection of records is called a *file.* For example, a company may store information about each employee in a single record consisting of a field to represent the name, a field to represent the Social Security number, and so on.

Below is a program illustrating the use of the Pascal record data type. Suppose we are keeping track of the charge account balances for customers at a very small store. We will define a customer record consisting of four fields: name, address, customer class, and account balance. The information on all of the customers is stored in an array of records. This simple program provides three options: entering the information for a new customer, updating a customer's balance, and printing a list of all customers. (Note that a real customer records program must have provisions for storing and retrieving data from a disk or other memory device.)

```
PROGRAM account (INPUT, OUTPUT);
   { This program illustrates the use of records in
   Pascal. It keeps track of the accounts of customers
   at a very small store. }
CONST
   number = 5; { number of customers }
      { Each customer record contains four fields:
      name, address, class, and balance: }
TYPE
   customer = RECORD
      name : STRING;
      Address : STRING;
      class : INTEGER;
      balance : REAL
   END;
VAR
   list : ARRAY[1..number] OF customer;
   continue : BOOLEAN;
   query : CHAR;
PROCEDURE readin;
   VAR cnum : INTEGER;
       newname : customer;
   BEGIN
      WRITELN ('Enter customer number');
      WRITELN ('for new customer:');
```

```
    READLN(cnum);
    WRITELN ('Enter name:');
    READLN(newname.address);
    WRITELN ('Enter class:');
    READLN(newname.class);
    newname.balance := 0;
    { A new customer has a zero balance. }
    list[cnum] := newname
  END;
PROCEDURE update;
  VAR cnum : INTEGER; change : REAL;
      cname : STRING;
  BEGIN
    WRITELN ('Enter customer name:');
    READLN(cname);
    cnum := 0;
    REPEAT cnum := cnum + 1 UNTIL
    list[cnum].name = cname;
    WRITELN ('Enter change in account:');
    WRITELN ('Charges are positive');
    WRITELN ('payments are negative.');
    READLN (change);
    list[cnum].balance
              := list[cnum].balance + change
  END; { Note: A program that is used in actual
        operation needs a procedure to verify that
        the customer name typed in actually is on
        the list. }
PROCEDURE printout;
  VAR cnum : INTEGER;
      printrec : customer;
  BEGIN
    FOR cnum := 1 TO number DO
      BEGIN
        printrec := list[cnum];
        WRITELN(printrec.name);
        WRITELN(printrec.address);
        WRITELN(printrec.class);
        WRITELN('Balance:',printrec.balance:7:2);
        WRITELN
      END
```

```
    END;
BEGIN    { Main program block }
    continue := TRUE;
    WHILE continue DO
        BEGIN
            WRITELN ('Enter your choice:');
            WRITELN ('N-enter a new customer');
            WRITELN ('C-change balance');
            WRITELN ('P-list the customers');
            WRITELN ('S-stop');
            READLN(query);
            CASE query OF
                'N' : readin;
                'C' : update;
                'P' : printout;
                'S' : continue := FALSE
            END
        END
END.
```

RECOVERING ERASED FILES When you erase a file on a computer disk, the space that the file occupied is marked as free, but it is not actually overwritten until the space is needed for something else. If you erase a file accidentally, you can often get it back by using programs such as the Norton Utilities (on the IBM PC) or analogous programs on other machines. As soon as you realize you want to recover a file, remove the disk from the machine so that nothing else will be written in the space that the file occupied.

RECURSION Recursion occurs when a program calls itself while being executed. It is a programming technique that is useful in many cases where a problem can be broken into simpler problems that have the same form as the original. To allow recursion, a programming language must allow for local variables (thus, recursion is not easy to accomplish in most versions of BASIC). Each time the procedure is called, it needs to keep track of values for the variables that may be different from the values they had the last time the procedure was called. Therefore, a recursive procedure that calls itself many times can consume a lot of memory.

A recursive procedure can be used to calculate the factorial of an integer. (See **factorial**.) Here is a Pascal program to do so:

```
PROGRAM factcal(INPUT,OUTPUT);
   VAR x:INTEGER;
FUNCTION fact(x:INTEGER) :INTEGER;
   VAR z:INTEGER;
   BEGIN
     WRITELN('Now looking for factorial of',x);
     IF x > 0 THEN z :=x * fact(x-1)
              { Here is the recursion }
     ELSE z := 1;
     WRITELN('The factorial of ',x,'is',z);
     fact :=z
   END;
BEGIN   { main program block }
   READLN(x);
   WRITELN(fact(x))
END.
```

The recursion occurs when the function "fact" calls itself. Note that the ELSE clause is crucial. That clause gives a nonrecursive definition for the factorial of zero. If it was not there, the program would end up in an endless loop as the function fact kept calling itself until the computer ran out of memory. Any time recursion is used, it is necessary to make sure that there is some condition that will cause the recursion to halt. Following is an example of the output from this program when the number 4 is given as the input. In practice, you would want to remove the two WRITELN statements from the function, but they are included here to make it possible to see the order of execution.

```
Now looking for factorial of 4
Now looking for factorial of 3
Now looking for factorial of 2
Now looking for factorial of 1
Now looking for factorial of 0
The factorial of 0 is 1
The factorial of 1 is 1
The factorial of 2 is 2
The factorial of 3 is 6
The factorial of 4 is 24
```

The mathematical formula for calculating the determinant of a square matrix is another case where recursion is helpful, since the determinant for a matrix larger than 2 by 2 can be expressed in terms of smaller determinants. Here is an APL program to calculate determinants:

```
∇ Z ← DETERM A;N;M;B;I;S;T;N1;D;C
 [1]   N ← 1 ↑ ρA
 [2]   →(N = 2)/TWO
 [3]   M ← N - 1
 [4]   B ← (M,N) ρ N ↓ ,A
 [5]   I ← 1
 [6]   S ← 1
 [7]   T ← 0
 [8]   N1 ← A[1;]
 [9]   START:D ← N1[I]
[10]   C ← B[;((ιN) ≠ I)/ιN]
[11]   V ← DETERM C
[12]   T ← T + D x S x V
[13]   S ← -S
[14]   →((I ← I + 1) ≤ N)/START
[15]   Z ← T
[16]   ← 0
[17]   TWO:Z←(A[1;1]xA[2;2])-A[1;2]xA[2;1]∇
```

The recursion occurs in line ιι. Lines 2 and 17 avoid the infinite loop by giving an explicit solution for the determinant of a 2×2 matrix.

Recursion can also be used to construct iterative programs, and it is often used for that purpose in LISP and Prolog. Recursion can be used when determining the structure of a sentence in a human language, such as English (see **parsing**). Graphical recursive procedures can be used to draw interesting snowflake-like figures. For other examples of recursion, see **Quicksort** and **outline**.

REGISTER A register is a row of flip-flops used to store a group of binary digits while the computer is processing them. (See **flip-flop**.) A group of binary digits (bits) is called a *word*. A flip-flop can be in either of two states, so one flip-flop can store 1 bit. A register consisting of 16 flip-flops can store words that are 16 bits long. The accumulator is an example of a register.

RELATIONAL DATA BASE A relational data base is a data base in which some data items in one type of record refer to records of a different type.

Consider, for example, a data base of mailing addresses. Within each record, only the zip code is given, not the city and state. There is also a set of records containing zip code corresponds. To print out a complete address, the computer examines all the data in the address record and then looks up the appropriate city-and-state record to obtain additional information.

RELATIVE ADDRESS (1) A relative address is a computer address where it is necessary to add a base address in order to obtain the actual absolute address in the machine memory.

(2) In a spreadsheet program, a relative address is a cell address that indicates the position of a cell relative to another cell. If this formula is copied to another location, the address will be changed so that it refers to the cell in the same position relative to the new cell. In Lotus 1-2-3, a cell address is treated as a relative address unless it contains dollar signs. (See **absolute address**.) For example, if the formula 2*D7 is entered into the cell E9, the D7 really means, "the cell that is one column to the left and two rows above." If this formula is now copied to cell H15, the formula will now become 2*G13, since G13 is the cell that is one column to the left and two rows above the cell H15.

RELOCATABLE A relocatable machine-language program can execute correctly regardless of the location where it is loaded into the computer's memory. The loader changes the addresses referred to within the program to reflect the program's actual position. (See **COM file; EXE file**.)

REM The keyword REM in BASIC is used to signify the beginning of a comment. (See **comment**.)

REPEAT The keyword REPEAT is used to define one kind of loop in Pascal. The word REPEAT marks the beginning of the loop, and the word UNTIL marks the end. Here is an example:

```
x := 1;
REPEAT
   WRITELN(x);
   x := 2*x;
   WRITELN ('Type S if you want to stop.');
   READLN(query);   {Query is of type CHAR.}
UNTIL query = 'S';
```

The computer always executes the loop at least once, because it does not check to see whether the stopping condition is true until after it has executed the loop.

REQUIRED HYPHEN In word processing, a required hyphen is a hyphen that does not indicate a place where a word can be broken apart. For instance, if the hyphenated word "flip-flop" falls at the end of the line, then "flip-" may appear on one line, with "flop" at the beginning of the next. But if you type "flip-flop" with a required hyphen, it will not be split up.

In Word Perfect, a required hyphen is typed by hitting the Home key and then the hyphen key.

REQUIRED SPACE In word processing, a required space is a blank space that does not denote a place where words can be split apart at the end of a line. For example, if you type two words with an ordinary space between them, and the first word falls at the end of a line, the second word will be at the beginning of the next line. But if you put a required space between them, they will always stay together on the same line.

In Word Perfect, a required space is typed by hitting the Home key and then the space bar.

RESEDIT ResEdit, or Resource Editor, is a program distributed by Apple Computer for configuring and modifying the operating system of the Macintosh. (See **Macintosh**.)

RESERVED WORD A reserved word is a word that has a special meaning in a particular programming language and cannot be used as a variable name. For example, in BASIC and Pascal, IF is a reserved word. COBOL has dozens of reserved words; FORTRAN and PL/I have none, since in these languages it is always possible to tell from the context whether or not a word is a variable name.

RESISTANCE The resistance of an electronic component is a measure of how difficult it is for electric current to flow through the component. Resistance is measured in a unit called the *ohm*. (See **Ohm's law; resistor**.)

RESISTOR A resistor is an electronic component with a fixed amount of resistance to the flow of electric current. The symbol for a resistor is a zigzag line (see Figure 65).

Resistance is measured in a unit called the *ohm*. If V measures the voltage across the resistor, and *R* measures the resistance, then the current (*I*, measured in amperes) that will flow through the resistor can be found from Ohm's law: $I = V/R$.

FIGURE 65 resistor

RESOLUTION The resolution of a printer or screen is a measure of the sharpness of the images it can produce. For instance, many laser printers have a resolution of 300 dots per inch (DPI), meaning that they print characters using a grid of black or white squares each ⅟₃₀₀ of an inch across. This is equivalent to 150 lines per inch (LPI), because in order to distinguish two lines, the row of dots between them must be left blank.

The human eye normally resolves about 150 lines per inch at normal reading distance, but a person examining a page critically can distinguish two or three times this much detail.

The resolution of a screen is given as the total number of pixels in each direction (e.g., 640 x 480 pixels across the whole screen). The equivalent number of dots per inch depends on the size of the screen. Present-day video screens resolve about 80 dots per inch; they are not nearly as sharp as ink on paper.

RETURN The RETURN statement in BASIC marks the end of a subroutine. (See **GOSUB; subroutine.**)

RETURN KEY The return key on a computer terminal is the key that tells the computer that the end of a line has been reached. On some terminals this key is called the **enter key.**

REVERSE BIASED A diode is reverse biased when the voltage applied across it is in the wrong direction for it to conduct. (See **diode.**)

RFI PROTECTION Computers use the same kind of high-frequency electrical energy as radio transmitters. This often causes RFI (radio-frequency interference). All computers interfere with nearby radio and TV reception to some extent, and sometimes the problem is severe. On rare occasions, the opposite happens—a strong signal from a nearby radio transmitter disrupts the computer, or two computers interfere with each other.

Here are some suggestions for reducing RFI:

1 If possible, move the radio or TV receiver away from the computer, and plug it into an outlet on a different circuit.
2 Supply power to the computer through a surge protector that includes an RFI filter (see **surge protector**).
3 Ground the computer properly (again, see **surge protector**).
4 Use high-quality shielded cables to connect the parts of the computer system together. Make sure all cable shields and ground wires are connected properly. This is especially important for the monitor cable and the printer cable. If possible, wind the cable into a coil to increase its inductance.
5 Check that the computer has the appropriate approval from the FCC (Federal Communications Commission). Some computers are not approved for use in residential areas.

RGB MONITOR An RGB monitor is a color monitor that uses separate signals for the three additive primary colors (red, green, and blue). Each primary color is either on or off at any moment. For example, yellow is displayed by turning red and green on and blue off. Only eight colors can be displayed using this system.

Most RGB monitors have an additional signal, called *intensify*, that makes the color brighter. For instance, light red is the same as dark red except that the intensify signal is also on. This gives a total of 16 colors that can be displayed. An RGB monitor with an intensify signal is sometimes called an RGBI monitor; RGBI monitors are used with the IBM Color/Graphics Adapter (see **CGA**).

The monitors used with the IBM Enhanced Graphics Adapter (EGA) have two level signals for each color, giving a total of 64 combinations. (See **EGA**.)

See also **analog monitor**.

RGBI MONITOR See **RGB monitor**.

RIVER A river is a series of white spaces between words that appear to flow from line to line in a printed document. Rivers result from trying to justify type when the columns are too narrow or the available software or printer are not versatile enough. (See **justification**.)

RLL An RLL (run-length-limited) hard-disk controller gets about 50% more data on the same disk as a conventional hard-disk controller. Thus, the Seagate ST-225 hard disk has 20 megabytes of capacity with a conventional controller, or 30 megabytes with an RLL controller.

When a hard disk is converted from conventional to RLL usage, it must be reformatted; this operation erases all the data on it.

ROLL OUT See **timesharing**.

ROM ROM is an acronym for Read-Only Memory. A ROM contains computer instructions that do not need to be changed, such as the instructions for calculating arithmetic functions. The computer can read instructions out of ROM, but no data can be stored in ROM.

ROOT DIRECTORY The root directory is the main directory of a disk, containing files and/or subdirectories. (See **directory**.)

RPG RPG (Report Program Generator) is a programming language developed by IBM in the 1960s in an attempt to simplify programming for business applications. RPG is based on the principle that most business computer programs have the same structure: a large file is read one record at a time, some actions are performed for each record (e.g., adding numbers to running totals, or perhaps writing an altered form of the record onto another file), and other actions are performed only at the end (e.g., printing out the totals). The RPG programmer specifies only the details of these actions, not the overall structure of the program.

Because RPG programming can be reduced to a fixed procedure for filling out forms, RPG is often the first programming language taught to trainees. However, RPG programs are markedly less readable than programs in other languages, and complex algorithms are difficult to express in RPG.

Figure 66 shows a fragment of an RPG program that subtracts EXPENSE from GROSS, giving NET, and then adds NET to PROFIT if NET is positive, or to LOSS if NET is negative. The subtraction in the first line sets indicator 27 if the result is negative and indicator 28 if it is zero. The second line executes only if neither indicator 27 nor indicator 28 is set; the third line executes only if indicator 27 is set.

FIGURE 66 Part of an RPG Program

RPN See **Polish notation.**

RS-232 Electronics Industries Association (EIA) Recommended Standard 232-C (RS-232C, or RS-232 for short) defines a standard way of transmitting serial data by wire. Almost all modems,

Normal terminal-to-modem or computer-to-modem connection
(All 25 pins may be connected straight through. Minimally,
pins 1-8 and 20 should be connected in order to pass all
commonly used control signals.)

```
GND ——— GND
TD  ——— TD
RD  ——— RD
RTS ——— RTS
CTS ——— CTS
DSR ——— DSR
CD  ——— CD
DTR ——— DTR
SG  ——— SG
```

Simplest terminal-to-modem or computer-to-modem connection
(Some control signals are ignored; "fake" control signals are
generated by looping back outputs to inputs.)

```
TD  ——— TD
RD  ——— RD
RTS ⌐   ⌐ RTS
CTS ⌙   � CTS
DSR ⌐   ⌐ DSR
CD  ⌙   ⌐ CD
DTR ⌙   ⌐ DTR
SG  ——— SG
```

Full-featured "modem eliminator" for connecting computer to
computer or terminal to terminal

```
GND ——————— GND
TD  ⟍   ⟋ TD
RD  ⟋   ⟍ RD
RTS ⟍   ⟋ RTS
CTS ⟋   ⟍ CTS
DSR ⌐   ⌐ DSR
CD  ⟍ ·· ⟋ CD
DTR ⟋   ⟍ DTR
SG  ——————— SG
```

Simplest modem eliminator, sacrificing some control signals

```
TD  ⟍   ⟋ TD
RD  ⟋   ⟍ RD
RTS ⌐   ⌐ RTS
CTS ⌙   ⌙ CTS
DSR ⌐   ⌐ DSR
CD  ⌙   ⌙ CD
DTR ⌙   ⌙ DTR
SG  ——— SG
```

FIGURE 67 Solutions to Some RS-232 Cabling Problems

asynchronous computer terminals, and serial printers follow the RS-232C standard at least partly.

The connection includes lines for sending and receiving data, ground connections, and, usually, one or more control lines such as Carrier Detect or Data Terminal Ready (see below). The data are sent as a stream of bits at a constant speed. Each character is preceded by a start bit and followed by one or two stop bits.

The signal voltages are +5 to +15 volts (binary 0 on the data lines, "high" or "true" on the control lines) and −5 to −15 volts (binary 1 on the data lines, "low" or "false" on the control lines). In principle, a disconnected wire can be recognized because it is neither positive nor negative, but few RS-232 ports do this.

RS-232 ports usually have 25-pin connectors, but the connector is not part of the standard and its usage varies somewhat. Table 15 shows the usual pin assignments. Table 16 shows the 9-pin connector used on the IBM PC AT. (The Macintosh follows the RS-422 standard; see **RS-422.**) Figure 67 shows the solutions to some common cabling problems.

See also **serial; parallel; baud; RS-422; RS-423.**

RS-422 This Electronics Industries Association standard defines a format for serial data communication by wire. It is intended to supersede RS-232 and offers higher data rates and greater immunity to electrical noise.

The Apple Macintosh computer has an RS-422 port that is also RS-232 compatible. Table 17 shows the pin connections. For RS-232 compatibility, use only the "−" line in each pair.

RS-423A This Electronics Industries Association standard defines a format for serial data communication by wire. With appropriate cable adapters, RS-423A equipment is compatible with both the older RS-232 and the newer RS-422A standard.

RUN The RUN statement in BASIC causes execution of the currently stored program to begin.

RUN-TIME ERROR A run-time error is an error that occurs when a program is being executed. For example, a run-time error might occur if division by 0 is attempted, or if the subscript for an array is outside the allowable bounds for that array. A run-time error may cause the program to stop execution, or it may be handled by an error-trapping routine (see **trapping**). For contrast, see **compile-time error.**

TABLE 15 RS-232 Pin Assignments on Commonly Used 25-Pin Connectors (Pin numbers are embossed on the connector.)

Pin	Signal	Direction	Explanation
1	GND	Both	Frame ground—ties together chassis of terminal and modem often omitted
2	TxD	To modem	Transmitted data
3	RxD	To terminal	Received data
4	RTS	To modem	Request to send—high when terminal is on and able to communicate
5	CTS	To terminal	Clear to send—high when computer on other end is able to receive
6	DSR	To terminal	Data set ready—high when moden is on and functioning
7	SG	Both	Signal ground—reference point for all signal voltages
8	CD	To terminal	Carrier detect—high when a connection to another computer has been established
12	CD 2	To terminal	On Hayes modems this is high when high speed (1200 baud) is being used. Other usage varies.
20	DTR	To modem	Data terminal ready—high when terminal is on and functioning. Most modems hang up phone when DTR goes low.
22	RI	To terminal	Ring indicator—high when telephone is ringing

TABLE 16 Pin conneections for IBM PC AT Serial Port

Pin	Signal
1	Carrier detect
2	Receive data
3	Transmit data
4	Data terminal ready
5	Signal ground
6	Data set ready
7	Request to send
8	Clear to send
9	Ring indicator

TABLE 17 Pin conneections for Macintosh RS-422 Port
(Pin numbers are embossed on the connector.)

Original Macintosh (9-pin D-connector):

Pin	Signal
1	Frame ground
2	+5V power to external device
3	Signal ground
4	Transmit +
5	Transmit −
6	+12V power to external device
7	Clear to send
8	Receive +
9	Receive −

Macintosh SE, Macintosh II (8-pin mini-DIN connector):

Pin	Signal
1	Data terminal ready
2	Clear to send
3	Transmit −
4	Signal ground
5	Receive −
6	Transmit +
7	Carrier detect or clock input (Not used on Macintosh Plus)
8	Receive +

S

SANS-SERIF Sans-serif type does not have serifs; for example, the letter "I" is a vertical line with no ornaments at the top or bottom. For illustration, see **serif; typeface.**

Use sans-serif type with caution. It is not as readable as type with serifs.

SCANNER A scanner is a device that enables a computer to read a printed or handwritten page. The simplest scanners give the contents of the page to the computer as a graphic image—a handy way of putting pictures into the computer (see **desktop publishing**). More advanced scanners can read the letters of typewritten text, transmitting them into the computer as if they were typed on the keyboard. This process is seldom 100% accurate.

Several other kinds of electronic devices are called scanners, including bar code readers (see **bar code**) and devices for scanning the radio spectrum.

SCROLLING Scrolling refers to the movement of data on a computer screen. (See **editor.**)

SCSI The <u>S</u>mall <u>C</u>omputer <u>S</u>ystems <u>I</u>nterface (SCSI) is a standard bus for connecting devices such as disk drives to computers. It is not the same as the internal bus by which the CPU communicates with memory. SCSI is used on a variety of machines, including the Macintosh II. (See **bus; Macintosh.**)

SEARCH AND REPLACE To search and replace is to work through a file, changing every occurrence of a particular sequence of characters into some other sequence of characters. (See **editor.**)

SECOND-GENERATION COMPUTERS The term *second-generation computers* refers to computers made with transistors in the 1950s and 1960s.

SECTOR A sector is a part of track on a disk. For example, a typical floppy disk system partitions the disk into 40 circular tracks with each track having 10 sectors. (See **track; disk.**)

SEGMENT On a microprocessor such as the 8088, the segment address is one of two numbers that define a memory location. (See **offset.**)

On the 80286 and 80386, in protected mode, the segment address itself is not added to the offset; rather, it serves as a pointer to a table of segment descriptors that define the locations to which offsets are added.

SELECTION SORT Selection sort is an algorithm for sorting the elements of an array by first selecting the lowest-valued item, then the next lowest, and so on. In practice, the lowest valued item is exchanged with the first item in the part of the array being searched, and the search is confined to the remainder of the array from then on.

Selection sort is probably the easiest to remember of the many general-purpose sorting algorithms. The following program implements selection sort in BASIC:

```
10    REM Selection sort in BASIC
20    REM Assume X has been dimensioned
30    REM and contains N values
40    FOR I = 1 TO N
50       M = I
60       FOR J = I + 1 TO N
70          IF X(J)>= X(M) THEN 90
80          M = J
90       NEXT J
100      Y = X(M)
110      X(M) = X(I)
120      X(I) = Y
130   NEXT I
```

SEMICONDUCTOR A semiconductor is a material that is neither a good conductor nor a good insulator. Semiconductor devices, such as diodes, transistors, and integrated circuits, are the essential parts that make it possible to build small, inexpensive electronic machines.

The most common semiconductor material is silicon. Each atom in a silicon crystal contains four outer-level (or valence) electrons. A pure silicon crystal is not a very good conductor, because these electrons will normally stay bound to their atoms. An N-type semiconductor region is formed by adding a bit of impurity to the pure silicon. This process is known as *doping*. The impurity added is a material such as phosphorus, where each atom has five valence electrons. The result is a crystal very much like the original one, except that there are now a few extra electrons floating around (one for each atom of phosphorus that was added). The whole crystal is called an *N-type* region, because it contains free negative charges. If an impurity with only three valence electrons, such as boron, is added to the silicon crystal, gaps are left in the crystal structure because there are not enough electrons to fill all the spaces in the crystal. Each gap is called a *hole*. Even though a hole is nothing but the absence of an electron, it can be thought of as carrying a mobile positive charge. A semiconductor region with an excess of holes is called a *P-type* semiconductor region.

Electric current can flow in an N-type region in much the same way that it flows in a regular conductor. In a conductor, the current is made up of outer-level valence electrons that are not too tightly bound to their atoms. When a negative voltage is applied to one end of the N-region and a positive voltage is applied to the other, the loose electrons will be repelled by the negative voltage and attracted by the positive voltage.

Current can flow in the P-type region, but the process is quite different. If a negative voltage is applied to one end of the P-type region, the electrons will be repelled. However, the P-type region does not contain any mobile electrons. What an electron can do is jump into one of the holes. This process creates a new hole where the original electron used to be. We can think of the hole itself as moving toward the negative voltage, carrying a positive charge with it.

A semiconductor diode is formed by joining a P-type region and an N-type region. A transistor consists of a thin layer of one type of semiconductor between two layers of the opposite type. A semiconductor integrated circuit is made by placing many P and N regions on a single chip, so as to form a complex circuit containing many miniature transistors and other circuit elements.

SEND TO BACK In some graphical editing environments, the Send to Back command puts an object or window "at the back," so that other objects or windows are allowed to overlap it. See also **overlaid windows; Bring to front.**

SEQUENTIAL-ACCESS DEVICE A sequential-access (or serial-access) device is a memory device in which it is necessary to read through all preceding records before the computer finds the record it is looking for. Tape storage devices are examples of sequential-access devices. For contrast, see **random-access device.**

SERIAL To transmit data serially is to transmit it one bit at a time over a single wire. Serial transmission is the normal way of linking computers to terminals and is often used to link microcomputers to printers, especially relatively slow ones. (See **baud; parallel; RS-232.**)

SERIAL-ACCESS DEVICES See **sequential-access** device.

SERIES Two electronic components are connected in series if they are joined one right after the other (see Figure 68).

FIGURE 68 Series

SERIF Serifs are small ornaments at the ends of the lines that constitute a letter or digit, such as the flat parts on the top and bottom of the letter "I" (see Figure 69). Serifs originated as the points at which Roman stonecutters inserted their chisels into the stone. Today, serifs make type more readable by helping the reader's eye stay on the line.

FIGURE 69 Serifs on "T" at Left. There are no serifs on "T" at Right.

SERVER A server is a machine on a network that provides a particular service to other machines; for instance, a disk server manages a large disk, and a print server manages a printer. (See **local-area network.**)

SET (1) Pascal provides for a data type known as a set, which consists of a group of objects of a specified type. For example, a set can be declared with a statement such as

VAR smallnum : SET OF INTEGER;

and then it can be assigned a set of values with an assignment statement such as:

smallnum := [1,2,3,4];

Now you can test to see whether a given integer x is contained in this set. The expression x **IN smallnum** will be true if x has the value 1, 2, 3, or 4; otherwise, it will be false. Pascal also provides for standard set operations, such as union (symbolized by +), intersection (*), and set difference (−).

(2) The set input of a flip-flop causes the state of the flip-flop to become 1. (See **flip-flop**.)

(3) In MS-DOS (PC-DOS) and OS/2, the SET command stores information in the operating system's *environment area* (see **environment**). In UNIX, it has a similar effect. In other operating systems (e.g., VM/CMS and VAX/VMS), the SET command allows the user to customize many aspects of the operating system.

SEVEN LAYERS See **data communication**.

SHAREWARE Shareware is software that is copyrighted but can be distributed free of charge to anyone. Users are asked or required to make a payment directly to the author if they use the program regularly. Shareware is often misleadingly described as "free" (see **free software**).

Shareware has been criticized for relying on the unpaid work of users to do much of the advertising and distribution while the income goes only to the author. On the other hand, shareware products can be much less expensive than comparable commercial products.

SHELL In MS-DOS (PC-DOS), a shell is a second copy of DOS, loaded into unused memory on top of an application program (such as a word processor or spreadsheet). By using a shell, the application program can pass commands to DOS or allow the user to use DOS without leaving the application program, provided enough memory is available.

The SHELL statement in IBM PC BASIC (GW-BASIC) creates a shell. To leave a shell, type the DOS command EXIT.

SHELL SORT The Shell sort algorithm is a variation of the insertion
sort algorithm (see **insertion sort**). A Shell sort is a series of
insertion sorts in which each item, instead of being compared with
the items next to it, is compared with items a certain number of
elements away. On each pass, this number (the "skip count")
becomes smaller until it reaches 1; thus, the last pass is an
ordinary insertion sort. The earlier passes take care of large
moves that would be time-consuming in a pure insertion sort.

Here is a Pascal program that reads 10 numbers and performs
a Shell sort:

```pascal
PROGRAM shellsort;
  { Demonstration of Shell sort. }
  { Based on R. Sedgewick, ALGORITHMS
    (Addison-Wesley, 1983). }
LABEL 1;
CONST
  n = 10;
VAR
  a : ARRAY [1..n] of INTEGER;
  i, value, position, skipcount : INTEGER;
BEGIN
  { Read in the data }
  FOR i := 1 TO n DO
    BEGIN
      WRITE('Enter item ',i:2,':');
      READLN(a[i])
    END;
  { Choose a skip count for the first pass }
  skipcount := 1;
  REPEAT
    skipcount := 3*skipcount + 1
  UNTIL skipcount > n;
  { Perform the Shell sort }
  REPEAT
    skipcount := skipcount DIV 3;
    FOR i := skipcount + 1 TO n DO
      BEGIN
        value := a[i];
        position := i;
        WHILE a[position-skipcount] > value DO
```

```
        BEGIN
            a[position] := a[position-skipcount];
            position := position-skipcount;
            IF position <= skipcount THEN GOTO 1
        END;
   1: a[position] := value
        END
   UNTIL skipcount = 1;
   { Print the results }
   FOR i := 1 TO n DO WRITE(a[i]:5);
   WRITELN
END
```

SHIFT REGISTER A shift register is a register in which all the bits
can be moved one place to the left (or the right) when a particular
control signal is pulsed. For example, the register containing 0 0
0 0 1 1 0 1 when shifted left once is 0 0 0 1 1 0 1 0, and when shifted
twice is 0 0 1 1 0 1 0 0. A shift register can be constructed using
flip-flops and AND gates (see Figure 70). If the control line is at
0, then each flip-flop will stay the way it is. If the control line is

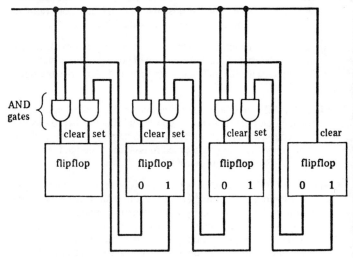

FIGURE 70 Shift Register

pulsed, then each flip-flop will acquire the state of its neighbor one place to the right. For an application, see **binary multiplication**.

SIDE EFFECT A side effect occurs when the execution of a program or subprogram causes unanticipated effects on the computer system. For example, this Pascal procedure

```
PROCEDURE swap (VAR a,b : INTEGER);
   BEGIN
      t := a;
      a := b;
      b := t
   END;
```

will swap two values. For example, if it is called by the statement swap(x, y), it will cause the variables x and y to swap values. However, in addition to this intended effect, the procedure will also have the unintended effect of changing the value of the global variable t, if there is one, which may cause errors to arise elsewhere in the program. This problem could be avoided by declaring t to be a local variable within the procedure. Then there would be no side effect because the value of the global variable t would not be affected. (See **local variable**.)

SIDEKICK SideKick is a memory-resident program marketed by Borland International. It offers a set of pop-up utilities including a notepad, calendar, calculator, and phone dialer. (See **memory resident**.)

SILICON Silicon is the primary material used to make semiconductor devices. Each atom in a silicon crystal contains 14 protons and 14 electrons. Ten of the electrons are tightly bound to the nucleus, while the outer four valence electrons can be dislodged relatively easily. (See **semiconductor**.)

SIMULATION Simulation is the process of representing one system by another. In computer science, simulation means representation of the real world by a mathematical model solved by a computer. A mathematical model of population growth can simulate a real population. A *deterministic* simulation occurs when the future path of the system is exactly determined by the parameters of the system. A *Monte Carlo* simulation occurs when probabilities are known and a selection of random numbers is used to guide the system.

SIN If *A* is an angle in a right triangle, then the sine of *A* (written as sin *A*) is given by

$$\sin A = \frac{\text{length of opposite side}}{\text{length of hypotenuse}}$$

The function SIN(A) on most computers calculates the value of sin *A*. Many computers require that the value of *A* be expressed in radians. (See **radian measure**.)

SINGLE-SIDED DISK A single-sided disk can have data stored on only one side of the disk. Therefore, single-sided disks have less storage capacity than do double-sided disks.

SITE LICENSE A site license is a software license that allows unlimited copying of a computer program for use by a single organization at a specified site. A site license is often much cheaper than the purchase of multiple copies. See also **software license.**

SLOT A slot is a socket in a microcomputer designed to accept a plug-in circuit board. (See **card**.)

SNOBOL SNOBOL is a language for processing character-string data, developed at Bell Telephone Laboratories in 1962. It is based on the theory of finite-state Markov processes, and surprisingly concise and powerful programs can be written in it. However, since nearly every SNOBOL statement contains at least one conditional jump, structured programming in SNOBOL is impossible and nowadays the language is little used.

SNOW Small flickering white spots on a computer screen are called snow. The IBM Color/Graphics Adapter (CGA) produces snow when the contents of video memory are changed rapidly. Compatible video adapters from other manufacturers can run the same software without producing snow. (See **CGA; video modes [IBM PC].**)

SOFT-SECTORED DISK When a soft-sectored disk is formatted, the computer writes a magnetic pattern onto the disk to mark the boundaries of each sector. (See **disk**.)

SOFTWARE The software of a computer system is the set of programs that tell the computer what to do. The term *software* is contrasted with *hardware*, which refers to the actual physical machines that make up a computer system. The hardware by itself is of little value without the instructions that tell it what to do.

Common types of software available for microcomputers include programming language interpreters and compilers (which allow you to write your own software in languages such as BASIC and Pascal), word processing programs, financial-decision-making packages such as spreadsheets, data base management programs, and games. You may also obtain software designed to fulfill a specific task, such as maintaining a firm's general ledger or solving a particular type of scientific problem.

SOFTWARE INTERRUPT See **interrupt**.

SOFTWARE LICENSE A software license is an agreement between the publisher of a computer program and the person who buys a copy of it. Some licenses specify that when you buy a copy of a program, you do not really own the copy but have merely bought the right to use it in certain ways. Other licenses allow you to make a working copy of the program, which would otherwise be forbidden by copyright law (see **copyright**).

Most licenses allow a single copy of the program to be used on only one machine at a time. It can be copied for backup purposes, and it can be moved from one machine to another, but it cannot be actually in use in two places at once. Thus you are forbidden to load the same program into more than one machine through a network (see **local-area network**). However, it is usually permissible for several people to use the same program on a multi-user machine with a single CPU.

A *site license* allows unlimited copying of a program for use by a single organization at a specified site. A site license is often much cheaper than the purchase of multiple copies. Another alternative for schools and colleges is the use of *student editions* of software; these are less powerful than the commercial version and are sold at much lower prices.

Many aspects of software licenses have not yet been tested in court. In particular, the license document is often packed where the user cannot see it until after buying and opening the software package. In such cases, it can hardly be described as a valid contract. When dealing with unclear or unreasonable licenses, users should make a good-faith effort to obey copyright law and to avoid depriving the publisher of income.

See also **free software**.

SORT To sort a group of items, such as the elements in an array or the records in a file, is to arrange them in numerical or alphabetical order. There are many different algorithms that can be used to sort a group of items. If the number of items is small, it is probably best to use an algorithm that can be represented by a short program. If the number of data items is large, then it is more important to use a more complicated algorithm that executes more quickly. Some algorithms assume that the data items have been read into the memory of the computer. However, if there is a very large number of items, it will be necessary to use an algorithm that works when the data are stored on an auxiliary storage device. Since sorting is such a common operation, many operating systems include built-in sorting algorithms. For examples of specific sorting algorithms, see **bubble sort; insertion sort; merge sort; Quicksort; radix sort; selection sort;** and **Shell sort**.

SOURCE (1) In a copy operation, the source refers to the place where the information is coming from. (See **target**.)

(2) The source is one of the three parts of a field-effect transistor (see **field-effect transistor**).

SOURCE, THE The Source is a computer data bank that can be accessed by subscribers with microcomputers and modems. It is a subsidiary of the *Reader's Digest*.

SOURCE PROGRAM A source program is a program written in a programming language (such as FORTRAN) and fed into a computer. The computer translates the program into a machine language object program.

SPOOLING Spooling is the process of storing the computer output before sending it to the printer.

SPREADSHEET A spreadsheet is a table of numbers arranged in rows and columns. Spreadsheets have long been used for business calculations. However, spreadsheet calculations can be very tedious; changing a single number can affect the results in many different rows and columns. Therefore, it helps greatly to have a computer perform spreadsheet calculations. Several software packages are available that turn the computer into an electronic spreadsheet. Some of the popular spreadsheet packages are Lotus 1-2-3, Excel, Multiplan, and Quattro.

When you first start working with a spreadsheet program, your screen will be filled with an array of zeros. You will probably want to define a label for each row and each column. Then you will want to enter some numbers into the table. Each location in the spreadsheet is called a *cell*. By using the appropriate cursor movement keys, you can enter values in whichever cells you choose. Suppose you would like one column to consist of values that grow at 5 percent per year. You can use a command that causes the values in the column to increase automatically by 5 percent.

To do calculations, you must use the commands that define formulas for all the rows and columns. For example, you might want one row to consist of the totals of the values in all of the rows above it, or you might want a column labeled "profit" to be equal to the difference between the column labeled "revenue" and the column labeled "cost." The important feature about spreadsheets is that the computer can remember the formulas associated with a particular row or column even when the numerical values change. For example, suppose you calculate a revenue forecast based on the assumption that sales grew by 5 percent per year. If you now change the sales column so that it grows by 8 percent per year, you can execute the "recompute" command and the computer will automatically fix all of the other values in the table to correspond to the new value for sales.

Here is a very simple example of a spreadsheet calculation. Let's keep track of the statistics for the players on a basketball team. We will label the columns "FG," "FGA," "FT," "FTA," "PTS," "FG PCT," and "FT PCT." The rows will be labeled with the names of the players. The bottom row will calculate the totals for the team. Column 5 (points) is defined by the formula

(column 5) = 2 * (column 1) + (column 3)

Columns 6 and 7 are defined by the formula

(column 6) = (column 1)/(column 2)
(field goal percent)
(column 7) = (column 3)/(column 4)
(free throw percent)

Here is an example of how the spreadsheet looks on the screen:

	FG	FGA	FT	FTA	PTS	FG PCT	FT PCT
	—1—	—2—	—3—	—4—	—5—	—6—	—7—
1 JONES	7	14	0	4	14	0.500	0.000
2 SMITH	9	20	5	5	23	0.450	1.000
3 JOHNSON	11	24	1	4	23	0.458	0.250
4 HERNANDEZ	18	25	1	4	37	0.720	0.250
5 RUSSELL	8	17	1	2	17	0.471	0.500
6 TOTAL	53	100	8	19	114	0.530	0.421

After we have printed the report we can erase all of the current data (but not the formulas) and then enter the statistics for the next game. The computer will automatically calculate the totals and the last three columns.

More elaborate spreadsheet packages can also fulfill other functions. For example, Lotus 1-2-3 provides graphic capabilities that make it possible to create graphs based on the spreadsheet data.

SPRITE A sprite is a moving element in a graphical display. Most video games use sprites.

STACK (1) A stack, also called a *pushdown stack* or *pushdown store*, is a data structure from which items are removed in the reverse order from which they were inserted. For example, when a program calls a subroutine, information about how to return to the main program is usually placed on the stack. If the subroutine then calls another subroutine, information about how to return to the first subroutine is placed on the stack. Since this information is retrieved from the stack in the opposite order from which it was placed there, each subroutine returns control to the right place. Stacks are very useful for dealing with one operation nested inside another.

To *push* a data item is to place it on a stack; to pop the stack is to remove an item from it.

(2) A stack is a collection of information used by HyperCard. (See **HyperCard**.)

START BIT The start bit indicates the beginning of an asynchronous RS-232 character. (See **RS-232**.)

STATEMENT A statement is a set of instructions that make up one unit of a computer program. (See **programming language**.)

STATISTICS PROGRAM A statistics program is a software

package designed especially for performing statistical calculations. A statistics program works with lists of numbers instead of single values. It should have built-in commands for calculating the average and standard deviation of the elements of a list, for testing hypotheses about the relationships between variables through methods such as multiple regression, for performing transformations (such as taking the logarithm of the elements in a list), and for drawing graphs of the data. Examples of statistics programs include SAS (Statistical Analysis System) and SPSS (Statistical Program for the Social Sciences).

STOP BIT The stop bit indicates the end of an asynchronous RS-232 character. (See **RS-232**.) Normal practice is to use two stop bits at 110 baud and one stop bit at higher baud rates.

STORE To store an item of data is to transmit the data from the computer to a memory device.

STORED PROGRAM COMPUTER A stored program computer is a computer that can store its own instructions as well as data. In current usage the term *computer* usually refers to a stored program computer. The concept was originated by Babbage in the nineteenth century and was developed by von Neumann. The ability of a computer to store instructions allows it to perform many tasks without human intervention. The instructions are usually written in a programming language. (See **computer**.)

STRING A string (or *character string*) is a group of characters stored in a computer. For example, the surname of the first president can be stored as a string 10 characters long: "WASHINGTON."

In BASIC character string variable names end in a dollar sign, \$. Here are three examples of character string variables:

```
P1$ = "WASHINGTON",
P2$ = "ADAMS",
P3$ = "JEFFERSON"
```

See **string operations.**

STRING OPERATIONS There are several operations that are typically performed on character string data. A programming language that is capable of working on string data will normally include built-in commands to perform the functions listed below.

Here are some examples from Microsoft BASIC, where A$ represents the string "GEORGE" and B$ represents "WASHINGTON."

1 Compare two strings to see if they are the same (often symbolized by an equal sign) or if one string comes before the other in alphabetical order (often symbolized by a less than sign). Alphabetical order is determined on the basis of ASCII codes, so lower-case letters come after upper-case letters (see ASCII).

2 Join two strings together (concatenation). This is often symbolized by a plus sign. For example, A$ + ' ' + B$ is "GEORGE WASHINGTON."

3 Calculate the length of a string. In BASIC, this is symbolized by LEN. For example, LEN (B$) is 10.

4 Select specified characters from the middle of the string. In BASIC, this is symbolized by MID$. For example, MID$(A$,3,2) is "OR," which means select two characters starting at position 3. BASIC also provides LEFT$ and RIGHT$ to automatically select a specified number of characters from the left or right end of the string, respectively.

5 Determine if one string is contained in another string, and if so, at what position it starts. In BASIC, this is written INSTR. For example, INSTR("OR",A$) is 3; INSTR("AND",A$) is 0.

6 Determine the ASCII code of an individual character. In BASIC, this is written ASC. For example, ASC("A") is 65.

7 Determine the character associated with a given ASCII code. In BASIC, this is written CHR$. For example, CHR$(65) is "A".

8 Determine the numerical value of a string that represents a number. In BASIC, this is written VAL. For example, VAL("86") is the number 86. If the string does not represent a number, then the result is 0 (for example, VAL(A$) is 0.)

9 Convert a numeric value into a string. In BASIC, this is written STR$. For example, STR$(86) is the string "86."

STRUCTURED PROGRAMMING One of the most important barriers to the development of better computer software is the limited ability of human beings to understand the programs that they write. Structured programming is a style of programming designed to make programs more comprehensible and programming errors less frequent. Because it is more a popular movement than a precise theory, structured programming can be defined in several ways, but it usually includes the following:

1 Block structure. The statements in the program must be organized into functional groups. For example, of the following two Pascal program fragments, the first is structured, while the second is not:

```
Structured:
IF x<=y THEN
   BEGIN
      z := y-x;
      q := sqrt(z)
   END
ELSE
   BEGIN
      z := x-y;
      q := -sqrt(z)
   END;
WRITELN(z,q);
Unstructured:
   IF x>y THEN GOTO 2;
   z := y-x;
   q := sqrt(z);
   GOTO 1;
2: z := x-y;
   q := -sqrt(z);
1: WRITELN(z,q);
```

Note that it is much easier to tell what the first example does.

2 The avoidance of jumps ("GOTO-less programming"). It can be proved mathematically that, if a language has structures equivalent to the (block-structured) IF-THEN and WHILE statements in Pascal, it does not need a GOTO statement. Moreover, GOTO statements are often involved in programming errors; the programmer becomes confused as to the exact conditions under which a particular group of statements will execute. Advocates of structured programming allow GOTO statements only under very restricted circumstances (e.g., to deal with error conditions) or not at all.

3 Modularity. If a sequence of statements continues uninter-

rupted for more than about 50 lines, human beings have a hard time understanding it because there is too much information for them to keep track of. As an alternative, programs should be broken up into subroutines, even if some of the subroutines are called only once. Then the main program will read like an outline, and the programmer will never need to understand more than about one page of code at a time. (He must know what the subroutines do, but not how they do it.) This principle is sometimes called *information hiding*—irrelevant information should be kept out of the programmer's way.

STYLE A style of type is a particular size, either plain, boldface, or italic. (See **font; typeface.**)

SUBDIRECTORY A subdirectory is a disk directory that is stored in another directory. (See **directory.**)

SUBROUTINE A subroutine is a set of instructions, given a particular name, that will be executed when the main program calls for it. In BASIC, a subroutine is labeled by the statement number of its first line and is executed when a GOSUB command is reached. For example, suppose that X is a real number between 0 and 24 that tells the number of hours after midnight that a particular event occurs. Here is a BASIC program that uses a subroutine to convert X into hours:minutes:seconds and tell whether it is A.M. or P.M.:

```
10    INPUT "NUMBER OF HOURS AFTER MIDNIGHT:";X
20    GOSUB 100
30    PRINT H;":";S;D$
40    END                 :REM END OF MAIN PROGRAM
100   REM START OF SUBROUTINE
110   H = INT(X)          :REM NUMBER OF HOURS
120   F = 60*(X - H)
130   M = INT(F)          :REM NUMBER OF MINUTES
140   S = 60*(F - M)      :REM NUMBER OF SECONDS
150   IF X>=12 THEN D$ = "P.M."
160   IF X<12 THEN D$ = "A.M."
170   IF H>12 THEN H = H - 12
180   IF H = 0 THEN H = 12
190   RETURN              :REM END OF SUBROUTINE
```

The command RETURN marks the end of the subroutine and

tells the computer to return to the main program.

There are two main advantages to using subroutines when writing programs. If a complicated set of instructions is needed at different locations in the program, then making the instructions into a subroutine can save considerable work since it will be unnecessary to type the instructions more than once. Also, a complicated program is best written as a collection of smaller parts, each with a well-understood purpose. (See **top-down programming; procedure**.)

SUBSCRIPT A subscript is a number or letter used to identify a particular element in an array. In mathematics, subscripts are written below the main line, as in x_1 or a_{23}. In most computer languages, however, subscripts are surrounded by parentheses, as in X(1) or A(J). (See **array**.)

SUBSCRIPTED VARIABLE A subscripted variable is another name for an array, since it is necessary to use subscripts to identify a particular element. (See **array**.)

SUPERCOMPUTER A supercomputer is designed to be markedly larger and/or faster than ordinary mainframe computers. Examples are the Cray-1 and ETA-10 vector processors and the Intel iPSC parallel processor.

SURGE PROTECTOR A surge protector absorbs brief bursts of excessive voltage coming in from the AC power line. These surges are created by lightning or by electric motors switching off. Early microcomputers were easily damaged by surges, but present-day personal computers usually have adequate surge protection built in.

Surge protectors do little good unless the power line is properly grounded. Always plug the computer into a three-wire outlet that meets modern wiring standards. Never try to use a two-wire outlet with an adapter.

Many surge protectors also incorporate RFI protectors to help reduce radio and TV interference emitted by the computer into the power line. (See **RFI protection**.)

A surge protector cannot do anything about momentary power failures. See also **power line protection**.

SWAPPING Swapping is the temporary copying of data from RAM to disk so that the RAM can be used for something else. Swapping is practiced by operating systems such as OS/2 and VAX/VMS, but not MS-DOS or CP/M.

SYMBOLIC ALGEBRA A symbolic algebra program on a computer is a program that is capable of performing operations on symbols representing variable names (for example, calculating that (A+B) times (C+D) is equal to the expression AC + AD + BC + BD). In this type of program, a variable can represent an expression as well as a value. For example, the variable Y could represent the expression $AX^2 + BX + C$. Then there are three possible ways in which a user might wish to use Y: (1) use it as a literal, for example, having 2Y appear as 2Y; (2) replace it with the expression it represents, for example, having 2Y appear as $2AX^2 + 2BX + 2C$; or (3) replace it with the numerical value of the expression it represents, for example, if X has the value 3, A = 2, B = 7, and C = 10, then 2Y would appear as 98. The programming language LISP is suited for symbolic computation such as this. By contrast, a language such as BASIC is designed only to work with the numeric value of mathematical variables.

SYMBOLIC DEBUGGER A symbolic debugger allows you to step through a compiled program, interrupting it at any point and examining or changing the values of variables. A symbolic debugger analyzes the source code and the object code together, so that even though the program has been compiled, you can work with it as if you were editing the source program. See also **CodeView**.

SYNTAX The syntax of a programming language is the set of rules that specify how the language symbols can be put together to form meaningful statements. Syntax rules are like grammar rules. If a program violates the language syntax rules, a syntax error has occurred.

SYS REQ KEY On IBM mainframe terminals, the Sys Req (system request) key enables the user to communicate with the communications system itself rather than the application program. The IBM PC AT and PS/2 have a Sys Req key, but little or no software has been written to make use of it.

SYSOP The SYSOP (system operator) is the person who manages a bulletin-board system. (See **BBS**.)

SYSTEMS PROGRAMMER A systems programmer is a person

TABLE **298**

who writes the programs needed for a computer system to function. Some of the programs that systems programmers write include operating systems, language processors and compilers, and data file management programs. Systems programming, which is usually done in an assembly language, requires considerable knowledge of the particular computer system being used. By way of contrast, see **application programmer.**

t

TABLE A table is a two-dimensional array (or matrix). For example, the results of an election can be stored in a table:

County	Candidate Smith	Condidate Jones	Other
1	5,402	4,501	2
2	362	5,481	3
3	10,601	2,805	10
4	4,502	4,666	0

(See **array.**)

TAN If A is an angle in a right triangle, then the tangent of A (written as tan A) is defined to be

$$\tan A = \frac{\text{length of opposite side}}{\text{length of adjacent side}}$$

The function TAN (A) on many computers calculates the value of tan A. Many computers require that the value of A be expressed in radians. (See **radian measure.**)

TAPE Magnetic tape can be used to store information in a form that can be easily read by a computer. Magnetic tape is much the same as ordinary tape recorder tape, and some personal computers can even store information on ordinary cassette tapes. It is much cheaper to store information on tape than in the computer main memory or on a disk memory device, but a longer time is required to locate a particular data item if it is stored on tape. (See **memory.**)

TAPE DRIVE A tape drive is a device that converts information stored on magnetic tape into signals that can be sent to a computer.

TARGET (1) The target is the place to which information is supposed to be copied (e.g., the "target disk" when copying disks) (See **source**.)

(2) A target is something that is being searched for (as when searching for a word in a document).

TBBS TBBS is a popular program for implementing bulletin-board systems. (See **BBS**.)

TCP/IP TCP/IP (Transport Control Protocol/Interface Program), developed by the U.S. Department of Defense, is one of several software protocols that can be used to connect computers together. It is widely used in Ethernet systems and packet radio systems.

TELEX TELEX (Teletypewriter Exchange) is an international system similar to the telephone system, but linking teletypewriters. TELEX messages can be sent and received by computer using carriers such as MCI Mail (MCI Communications, Inc.).

TEMPLATE (1) A template is a plastic card with flowchart symbols cut out of it. A programmer using a template card can easily trace out the symbols that are needed in drawing a flowchart.

(2) A template is a particular pattern for a spreadsheet program or a data base program that is frequently used. Therefore storing the template will save you from having to retype the specifications each time.

TERMINAL A computer terminal is an input-output device whereby a user is able to communicate directly with a computer. A terminal must have a keyboard, so that the user can type in instructions and input data, and a means of displaying output, such as a CRT (television) screen or a typewriter. The earliest terminals were teletype machines. Today, personal computers are often used as terminals on larger computers. (See **data communication; modem; upload; download**.)

TERMINAL-NODE CONTROLLER See **packet radio**.

TERMINATE-AND-STAY RESIDENT See memory **resident**.

TEX TeX (pronounced "tek"), by D.E. Knuth, is a computer typesetting program used by the American Mathematical Society and many book publishers and educational institutions. Unlike most desktop publishing systems, TeX does not attempt to show you the appearance of the finished document on the screen as you edit it (though screen previews can be generated). Instead, you type a document with codes in it that indicate boldface, italics, special characters (e.g., "\integral" for an integral sign), and the like.

The rationale is that correct typesetting relies on distinctions that are too subtle to see on a computer screen. A user who wants an em dash rather than an en dash should say so with explicit codes, rather than trying to make a mark that appears the right length on the screen. Likewise, large-scale aspects of design should be automated; you should be able just to give the title of a chapter, and let the computer take care of numbering the chapter and putting the title in the right place on the page.

TeX is generally considered the most sophisticated computer typesetting system, as well as (for an experienced user) one of the easiest to use. It sets a standard that other desktop publishing systems try to emulate.

TEXAS INSTRUMENTS (TI) A manufacturer of semiconductors and computers, TI is headquartered in Dallas, Texas. Jack S. Kilby developed the first working integrated circuit ("silicon chip") at TI in 1958, making it possible to miniaturize electronic equipment to a degree far beyond earlier expectations. Currently, TI produces parts for practically all makes of computers, as well as a number of micro- and minicomputers of its own.

TEXT EDITOR A text editor is an editor designed primarily or exclusively for handling textual material (letters, manuscripts, etc.) rather than programs. (See **editor**.)

TEXT FILE A text file is a file that contains lines of written information that can be sent directly to the screen or printer by using ordinary operating system commands.

The files produced by word processors are usually not text files. Although they contain text, they also contain special codes (for margins, underlining, etc.) whose meaning is known only to the word processing software. Many word processors can, however, produce text files ("nondocument mode" in WordStar, "DOS text files" in Word Perfect).

On machines that use the ASCII character set, text files are often called ASCII files.

To create a text file on the Macintosh, save a document as "text only."

THERMAL PRINTER A thermal printer prints by heating spots on the paper with an array of tiny, fast-acting heating elements. Thermal printers are among the least expensive printers and are often used on calculators and very low-priced computers. However, they require special paper that may discolor with age.

THIRD-GENERATION COMPUTERS The term *third-generation computers* refers to computers made with integrated circuits. Current computers built with circuits that have large-scale integrations are often called *fourth-generation computers*.

THREADED INTERPRETIVE LANGUAGE See **FORTH**.

THREE-DIMENSIONAL GRAPHICS In CAD/CAM systems, it is frequently helpful to be able to see representations of three-dimensional objects that can be viewed from different angles. Suppose that you wish to build a cube. Here is a BASIC program that keeps track of the coordinates of the vertices of the cube (in three dimensions) and then figures out how to display the appearance of the cube in two dimensions. In this program the user can choose which direction to rotate the cube, and then a coordinate rotation formula from trigonometry is used to shift the coordinates of the vertices to their new locations.

```
1    REM This Microsoft BASIC program draws a
2    REM cube on the screen and makes it possible
3    REM for the user to rotate the cube to make it
4    REM possible to view it from different angles.
100  DIM A(8,3) ' THE ARRAY A CONTAINS THE
        COORDINATES
101    ' OF THE 8 VERTICES OF THE CUBE
110  REM — READ IN INITIAL COORDINATES
120  FOR I=1 TO 8:FOR J=1 TO 3
        :READ A(I,J):NEXT J:NEXT I
129  REM X Y Z
130  DATA 1, 1,  1
140  DATA -1, 1, 1
150  DATA -1, -1, 1
160  DATA 1, -1, 1
170  DATA 1, 1,  -1
```

```
180 DATA -1, 1, -1
190 DATA -1, -1, -1
200 DATA 1, -1, -1
210  H=100 : SCALE=40
220 FOR I=1 TO 8:FOR J=1 TO 3
       :A(I,J)=A(I,J)*SCALE:NEXT J:NEXT I
230  GOSUB 300 'DRAW CUBE
240  GOSUB 400 'INPUT COMMAND
250  GOSUB 500 'PERFORM ROTATION
260  GOTO 230
299
300 REM – DRAW CUBE
305 SCREEN 1:CLS
307 REM IT TAKES 12 LINES TO DRAW THE CUBE
310  FOR I=1 TO 3
320  LINE((H+A(I,1)),(H+A(I,3)))-((H+A(I+1,1)),(H+A(I+1,3)))
330  LINE((H+A(I+4,1)),(H+A(I+4,3)))-((H+A(I+5,1)),(H+A(I+5,3)))
340  NEXT I
350  LINE((H+A(1,1)),(H+A(1,3)))-((H+A(4,1)),(H+A(4,3)))
360  LINE((H+A(5,1)),(H+A(5,3)))-((H+A(8,1)),(H+A(8,3)))
370  FOR I=1 TO 4
320  LINE((H+A(I,1)),((H+A(I,3)))-((H+A(I+4,1)),((H+A(I+4,3)))
390  NEXT I
395 RETURN
399
400 REM INPUT COMMAND
401 REM THE COMMAND IS ENTERED IN THE
        FORM "L #" OR "D #"
402 REM L MEANS ROTATE LEFT, D MEANS
        ROTATE DOWN
403 REM # REPRESENTS THE AMOUNT OF ROTATION
        (IN DEGREES)
410 LOCATE 24,1
420 INPUT X$
430 IF X$="S" THEN END 'S MEANS TO STOP
440 DIRECTION$=LEFT$(X$,1) 'DIRECTION OF
        ROTATION, L OR D
450  ANGLE = (3.14159/180)
        *VAL(MID$(X$,2,LEN(X$)-1))
451 REM NOTE - THE ANGLE IS CONVERTED TO
        RADIANS
460 RETURN
```

```
499
500  REM PERFORM ROTATION
510  IF DIRECTION$="L" THEN GOTO 520 ELSE
       GOTO 600
600  REM
520  REM - ROTATE TO THE LEFT
530  FOR I=1 TO 8
540    X=A(I,1):Y=A(I,2)
         'Z COORDINATE IS UNCHANGED
550    X2=X*COS(ANGLE)+Y*SIN(ANGLE)
560    Y2=Y*COS(ANGLE)-X*SIN(ANGLE)
570    A(I,1)=X2:A(I,2)=Y2
575  NEXT I
580  RETURN
599
600  REM - ROTATE DOWN
610  FOR I=1 TO 8
620    Y=A(I,2):Z=A(I,3)
         'X COORDINATE IS UNCHANGED
630    Y2=Y*COS(ANGLE)+Z*SIN(ANGLE)
640    Z2=Z*COS(ANGLE)-Y*SIN(ANGLE)
650    A(I,2)=Y2:A(I,3)=Z2
660  NEXT I
670  RETURN
```

TILDE The tilde is the mark "~" written above the letter N in Spanish (e.g., ñ). The ASCII character "~" is also called a tilde.

TILED WINDOWS Tiled windows divide the screen into sections without overlapping one another. By contrast, see **overlaid windows**.

TIMESHARING Timesharing is a way of running more than one program on the same computer at the same time, so that, for example, the computer can serve many users at different terminals simultaneously.

Timesharing is based on the idea that a computer spends most of its time waiting for things to happen. Almost all input-output devices (printers, card readers, disks, etc.) operate much more slowly than the CPU itself; the extreme case is a terminal or console, where the computer may spend minutes or hours waiting for someone to type something. In a timesharing system, more than one program is loaded into memory at once, and when the computer is unable to proceed with one program, it jumps to another.

In practice, the computer does not stay on one program more than a fraction of a second even if there is nothing to wait for; to do so would prevent other, possibly shorter, programs from being executed. Also, programs that are not executed are frequently "rolled out" of memory (i.e., copied to disk) to make memory space available to programs that are actually running.

TITLE BAR The title bar is the label at the top of a window, usually identifying the program or file to which it belongs. (**See window.**)

TNC See **packet radio.**

TOGGLE To toggle something is to switch it back and forth from one state to another. For instance, in some editors, the Ins key "toggles" insert mode; that is, it turns insert mode on if it is off, or off if it is on.

TOKEN RING A token-ring network is one in which the computers are connected together in a ring. A special message, called the *token*, is passed from one machine to another around the ring, and each machine can transmit only while it is holding the token. IBM markets a token-ring network for the PC family of computers. (See **local-area network.**)

TONER CARTRIDGE The toner cartridge of a laser printer contains the toner (ink) that will be used to make marks on the paper.

TOP-DOWN PROGRAMMING The top-down approach to programming means to first look at the broad outline of a programming problem; then to divide the problem into a collection of separate tasks, each with a well-defined purpose; and finally to write the separate parts and put them all together into one program. The top-down approach is usually the best way to write complicated programs. Detailed decisions are postponed until the requirements of the large program are known; this is better than making the detailed decisions early and then forcing the major program strategy to conform to them. Each part of the program (called a **module**) can be written and tested independently.

TRACK Data that are recorded on a disk are arranged in many concentric circles, each of which is called a track. (See **disk.**)

TRACTOR FEED A tractor feed is a mechanism that uses toothed gears to pull the paper forward in a computer printer. The teeth fit into the feed holes in the side of the paper.

TRANSISTOR A transistor is an electronic device formed by sandwiching a thin layer of semiconductor material between two layers of the opposite type of semiconductor. A PNP transistor has a thin layer of N-type semiconductor between two P-type regions. An NPN transistor has just the opposite construction. (See **semiconductor**.) The symbol for a transistor is shown in Figure 71.

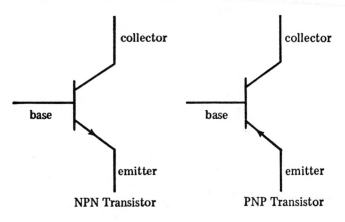

NPN Transistor   **PNP Transistor**

FIGURE 71

The middle section is called the *base*, and the other two regions are the *emitter* and the *collector*. The base-to-emitter voltage controls the collector-to-emitter current. In radios, transistors are used as amplifiers. The output signal, measured at the collector, is much larger than the input signal, which is applied to the base. In computers, transistors are used as switches. The nature of the voltage applied to the base determines whether or not current will flow from the collector to the emitter.

Consider an NPN transistor with the emitter connected to ground (0 volts), and the collector connected to a large positive voltage (see Figure 72). (A PNP transistor works in exactly the same way, except that all voltage polarities are reversed.) If a positive voltage is now applied to the base, the base-emitter junction will be forward biased. This means that the base-emitter junction will act like a conducting diode. (See **diode**.) Electrons in the emitter and holes in the base will be driven toward the junction. The result is that electrons will flow from the emitter to the base. So far, this is exactly what happens in a regular diode. The difference between a transistor and a diode is due to the fact that the base in the transistor is very thin. Some of the electrons that are pushed into the base will be pushed so hard that they travel all the way across the base to the collector. These electrons make up a current flow from the emitter to the collector. An amplifier transistor is designed so that the current flow from the emitter to the collector is actually much greater than the current flow from the emitter to the base.

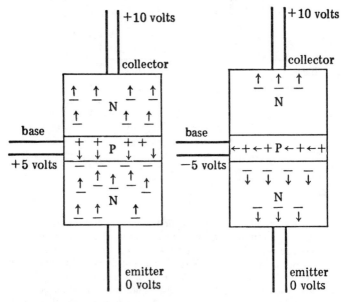

FIGURE 72

In computers, transistors act as switches (see Figure 73). If a positive voltage is applied to the base, current will flow from the

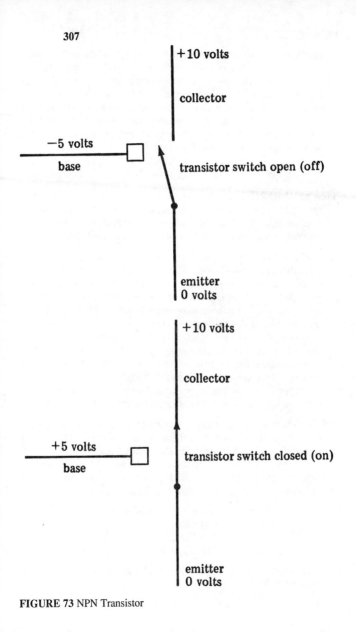

FIGURE 73 NPN Transistor

emitter to the collector, and the transistor acts like a switch that is on (or closed). If a negative voltage is applied to the base, the base-emitter junction is reverse biased, causing the flow of electrons from the emitter to the base to stop. Since no more electrons are being driven into the base, there are no electrons to sneak across the base into the collector. This means that the current from the emitter to the collector stops, so the transistor acts like a switch that is off (or open).

This type of transistor is called a *bipolar*, or *junction*, *transistor*. Another type of transistor is the field-effect transistor.

TRANSPARENT In computing, something is transparent if it has no visible effect. For instance, if a print-spooling program is transparent, all other software works exactly as if the print-spooling program were not installed. This is a desirable feature.

TRAPPING To trap an event is to perform a special action when something happens that would ordinarily interrupt the operation of the computer. For instance, some programming languages provide "error trapping," which means that when the program attempts to do something impossible (such as divide by zero or read a file that doesn't exist), control will be transferred to an error-handling routine supplied by the programmer. If no error trapping were provided, the program would simply end with an error message that might puzzle the user. In BASIC, trapping is activated by statements such as ON ERROR.

Trapping also refers to special actions activated by the system clock or by events such as data arriving through a serial port.

TREE A tree is a data structure similar to a linked list, except that each element carries with it the addresses of two or more other elements, rather than just one. (See **linked list**.)

Trees are a very efficient way of storing items that must be searched for and retrieved quickly. Suppose, for example, that you want to store the following names in a computer:

Jones	Voss
Steinfeld	Marino
Alexander	Williams
Bateman	Rodriguez

The names can be arranged into a tree by using the following two-step procedure:

1 Use the first name on the list as the root of the tree.

2 To find where to put each subsequent name, start at the root of the tree. If the name you are dealing with precedes the root name alphabetically, follow the left pointer; otherwise follow the right pointer. Proceed in this way until you come to an empty pointer; attach the new name to it.

The result is the tree shown in Figure 74. Step 2 in the procedure above can be used to locate names already in the tree in a minimum of steps (in this case, no more than four steps even though there are eight names in the list). The search sequence that results is not quite as good as a binary search, but it is much better than having to work through the whole list. Furthermore, as with linked lists, new nodes can be added at any time without requiring that existing nodes be moved.

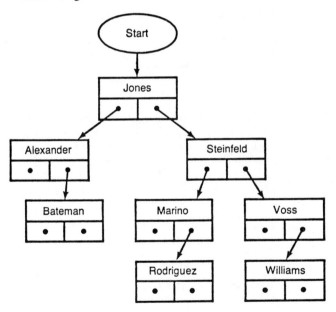

FIGURE 74 A Search Tree

TROJAN HORSE A Trojan horse is a computer program with a hidden destructive function, such as erasing the disks on a specified date. Trojan horses are often distributed as counterfeit "new" versions of shareware products.

Knowingly distributing a destructive computer program is a crime under common law and under specific laws of various states. See also **virus**.

TRUNCATION In truncation, all the digits of a number that are to the right of the decimal point are dropped. For example, the truncation of 6.45 is 6, and the truncation of 737.984 is 737. In PL/I this operation is symbolized by TRUNC; in BASIC, by INT.

TSO TSO (timesharing option) is the part of OS/360 and related IBM operating systems that supports timesharing terminals.

TSO data set names consist of one or more fields joined by periods, such as

JONES.MATRIX.MULT345.PLI

where each field consists of one to eight alphnumeric characters, beginning with a letter, and the overall length of the name does not exceed 40 characters. Under TSO, the first field is normally the user ID and the last field indicates the type of file: PLI for a PL/I source program, OBJ for an object program, DATA for all-upper-case, fixed-record-length data, or TEXT for data with variable record length and both upper- and lower-case letters. (Only a few commands are sensitive to the last field; changing the name of a file does not automatically change its type.)

Some commonly used TSO commands are as follows:

HELP	Display information about other commands.
EDIT	Edit a data set. (Within EDIT, type HELP for more information.)
LISTCAT	Display the names of a user's data sets.
LIST	Display the contents of a data set.
DELETE	Get rid of a data set.
ALLOCATE	Assign a file name or other attributes to a data set (like the JCL DD card).
FREE	Cancel a previous ALLOCATE command.
SUBMIT	Submit a data set to OS as a batch job.
LOGOFF	End the session. Data sets are permanent, but they may be erased after a few hours, depending on local policy.

The details of TSO vary considerably from installation to installation; for more information, consult local manuals.

TSR See **memory resident**.

TTL TTL (Transistor-Transistor Logic) is a type of integrated circuit that operates at very high speeds and requires relatively large amounts of power at an accurately regulated voltage (5 volts). Most microcomputers use TTL devices for input-output and control functions. TTL integrated circuits are recognizable because their type numbers contain "74" or "74LS" followed by two or three digits (e.g., SN7402N).

TURBO BASIC Borland International's Turbo BASIC is a high-performance compiler for essentially the same language as Microsoft QuickBASIC, with minor differences in the syntax of a few of the newest features. Turbo BASIC is a conventional compiler similar in spirit to Turbo Pascal.

TURBO PASCAL The Turbo Pascal compiler, the first major product of Borland International, is one of the most popular compilers ever written (see **Borland International**). Turbo Pascal compiles Pascal programs 50–100 times faster than conventional compilers, and it includes a built-in full-screen editor for writing programs. If the compiler finds a syntax error, it immediately calls up the editor and places the cursor on the offending character so that the programmer can correct the error. This makes it possible to develop and refine programs very quickly.

The Turbo Pascal language is close to the ISO standard (see **ISO**) but does not include the predefined procedures GET and PUT, nor is the behavior of READ, EOF, and EOLN entirely standard. Many extensions to the language have been added, including "typed constants" (actually variables initialized at compile time), additional ways of using pointers, and predefined procedures for screen control, graphics, and operating system services.

Turbo Pascal obtains its remarkable compilation speed partly because it is extremely well designed, and partly because it takes a number of shortcuts. The compiler does not produce object listings nor does it have to recover from syntax errors, since it calls up the editor as soon as the first error is found.

The first versions of Turbo Pascal were released in 1984 for computers running the CP/M and MS-DOS operating systems. Priced at $49.95, and outperforming compilers in the $300 to $800 range, Turbo Pascal almost drove its competitors off the market. Turbo Pascal is now available for the Macintosh, and Borland has released similar compilers for C and BASIC on the IBM PC. Turbo Pascal 5.0 includes a symbolic debugger.

TURBO PROLOG Borland International's Turbo Prolog is a Prologlike language that sacrifices some versatility in order to get programs to run very fast. It is not compatible with any other dialect of Prolog, and the ability of programs to modify themselves—a key requirement for artificial intelligence programming—is severely limited. However, Turbo Prolog is powerful enough for many kinds of expert systems, and an excellent development environment is provided.

TURING MACHINE A Turing machine is an imaginary machine conceived by A.M. Turing in the 1930s to help identify the kinds of problems that are potentially solvable by machines. The machine is a kind of simple computer. It consists of a long string of paper tape and a machine through which the tape can be fed. The machine can do four things; it can move the tape one space, it can place a mark on a space, it can erase a mark, or it can halt. Turing's thesis states that this simple machine can solve any problem that can be expressed as an algorithm (if it has an unlimited supply of paper tape). As you might imagine, in practice it would be difficult to give instructions to a Turing machine so that it could solve a particular problem. The Turing machine is important theoretically, however, because it provides an indication of what kinds of problems computers can solve, and what kinds they can never solve.

TURNKEY SYSTEM A turnkey system is a computer system that is ready to perform a particular task with no further preparation. A turnkey system is sold as a complete package from a single vendor. By contrast, most computer systems are assembled step-by-step by users who obtain hardware and software from various suppliers.

TURTLE A turtle is a device used for computer-controlled graphics in some computer systems, especially those using the LOGO language (see **LOGO**). The computer gives commands to the turtle, telling it when to move in certain directions and when to raise or lower its paintbrush. By giving the proper commands, a programmer can draw many kinds of patterns. Some LOGO systems use an actual mechanical turtle that moves along the floor and draws pictures on large pieces of paper. Other systems use imaginary turtles that move around the screen.

TWISTED PAIR A twisted pair of wires provides a cheap and relatively noise-free way to transmit signals. The two wires carry equal and opposite signals. Any electrical noise that they pick up will be the same (rather than the opposite) in the two wires, and the circuitry on the receiving end can be designed to ignore it. By contrast, see **coaxial cable**.

TYPE Under CP/M, MS-DOS (PC-DOS), OS/2, VAX/VMS, or VM/CMS, the command TYPE causes the contents of a text file to be displayed. For example:

```
TYPE LETTER.DOC
```

causes the file LETTER.DOC to be displayed on the screen. The equivalent UNIX command is CAT.

TYPEFACE Most of the typefaces used on computer printers today fall into the following categories (see Figure 75):

1 *Roman type, proportionally spaced, with serifs.* This kind of type originated with the stone engravers of ancient Rome. "Proportionally spaced" means that different letters are different widths (e.g., "M" is wider than "I"); serifs are the marks at the ends of the strokes (e.g., the horizontal marks at the top and bottom of "I"). Times Roman is a popular Roman typeface.

Roman type is the most readable kind of type and is used for the text of most books. *Blocks of Roman type should never be underlined*; use italics instead (or boldface in some situations). Underlining on typewriters was originally a substitute for italics.

Roman type usually includes some characters that are not on a typewriter, such as the dash (—) and distinct opening and closing quotation marks (" "). Be sure to use these where appropriate. (See **typesetting mistakes**.)

2 *Sans-serif type, proportionally spaced.* Two popular typefaces of this kind are Geneva and Helvetica. This kind of type is better for short captions, posters, or labels, but can be tiring to read for long periods.

3 *Fixed-pitch, typewriter-like typefaces.* Courier and similar "faces" are used when all characters must be the same width in order to line up properly, such as in computer program listings (see **COBOL** in this book for an example), when presenting financial tables, or when printing documents that were laid out for a simpler kind of printer.

4 *Novelty typefaces* such as Old English (not shown in the figure, but often used in ecclesiastic settings). These should

Times Roman
Proportional pitch, with serifs
24 point 18 point

14 point 12 point 10 point 9 point
ABCDEFGHIJKLMNOPQRSTUVWXYZ
abcdefghijklmnopqrstuvwxyz 1234567890
Plain **Boldface** *Italic*

Helvetica
Proportional pitch, without serifs
24 point 18 point

14 point 12 point 10 point 9 point
ABCDEFGHIJKLMNOPQRSTUVWXYZ
abcdefghijklmnopqrstuvwxyz 1234567
Plain **Boldface** *Italic*

Courier
Fixed pitch (all letters same width)
24 point 18 point

14 point 12 point 10 point 9 pt
ABCDEFGHIJKLMNOPQRSTUVWXYZ
abcdefghijklmnopqrstuvwxyz 123
Plain **Boldface** *Italic*

FIGURE 75 Samples of Various Typefaces on an Apple Laserwriter

be used very sparingly to make dramatic-looking titles or mastheads.

See also **font; serif; pitch; point; leading; desktop publishing.**

TYPESETTING MISTAKES The following pointers will help you avoid common mistakes in designing documents with desktop publishing software.

1 Notice the differences between typesetting and the typewriter: (a) left and right quotation marks are different characters ("like this"); a dash is not the same as two hyphens; underlining is rarely used—where you would underline on a typewriter, use italics (or possibly boldface) in type.

2 Remember that your type is proportionally spaced; letters are not all the same width. You can't count letter spaces the way you do on a typewriter; you must use other means of lining things up.

3 Always align columns with the tab key, not the space bar.

4 Type carefully. Be sure not to hit the space bar more than once between words. It's hard to tell the difference between one space and two spaces by just looking at the screen.

5 Don't justify everything. Justified type looks good only when the columns are rather wide. Flush-left type with a ragged right margin is easier to read if the columns are narrow; with narrow columns, justification puts excessive space between words. (See **justification**.)

6 Don't use more than one or at most two fonts in a single document. (Italics, boldface, and different sizes count as a single font.) Multiple-font documents are almost always ugly. Odd typefaces (such as Old English) can be *very* hard to read.

7 Make sure your document is not missing any essential features such as adequate margins or page numbers. If in doubt, find a well-designed document or book and imitate it.

8 Use appropriate features of your software. When you type a footnote, use the footnote instruction if there is one, rather than just moving the cursor to the foot of the page. That way, if you change the layout later, the software will probably still handle the footnote correctly.

9 *Standardize*. Don't face each document as an original design problem. Develop a standard format that you like, and stick with it.

UCSD P-SYSTEM The UCSD P-system is an operating system that was developed at the University of California at San Diego (UCSD) and implemented on many different microcomputers. The P-system itself and the object code produced by its compilers are written, not in machine language, but in a language called P-code. Implementing the P-system on a computer consists of little more than writing a P-code interpreter in the computer's machine language.

UNDOCUMENTED A feature of a computer or of a program is undocumented if it is not described in the literature (documentation) provided by the manufacturer.

Some computer programs rely on undocumented features of the machine on which they run. The risk of using undocumented features is that they may not be the same in future versions of the program or machine.

Undocumented features exist for several reasons. Some are accidental omissions from the documentation. Others represent incompletely tested features that will be made reliable and documented in future versions. Still others may be kept secret in order to give the vendor a competitive advantage in making add-on products.

See also **documentation**.

UNERASE See **recovering erased files**.

UNINTERRUPTIBLE POWER SUPPLY An uninterruptible power supply uses batteries to continue providing electricity to a computer for a few minutes in the event of a power failure. This makes it possible to shut down the computer in an orderly way without losing data.

UNIX UNIX is an operating system, or family of operating systems, developed at Bell Laboratories in the early 1970s as a replacement for an earlier system called *Multics*. UNIX is noteworthy because, although developed by a small team of about four people, it is in many ways superior to operating systems developed by large teams at tremendous expense (e.g., OS/360).

The main features of UNIX include the following:

1 Highly modular, structured design. The entire system is defined in terms of a relatively small number of subroutines;

UNIX can be implemented on any machine by implementing those routines. Furthermore, the operation of the whole system is based on a relatively small number of principles carried through very consistently; there is little arbitrary detail for the user to learn.

2 Extensibility. In many operating systems, a user can create commands of his own that execute sequences of ordinary commands stored on files. UNIX, however, provides a full-fledged programming language for this purpose (the "shell"), with IF, WHILE, and CASE statements similar to those of Pascal, as well as extensive facilities for string handling.

3 Input-output redirection. Any program invoked by a command can be told to take its input from, and/or write its output onto, a file rather than the user's terminal. For example:

SORT <ALPHA >BETA

tells the SORT program to take its input from ALPHA and write its output onto BETA. UNIX also supports pipelines, which allow one program to transmit its output directly into the input of another program. (See **MS-DOS.**)

Many UNIX commands, called *filters*, read a file and output a copy of it that has undergone some simple transformation, such as removing repeated lines. Powerful operations can be accomplished by stringing filters together through pipelines.

4 Tree-structured directories. In all earlier operating systems, a user's files were kept in a single list called a *directory*. In UNIX, however, directories are handled like files and a user can have an unlimited number of them, each of which must be listed in a higher directory until the main ("root") directory is reached. This makes it possible to arrange files into logical groups—for example, to put all files related to a particular project into a single directory. Tree-structured directories are a virtual necessity if one user is to keep track of more than a few dozen files, as is required, for example, on a microcomputer with a hard disk.

The following are some common Bell Labs UNIX commands. They may be different in other versions of UNIX.

CC	Compile a C Program. (See **C.**)
CP	Copy a file onto a file or into a directory.
DIFF	Display the differences between two files.
ED	Edit a file.

GREP	Search a file for lines matching a pattern.
LS	List contents of a directory.
MKDIR	Create a directory.
PR	Print a file.
RM	Remove a directory entry. (This is the normal way to delete a file.)
RMDIR	Delete a directory (which must be empty).

UPLOAD To upload is to transmit a file to a central computer from a smaller computer or a computer at a remote location.

UPS See **uninterruptible power supply.**

UPWARD COMPATIBILITY Upward compatibility is the situation in which a computer program or accessory works not only on the machine for which it was designed but also on newer models. For instance, programs written for the IBM PC in 1981 will still run (considerably faster) on the IBM PS/2 Model 70, introduced in 1988. Thus we say that the PS/2-70 is upward compatible with the PC. By contrast, see **downward compatibility.**

USENET USENET is a worldwide network for computers that use the UNIX operating system. USENET has gateways to BITNET and ARPANET.

A distinctive feature of USENET is that access can be very expensive. Many USENET nodes send and receive their messages by automatically calling other nodes over ordinary phone lines in the middle of the night.

USER-FRIENDLY A user-friendly computer program is designed to be easy for people to use. In the days when computers were operated only by specialists, little attention was paid to making programs user-friendly. However, when computers became more popular, it became very important to write programs that could be easily understood by the people who use them. The most important requirement for making a program user-friendly is a clear, understandable manual that explains how the program works. Other features that can help make a program user-friendly are menus that clearly list the available choices, and command names that are easy to remember. However, a program should not contain so many on-screen explanatory messages that it becomes cumbersome to use for people who have already learned how the program works.

USER INTERFACE The user interface of a program or operating system is the way it communicates with the person who is using it. There are three important types of user interfaces:

1 *Command languages.* This is a common way to giving intructions to operating systems; for instance, in CP/M, MS-DOS (PC-DOS), OS/2, or VAX/VMS, the user can obtain a list of files by typing the command "dir". Command languages work well only if they are used constantly so that the user never forgets the commands.

2 *Menus.* The user chooses an item from a displayed list. Menus are ideal for software that is seldom used, but experienced users may find them too slow.

3 *Graphical environments.* The user performs operations by moving icons (pictures) with a mouse. Environments of this type can be highly productive. For examples, see **Macintosh; Windows; Microsoft**. A drawback is that there is no simple way to describe how something is done; you almost have to see someone else do it. By contrast, commands in a command language can be written down on paper and even embedded in computer programs.

UTILITIES Utilities are programs that assist in the operation of a computer but do not do the main work for which the computer was bought. For instance, programs that compress data or defragment disks are utilities (see **data compression; fragmentation; Norton Utilities**). By contrast, word processors, financial programs, engineering programs, and other programs that do actual work for the user are called *application programs*.

V _____

V.21 CCITT standard V.21 defines a format used for 300-baud data communication over phone lines in Europe and Japan. By contrast, the Bell 103 format is used in the United States for the same purpose. (See **Bell 103A; CCITT.**)

V.22 CCITT standard V.22 defines a format for sending 1200-baud data over phone lines designed to carry voice signals. A different format, Bell 212A, is more commonly used in the United States. (See **Bell 212A; CCITT.**)

V.22 BIS CCITT standard V.22 bis defines the worldwide standard format for sending 2400-baud data over telephone lines designed to carry voice signals. (*Bis* is Latin for "a second time" and indicates that this is an extension of standard V.22.) The standard specifies that if the phone line is of low quality, the modem will drop back to 1200-baud in V.22 format. Some 2400-baud modems either do not do this or drop back to Bell 212A format instead. (See **V.22; Bell 212A; CCITT.**)

V.24 This CCITT standard for data communication is essentially identical to the American RS-232C standard. (See **RS-232; CCITT.**)

V SERIES The V series of CCITT standards defines ways of sending high-speed digital data over telephone lines. (See **CCITT; V.22; V.29; V.32.**)

V.29 CCITT standard V.29 defines a format for sending 4800-baud and 9600-baud serial data over telephone lines. This format is half-duplex only. (See **CCITT.**)

V.32 CCITT standard V.32 defines a standard format for sending 4800- or 9600-baud data over telephone lines designed to carry voice signals. The modem automatically analyzes the sound quality of the line and adjusts its output as needed. In general, V.32 modems will drop back to 2400-baud (V.22 bis format) or 1200-baud (V.22 or Bell 212A format) when line conditions are poor. (See **CCITT.**)

VACCINE A vaccine is a computer program that offers protection from viruses (see **virus**) by making additional checks of the integrity of the operating system. No vaccine can offer complete protection against all viruses.

VACUUM TUBE A vacuum tube is an electronic component consisting of electrodes placed inside an evacuated glass tube. Vacuum tubes work by using electric and magnetic fields to control the movements of electrons that have been emitted by one of the electrodes.

A CRT (Cathode Ray Tube) television screen is one example of a vacuum tube. The vacuum tubes originally used in computers performed the same type of functions that semiconductor diodes and transistors perform now. A vacuum tube diode consists of two electrodes; a cathode, which emits electrons, and an anode, or plate, which collects electrons. The diode will conduct electricity only when a positive voltage is applied to the cathode. A vacuum tube triode contains an electrode called the *grid*, located between the cathode and the plate. The flow of electrons from the cathode to the plate is controlled by the electric field of the grid. (Similarly, the current flow from the emitter to the collector in a transistor is controlled by the voltage applied to the base.) Vacuum tube triodes can be used for amplifications and logic functions.

The first electronic digital computer, the ENIAC (see **computer**), consisted of 18,000 vacuum tubes. The disadvantages of vacuum tube computers are that they are very big, they consume a great deal of power, and they generate a lot of heat. Also, it is necessary to constantly replace burned-out tubes.

VALENCE A valence electron is an electron that is only loosely connected to its atom; hence it can be dislodged easily. (See **conductor; semiconductor**.)

VARIABLE A variable is a symbol that represents a data item, such as a numerical value or a character string, that can change its value during the execution of a program. Programming languages typically require that variable names start with letters. It is generally good practice when writing a program, to include variables instead of constants, even if the value of the variable is not intended to change during the execution of the program. The value may need to change at some future date when you are running that same program, and it would be much easier to change one assignment statement for that variable than to change the value of a constant everywhere it occurs in the program.

See also **data types; data structures**.

VAX Digital Equipment Corporation produces the popular VAX line of minicomputers. (See **Digital Equipment Corporation; VAX/VMS**.)

VAX/VMS VAX/VMS is the most widely used operating system of Digital Equipment Corporation VAX computers. The command language is similar to MS-DOS. Some important commands are:

`dir`	Display a list of files.
`type xxx`	Show what is file xxx (a text file).
`help`	Invoke the help system.

@xxxxx	Execute the commands on file xxxxx.com.
run xxxxx	Execute the machine language program on file xxxxx.exe.

An unusual feature of VAX/VMS is the way it keeps previous versions of files. If you create a file called XXXX.YYY, it will be known as XXXX.YYY;1. If you then edit it, you will create XXX.YYY;2, and XXXX.YYY;1 will still exist. Whenever you do not specify a version number, you will get the latest version of the file. To delete all versions, you must use an asterisk in place of the version number, thus:

del xxxx.yyy;*

The command

purge xxxx.yyy

will delete all but the latest version of xxxx.yyy.

VDT VDT is an acronym for <u>v</u>ideo <u>d</u>isplay <u>t</u>erminal, that is, a computer monitor.

VECTOR GRAPHICS Vector graphics is a method of creating pictures on a computer telling it to draw lines in particular positions. The lines may be displayed on a screen or plotted on paper by a motor-driven pen. An advantage of vector graphics is that a picture can easily be moved from one output device to another, since it makes no assumptions about the exact way the lines are drawn. For the same reason, a vector graphics picture can be enlarged or reduced without loss of sharpness. By contrast, see **bit-mapped graphics**. See also **draw program; paint program**.

VENTURA Xerox Ventura Publisher is a desktop publishing program for the IBM PC family of computers. It was developed by Xerox Corporation using the software technology of the Xerox Star typesetting and layout workstation. (See **desktop publishing**.)

VGA The IBM Video Gate Array (VGA) is the video circuit built into the PS/2 model 50 and higher. It provides high-resolution graphics modes and crisp text as well as emulation of the CGA, EGA, and MDA. (See **video modes [IBM PC]**.)

VIDEO ADAPTER See video card.

VIDEO CARD A video card (video adapter) is a plug-in circuit board that enables a computer to display information on a particular type of monitor (screen).

VIDEO MEMORY Video memory is where a computer keeps track of the present contents of the screen. On the IBM PC, video memory occupies various locations above 640K, which is why only 640K of memory is available for programs even though the processor can address a full megabyte (1024K).

A fast way to change what is on the screen is to store new values directly into video memory.

See also **snow**.

VIDEO MODES (IBM PC) The ability of an IBM PC or PS/2 computer to display graphics depends on the video adapter (video card) that is installed in the machine and on the type of monitor connected. Regardless of which video adapter is installed, all of these machines can display text, including special box-drawing characters. (See **IBM PC**.)

Table 18 lists all the video modes of the IBM PC and PS/2 (not counting the Hercules Graphics Card or special products such as the IBM 8514 video adapter). Table 19 lists which modes are available with each video adapter and monitor.

Software will not use a particular video mode unless it is designed to do so. If you change video adapters and/or monitors, you can easily get sharper text, but you will not get increased graphics capability unless you use software designed for your new equipment.

TABLE 18 Video Modes of the IBM PC and PS/2 Family of Computers

Mode	Description
0	Text, 40 columns, black and white
1	Text, 40 columns, 16 colors
2	Text, 80 columns, black and white
3	Text, 80 columns, 16 colors (most popular text mode)
4	Graphics, 320×200, 4 colors (widely used graphics mode)
5	Graphics, 320×200, black and white
6	Graphics, 640×200, 1 color (widely used graphics mode)

7	Text, 80 columns, monochrome, with ability to underline (ideal for word processing)
8, 9, 10	Used only on PCjr
11, 12	Not used
13	Graphics, 320×200, 16 colors
14	Graphics, 640×200, 16 colors
15	Graphics, 640×350, monochrome
16	Graphics, 640×350, 16 colors (most popular EGA graphics mode)
17	Graphics, 640×480, 2 colors
18	Graphics, 640×480, 16 colors
19	Graphics, 320×200, 256 colors (good for digitized photographs)

TABLE 19 Video Modes Available with Particular Video Adapters and Monitors

IBM Monochrome Display Adapter (MDA) with TTL monochrome monitor
  Mode 7 only
IBM color Graphics Adapter (CGA) with RGB color monitor
  0, 1, 2, 3, 4, 5, 6
IBM Color Graphics Adapter (CGA) with composite video monitor
  0, 1, 2, 3, 4, 5, 6
  (If the monitor is monochrome, colors are rendered as shades of gray or striped patterns.)
IBM Enhanced Graphics Adapter (EGA) with EGA-type color monitor
  0, 1, 2, 3, 4, 5, 6, 13, 14, 16
IBM Enhanced Graphics Adapter (EGA) with CGA-type color monitor
  0, 1, 2, 3, 4, 5, 6, 13, 14
  (but not 16, which is the most widely used EGA graphics mode)
IBM Enhanced Graphics Adapter (EGA) with TTL monochrome monitor
  7, 15
  (not the same as any of the modes available on a color monitor)
IBM Monochrome/Cclor Graphics Adapter (built into PS/2 25 and 30)
  All except 13, 14, 15, 16, and 18
IBM Video Gate Array (VGA) (built into PS/2 models 50 and higher)
  All modes are available.

VIRTUAL DISK See **RAM disk**.

VIRTUAL STORAGE The term *virtual storage* refers to a way of extending the effective size of a computer's memory by using a disk file to simulate additional memory space. Typically, the operating system keeps track of which memory addresses actually reside in memory and which ones must be brought in from disk when they are referred to. Virtual storage is divided into units called *pages*, and the operation of bringing in a page from disk is called a *page fault*.

VIRUS A virus is a computer program that automatically copies itself, thereby "infecting" other disks or programs without the user knowing it, and then plays some kind of trick or disrupts the operation of the computer.

Viruses have existed as academic pranks since the 1960s, but the first malicious viruses appeared around 1987, apparently the work of disgruntled programmers trying to sabotage their competition.

The best protection against viruses is to obtain all your software from reliable sources, make regular backup copies of your work, write-protect disks that you boot from and other disks that do not need to be written to, and reboot by turning the computer off and then on again.

Knowingly spreading a computer virus is a crime under common law and under specific laws in various states.

See also **vaccine; Trojan horse.**

VISICALC VisiCalc, developed for the Apple II in the late 1970s, was the first electronic spreadsheet program. (See **spreadsheet**.)

VLSI VSLI is an acronym for <u>V</u>ery <u>L</u>arge <u>S</u>cale <u>I</u>ntegration, which refers to chips containing 10,000 or more logic gates.

VM/CMS See **CMS; VM/SP.**

VM/SP VM/SP (<u>V</u>irtual <u>M</u>achine/<u>S</u>ystem <u>P</u>roduct), an operating system for large IBM mainframe computers, such as the 370, 4341, and 30B1, is based on the idea of one computer simulating multiple copies of itself.

There is a straightforward way to make one computer simulate another; simply program the first (real) computer to recognize the second (virtual) computer's instructions and respond appropriately. If the real computer is capable of interleaving several tasks, it can even simulate several virtual computers at once.

Under VM/SP, one IBM 370 (or the equivalent) simulates many separate IBM 370s at once. The user of each virtual 370 can then program it as if he had an entire 370 to himself; the effect is very much like using a large, fast personal computer that runs IBM 370 software. VM/SP creates and deletes virtual machines as users log on and off, keeps the virtual machines from interfering with each other, and allows them to communicate in controlled ways.

Most VM/SP virtual machines run CMS and serve only one user at a time. (See **CMS**.) However, within a VM/SP system it is quite possible to create a virtual machine that runs MVS (with TSO) and serves dozens of users at once, just as a real 370 does. This is particularly convenient for installations that are converting from MVS to CMS and want to support both at once. (See **MVS; TSO**.)

VOICE RECOGNITION See **natural language processing**.

VOLT The volt is the unit of measure of electronic potential. If a potential of 1 volt is applied to a resistor with a resistance of 1 ohm, then a current of 1 ampere will flow through the resistor. (See Ohm's law.)   One volt can also be defined as 1 joule/coulomb, where a joule is a measure of energy: 1 joule = 1 (kilogram) $(meter)^2/(second)^2$.

VON NEUMANN, JOHN John von Neumann was a twentieth century mathematician who worked on one of the earliest computers and developed the stored program concept.

VT-100 The Digital Equipment Corporation VT-100 has had a major impact on the computer industry because it provides convenient control codes for positioning the cursor, clearing the screen, and selecting normal, bold, or underlined type (See **ANSI screen control**.)   This makes it possible to implement full-screen, personal-computer-like software on an asynchronous terminal. Most present-day asynchronous terminals are VT-100 compatible, and most personal computers can emulate the VT-100.

VT-101, VT-102, VT-220, VT-320 The VT-101, VT-102, VT-220, and VT-320 are computer terminals made by Digital Equipment Corporation. They are upward compatible with the VT-100. (See **VT-100**.)

W_____

WAIT STATE A wait state is a brief delay introduced when a microprocessor reads data from memory, to allow extra time for the memory chips to respond. Wait states are used when a fast microprocessor is used with relatively slow memory chips. A processor with one wait state on each memory access will typically be 10% to 20% slower than the same processor with no (zero) wait states.

WANG Wang Laboratories of Lowell, Massachusetts, is a leading manufacturer of dedicated word processors and microcomputers.

WARM BOOT, WARM START See **boot.**

WATFIV WATFIV (<u>Wat</u>erloo <u>F</u>ORTRAN <u>IV</u>) is a FORTRAN compiler developed for teaching purposes at the University of Waterloo, Ontario. The WATFIV compiler is used on mainframe computers such as the IBM 370; it requires less CPU time and memory than a conventional FORTRAN compiler, making it cheaper to run large numbers of student programs.

The WATFIV language is based on FORTAN IV but contains a number of Pascal-like extensions, including a WHILE loop, a block-structured IF-THEN-ELSE statement, and a new type of subroutine, called a *remote block*, that is internal to the main program rather than being compiled as a separate unit.

WIDE-AREA NETWORK A wide-area network is a set of widely separated computers connected together. For example, the worldwide airline reservation system is a wide-area network. By contrast, see **local-area network.**

WIDOW The first line of a paragraph is called a widow if it appears by itself as the last line of a page. Some word processors automatically adjust page breaks so that there are no widows. (See also **orphan.**)

WILD CARD A wild card symbol is a symbol that matches any other symbol. For instance, the MS-DOS (PC-DOS) command

```
dir ab*.exe
```

means "Show me the files whose names begin with 'ab' and end with '.exe'." The symbol '*' is a wild card and stands for the middle part of the file name, whatever it may be.

WINCHESTER DISK See **hard disk**.

WINDOW A window is an area of the screen set aside for a special purpose. On the Macintosh and in Microsoft Windows, the screen is divided into windows for different pieces of software. The user can control the size, shape, and positioning of the windows. The *active window* is the one in which you are currently typing.

WINDOWS DRAW See **draw program**.

WINDOWS, MICROSOFT Microsoft Windows is a software package that gives the IBM PC or PS/2 a window-based working environment similar to that of the Apple Macintosh. (See **windows**.) Several pieces of window-oriented software are included with the package, including a draw program, a multifont word processor, and a VT-100 terminal emulator. Other software packages for Microsoft Windows are available commercially. In addition, Microsoft Windows can run conventional PC software by giving the entire screen to the program.

In Microsoft Windows, the user can switch among tasks but cannot run more than one task concurrently. A related product, Windows 386, allows concurrent execution of more than one task on machines that have an 80386 microprocessor.

WINDOWS, PAINT See **paint program**.

WORD A word is a group of bits stored in a computer memory. The number of bits in a word depends on the type of computer being used. A minicomputer typically may use words that are 16 bits long. Large computers may use words that are up to 64 bits long.

WORD PERFECT Word Perfect is a very popular word processor for the IBM PC. It is a product of Word Perfect Corporation, Orem, Utah. The two most widely used versions are 4.2 (for conventional printers) and 5.0 (for desktop publishing with laser printers).

Word Perfect is noted for its ability to handle a wide variety of document formats, including footnotes, legal citations, and foreign language characters (which it constructs by overprinting letters and accents if necessary). It displays the document on the screen as it will look on the printer. The user need not memorize many special keys because most special functions are accessed through the F keys, which are labeled on a template attached to the keyboard.

WORD PROCESSING Word processing is the act of using a computer to prepare a letter, manuscript, or other document. There are several advantages to using a computer word processing system for writing. Without a word processor, revision of a document is a lot of work because the entire document must be retyped. With a word processor you can make your revision and then have the computer print out the entire final document.

You need three parts of a word processing system. First, you need a computer. Second, you need a word processing program. Several word processing programs are available for microcomputers; some popular programs are Word Perfect, WordStar, Perfect Writer, and Microsoft Word. These programs have different characteristics, and the decision as to which program will work best for you depends on what type of writing you do. It is also possible to obtain dedicated word processor systems that do nothing but word process. Once you obtain a suitable program, you will need to learn how it works. That is the hardest part about word processing. Finally, you need a printer. Dot-matrix printers are fast and inexpensive. Daisywheel printers produce letter-quality results.

The process of initially typing a document on a computer is similar to typing a document on a typewriter. You type at the keyboard, and the results appear on the screen. The advantage of word processing becomes clear when you make a mistake. You can move the cursor back over something you have typed and either delete the character that is there, add a new character, or replace the existing character with a different one. The word processor will automatically realign the rest of the text.

Other special features that word processors often include are the following:

- the ability to delete an entire block of text, or else move the block to a new location
- the ability to search through the entire text and change a specified word to another word every time it occurs
- the ability to automatically number the pages and put headings at the tops of the pages
- the ability to include footnotes
- the ability to print specified words in boldface or to underline them

You may also be able to obtain a spelling checker program that reads through each word in your file and identifies the words that are not included in its dictionary, allowing you to type a correction if a word has been misspelled.

When you have finished working on a document, you must make sure that it is saved on a disk so that it will be available for you to use the next time you need. Once you have completed a rough draft of your document, you can print it and then review it further. After marking revisions on the printed copy, you can then use the word processor to make the same revisions on the text stored on the disk.

See also **desktop publishing**.

WORD WRAP Word wrap occurs when, as you reach the end of a line, the cursor automatically jumps to the next line, rearranging the placement of words as necessary to avoid breaking a word. This is a useful feature when you are using a computer as a word processor because it means that you do not need to hit the return key at the end of each line. It also makes it possible to "even up" the lengths of the lines when material has been added or deleted or margins have been changed.

WORDSTAR WordStar, a popular word processing program, is produced by MicroPro International Corporation of San Rafael, California. When you type something in WordStar, it is formatted on the screen; therefore, when a paragraph is printed, it will look very much as it does on the screen. A line is drawn on the screen at the end of each page. To give commands to WordStar, you type the control key simultaneously with the appropriate letter or letters. For example, typing "control-Y" deletes a line of text and typing "control-K-D" saves your document file on the disk. To help you in case you can't remember all the commands, WordStar contains several menus that appear on the screen to display some of the command options.

WORKSTATION A workstation is an extremely powerful microcomputer typically used for scientific and engineering calculations. Two of the largest manufacturers of workstations are Sun Microsystems and Apollo.

WORM WORM is an acronym for write once, read many storage, which refers to a type of optical disk where a computer can save information once, can then read that information, but cannot change it. By contrast, with CD ROM (compact disk read only memory), the computer cannot save any information on the disk and can only read the information provided by the supplier of the disk. (See **CD ROM**.)

WRITE WRITE is one of the PASCAL output commands. The command WRITE(x) causes the value of the variable x to be displayed on the screen.

WRITE PROTECT A diskette is write-protected when it is fixed so that data can be read from it but not written to it. This can be a way to protect valuable data from being accidentally written over. A diskette has a small notch on one side. When this notch is open, it is possible to write to the disk. When the notch is covered with tape, the computer will realize that it is not supposed to write any data to that disk. (This is the way that write-protect works for 5 ¼-inch disks; 8-inch disks are the other way around.)

Cassette tapes can be write-protected by breaking the tabs at the back of the cassette.

WRITELN WRITELN is one of the PASCAL output commands. WRITELN is similar to WRITE except that, after executing a WRITELN command, the computer will put the output from the next output statement on the next line. For example, the output from this program segment:

```
WRITE ('Hello!');
WRITELN (' How are you?');
WRITE ('Fine.');
WRITELN (' How are you?');
```

will look like this:

```
Hello! How are you?
Fine. How are you?
```

X _____

X.21 This CCITT standard defines a format for transmitting serial data by wire. It includes signals that enable computers to dial their own calls when connected to an all-digital telephone line. By contrast, present-day auto-dial modems are used on voice telephone lines. (See **CCITT**.)

X.21 BIS This CCITT standard is virtually equivalent to RS-232C (see **RS-232**). It is a temporary substitute for X.21. (*Bis*, which is Latin for "a second time," denotes an alternative or substitute. See **CCITT**.)

X-HEIGHT The x-height of a typeface is the height of the smallest letters (such as "x") which have no ascenders or descenders, compared to the height of the larger letters. For example, some typefaces make "x" half as high as "X"; some make it 40% as high; and some make it 60% as high.

    A typeface with a large x-height looks larger than a typeface of the same overall size with a small x-height.

X-OFF, X-ON X-OFF and X-ON are codes that respectively turn off and on the transmission of data from a computer to a terminal. Many computers are programmed so that, if the person at the terminal types CTRL S (X-OFF), the computer will stop transmitting until the person types CTRL Q (X-ON). This is convenient when the computer is transmitting information too fast for the user to read it. Moreover, when the terminal is actually another computer, X-OFF and X-ON signals can be used to keep information from being transmitted faster than it can be processed.

XMODEM XMODEM is a protocol for transmitting files from one microcomputer to another and detecting transmission errors if they occur. XMODEM was developed by Ward Christensen and is used extensively by microcomputer hobbyists.

    A computer using XMODEM transmits 128-byte blocks of data, each of which is followed by a checksum (a number derived mathematically from the ASCII codes of all the characters in the block). (See **ASCII; checksum**.) The receiving computer computes a checksum from the characters that it receives; depending on whether or not this checksum agrees with the checksum transmitted with the data, the receiving computer then either asks for the next block or asks for the same block to be retransmitted.

The technical specifications for XMODEM are as follows:

1 Both computers must be set to transmit and receive 8 data bits per character (instead of the usual 7).
2 The receiving computer starts by transmitting ASCII code 21 once every 10 seconds until transmission begins.
3 Each block transmitted by the transmitting computer consists of the following, in the order named: ASCII code 01; an ASCII character indicating the block (01 for the first block, 02 for the second, etc.); an ASCII character whose code is 255 minus the block number; 128 bytes of data; and, finally, a checksum obtained by adding the ASCII codes for all the characters and taking the sum modulo 256.
4 The receiving computer indicates successful reception by transmitting ASCII 06, or asks for retransmission by transmitting ASCII 21.

A number of similar protocols such as YMODEM and ZMODEM have been developed. They provide faster data transfers by using longer packets and allowing transmission of a packet to begin before acknowledgment of the previous packet has been received.

See also **Kermit**.

y

YMODEM See **XMODEM**.

Z

Z80 The Z80, produced by Zilog, Inc., is an 8-bit microprocessor found in most machines that run the CP/M operating system. (See **microprocessor**.)

ZILOG, INC. Zilog produces the Z80 microprocessor. (See **microprocessor**.)

ZMODEM See **XMODEM**.

More selected BARRON'S titles:

DICTIONARY OF ACCOUNTING TERMS
Siegel and Shim
Nearly 2500 terms related to accounting are defined.
Paperback, $8.95, Can. $11.95 (3766-9)

DICTIONARY OF ADVERTISING AND DIRECT MAIL TERMS
Imber and Toffler
Nearly 3000 terms used in the ad industry are defined.
Paperback, $8.95, Can. $11.95 (3765-0)

DICTIONARY OF BUSINESS TERMS
Friedman, general editor
Over 6000 entries define business terms.
Paperback, $8.95, Can. $11.95 (3775-8)

BARRON'S BUSINESS KEYS SERIES
Each pocket-sized reference explains nearly 50 "key concepts."
Each book: paperback, $4.95, Can. $6.50
ESTATE PLANNING AND TRUSTS, *Crumbley & Milam* (4188-7)
INCORPORATING, *Fox* (3973-4)
INVESTING IN MUTUAL FUNDS, *Boroson* (4162-3)
INVESTING IN REAL ESTATE, *Harris and Friedman* (3928-9)
MORTGAGE FINANCING AND REFINANCING,
Harris & Friedman (4219-0)
READING AN ANNUAL REPORT, *Friedlob and Welton* (3930-0)
UNDERSTANDING THE FINANCIAL NEWS,
Apostolou & Crumbley (4206-9)
UNDERSTANDING SECURITIES, *Jones Lee* (4229-8)

BARRON'S BUSINESS REVIEW SERIES
These guides explain topics covered in a college-level
business course.
Each book: paperback
ACCOUNTING, *Eisen.* $10.95, Can. $14.95 (3574-7)
BUSINESS LAW, *Hardwicke and Emerson.* $10.95, Can. $14.95 (3495-3)
BUSINESS STATISTICS, *Downing and Clark.* $9.95, Can. $13.95 (3576-3)
ECONOMICS, *Wessels.* $9.95, Can. $13.95 (3560-7)
FINANCE, *Groppelli and Nikhbakht.* $10.95, Can. $14.95 (3561-5)
MANAGEMENT, *Montana and Charnov.* $10.95, Can. $14.95 (3559-3)
MARKETING, *Sandhusen.* $10.95, Can. $14.95 (3494-5)
QUANTITATIVE METHODS, *Downing and Clark.* $10.95,
Can. $14.95 (3947-5)

TALKING BUSINESS SERIES: BILINGUAL DICTIONARIES
Five bilingual dictionaries translate about 3000 terms not found in
most foreign phrasebooks.
TALKING BUSINESS IN FRENCH, *by Le Gal.* $8.95, Can. $11.95
(3745-6)
TALKING BUSINESS IN GERMAN, *by Strutz.* $6.95, Can. $9.95
(3747-2)
TALKING BUSINESS IN ITALIAN, *by Rakus.* $6.95, Can. $9.95
(3754-5)
TALKING BUSINESS IN JAPANESE, *by Akiyama.* $8.95,
Can. $11.95 (3848-7)
TALKING BUSINESS IN KOREAN, *by Cheong.* $6.95, Can. $9.95
(3992-0)
TALKING BUSINESS IN SPANISH, *by Fryer and Faria.* $8.95,
Can. $11.95 (3769-3)

All prices are in U.S. and Canadian dollars and subject to change without notice.
At your bookseller, or order direct adding 10% postage (minimum charge
$1.50, Canada $2.00), N.Y. residents add sales tax.

Barron's Educational Series, Inc.
250 Wireless Boulevard, Hauppauge, NY 11788
Call toll-free: 1-800-645-3476, in NY 1-800-257-5729
In Canada: Georgetown Book Warehouse
34 Armstrong Ave., Georgetown, Ontario L7G 4R9